TEN YEARS AROUND THE TABLE:

WOMEN WRITE

THE TUDOR OAKS WRITERS GROUP

Ten Years Around The Table: Women Write
The Tudor Oaks Writers Group

As of the publication date of this book, all websites cited are current.

ISBN-13: 978-1508407034
ISBM-10: 1508407037
1. Anthology
2. Fiction
3. Poetry
4. Essay
5. Women's Lives
6. Women in America

A NOTE ON THIS BOOK

This compendium comes from the minds and hearts of a writer's group that has met weekly for about 10 years. We decided that the parade of work presented to us was too good to be kept locked away. We wanted copies. We wanted to show each other off. We wanted to have a palpable, physical, remnant of the journeys on which we had taken each other. So we decided to make a book.

We have given every author the right and opportunity to select her own work for presentation. In that way, this is not an edited anthology. Each piece has been vetted, however, in that each writer has brought her work to the group at one time or another, heart in hand, and received honest, careful, loving response. It is the way of our group.

The only task left was to figure out how to format everything so it looked like a single book. Some of us are Mac, some of us are PC. We use several different text editors. Because I spent the early part of my working life in offices, I offered to take on the task.

Several years ago, Sharon Schaefer (around whose dining room table we gather, and whose baked treats greet us every time) went on a journey to a far off land. She came home with a small green frog for each of us. Somehow the frogs took hold. And the next time someone went on a trip, she came home with bookmarks adorned with pictures of frogs. And then someone went on another trip and came home with little green plastic frogs. And so it went. We were forevermore to refer to ourselves as "The Frogs."

We hope that you will enjoy our chorus. We hope that you will read more than just the author you know. We hope that we inspire you to take up your own pen.

Kathie Olsen for The Tudor Oaks Writers Group
aka The Frogs

TABLE OF CONTENTS

WOMEN WRITE
ANNE BATZER

Although we no longer lift the sheltering flaps of the red tent for one another, or link elbows in a protective circle of privacy on the prairie, women, as always, continue to come together for sustenance. We gather for support when our hearts ache with unrequited dreams, when our minds grapple with unsolved puzzles and when our lives linger too long in unresolved limbo. We meet for inspiration when a dreamy abstraction needs reflecting light, the moonbeam of feminine feedback, to crystallize and become a brilliantly clear idea. And we come together to celebrate on great occasions for glorious reasons and on ordinary days for no apparent reason at all.

Some women still gather to share tasks elevated by our foremothers from the level of daily maintenance to "everyday sacred" like quilting with its intrinsic reward of color and pattern and canning with its earthy, sensory satisfactions. In our time, of course, women meet for the work of business, the reciprocity of education and the gritty idealism of political action.

Increasingly we come together to share something more: the written word. It's not the need to discuss the latest best seller or even a long-awaited feminist tome that compels us, but our own words put boldly, carefully and intentionally to paper. Women's writing groups abound. And they are fulfilling our primal, venerable need for support, inspiration, celebration and for connection to our deepest selves, other women and the world we inhabit. But just as Women's Groups in the '60s helped us formulate a change we could not fully predict or understand, today's women's writing groups are helping us create a new, emerging reality---a change not even we who love words can yet fully articulate.

###

SHORT
STORIES

THE AWKWARD RUNNER

ELLEN DAVIDSON LEVINE

Grace was awake. She blinked her eyes and squinted at the alarm clock on the nightstand.   Too early yet. Another quarter-of-an-hour until the Awkward Runner would appear at the right side of the window across from Grace's bed.

Unless the weather was pouring down rain or dropping piles of snow, the Awkward Runner showed up at exactly 6:42 AM. In mid-winter, when sunrise wasn't until after 7:00 AM, the Awkward Runner wore a headlamp. Grace would watch the runner clumsily progress to the left side of the window, the glow from the lamp bobbing up and down in an uneven rhythm.

Although she hadn't run since she was a child, Grace could easily see how uncoordinated the runner was, compared to others who ran on the road. It was the reason Grace had first noticed the Awkward Runner. But even after all this time, Grace never could decide for certain if the runner was male or female.

Billy had been positive right away. He'd used the binoculars and declared he could see the curve of breasts under a tee shirt.

"Your awkward runner is a woman," he declared. "She's got boobs."

He said Grace should go out on the road the next morning to get a better look. "You could run at least as good as her. I bet you could even beat her, going up the hill."

Billy had been a difficult man, but he knew how to make her laugh. She thought now maybe that was why she fell in love with him all those years ago. She'd married Billy after college. He was making good money as a logger then. She gave up the notion of teaching and happily got up at 4:00 AM to feed him breakfast and pack his lunch before he left for work at dawn. The children were born in quick succession – Jacqueline, Robert and Phillip – and Grace often was up until well after midnight, doing laundry, and rising the next day at 4:00 or 4:30 AM. to get all the chores done.

Phillip, the youngest, was in First Grade when the mill shut down. Without the mill to take the logs, Billy got laid off. A lot of men were let go then. When the bills were three months overdue, Grace dressed in her nicest skirt and jacket and walked the two miles into town. She went into the offices of Hart & Hart Insurance and came out three-quarters of an hour later with a job as file clerk. Over the next several years, she was promoted and promoted again, until she became John Hart's personal secretary. When he retired, Grace filled the same role for John Hart Jr. until she too retired a decade later.

Billy never really found good work again, but they'd managed to get by with her salary and what little bit he earned doing odd jobs. Grace knew how much it humiliated him. Their marriage suffered. He drank more beer then he used to and he got mean after he'd been drinking. Sometimes his meanness turned violent. When it did, Grace was the target. She was thankful he never hit the children, at least not until the day he punched seventeen-year-old Robert and Robert punched him back. Grace wondered then if she should have fought Billy off instead of simply absorbing his blows, because after Robert hit him, Billy stopped drinking.

Billy was gone now, gone almost a half a year. She'd missed him at first, but not as much since Peggy came. To be truthful, she preferred having Peggy around. Peggy was better-natured and more willing than Billy ever had been to sit and talk and look out the window with Grace. On his last visit, Phillip had set the TV up in the bedroom, but Grace much preferred window-watching. She enjoyed seeing the morning joggers and walkers and the hardy few who rode bikes up the steep road. She was entertained by the antics of jays and robins and crows, the nervous darting flight of hummingbirds, and the families of quail and cooing doves foraging her backyard. She even enjoyed watching deer graze in the flower garden she could no longer tend.

"She show up yet?" Peggy's booming voice announced her entrance into the room. Her footsteps were heavy as she crossed the floor.

"Not yet." Grace didn't turn around. She didn't want to chance missing sight of the Awkward Runner. Despite the uncoordinated gait, the runner made it up the hill every morning. You have to be inspired by that, thought Grace, you have to be inspired by the sheer determination. She'd even said as much to Billy one morning, but he didn't listen, did he? When he got pneumonia last winter, he simply gave up. And now he was gone.

"I don't know how you do it," Peggy said. "Waking up every day the same time without an alarm clock." She laughed. "Me, sometimes I need a cannon going off before I can drag myself awake."

Grace smiled. She'd always risen early. As a child, she'd had her share of farm chores to finish before the school bus came to pick her up, and again in the afternoon, after the bus brought her home again. After high school, she attended the teacher's college in Monmouth on scholarship and worked early morning shift in the dorm cafeteria for

6

room and board. Her habits didn't change then and they certainly didn't change when she had to look after a husband and three children.

Now she was an old woman, unable to do much of anything but sleep and stare out the window. And wait. Wait from one doctor appointment to the next. Wait for family and friends to visit. Wait for whatever time she had left to tick by. Wait for the Awkward Runner to appear.

She'd first seen the Awkward Runner – Grace always thought of the words as a name more than a description – two years and five months ago, on a Saturday. She'd awakened at sunrise. Out the window, she could see the light creeping over Old Blue Mountain. A movement on the road had attracted her eyes. A jogger dressed in a loose white tee-shirt and baggy red shorts appeared at the right hand side of the window. Even at a distance - the house was set back thirty or so feet from Hillside Road - Grace could see that this person had a unique style of running, with arms flapping like chicken wings, legs pounding the ground in an irregular stride, and torso slanted forward at a surprising angle. It was a surprise the runner could make any progress up the hill, let alone not topple over. Grace sat up and watched until the runner moved out of sight. From then on, she waited every morning for the Awkward Runner to pass by.

"That the AR?" Peggy said. For a big woman, her voice was high and girlish, and she had a nervous laugh that punctuated most of her sentences. She kept her carrot-colored hair in a pixie cut and usually wore a loose-fitting black shirt over baggy, dark-colored cotton pants.

"No," Grace said. "It's two people. The AR is always alone."

"I brought you some nice tea," Peggy said. "And oatmeal that'll get cold if you don't eat it right away. I'll be back after I get dressed." She bustled out of the room, slippers slapping on the hardwood floor.

Grace gobbled the tasteless mush Peggy called oatmeal and made a face as she set the bowl down. She turned to look at the clock. A minute to spare. She sat back against the pillows and sipped her tea, something named Herbal Blossoms. To Grace, who longed for a good, strong cup of coffee, the brew was barely more than plain hot water. She took another sip and sure enough, the Awkward Runner appeared, heading up the hill.

After lunch, Peggy announced she needed to go shopping. "Out of milk and eggs and such," she said, with a burst of laughter. Grace reassured her, for what felt like the hundredth time, that she remembered how to use the medic alert button and that she could reach the telephone on the nightstand if she had to call a neighbor. "I'm fine, I'm fine," she repeated.

She heard the sounds of Peggy's departure – the back door banging shut, an engine starting, and the crunch of gravel as Peggy's car pulled down the driveway. And finally, there was quiet, the kind of quiet she used to treasure in the years when Billy went off to work and the children were at school, and later, when she stayed late at work and had the whole suite of Hart & Hart offices to herself. "I like to hear myself think," she used to say. Now, in the quiet, Grace drifted into sleep.

She woke up with a start. There'd been a loud noise. Grace felt her heart quicken with fear. And then, thank goodness, she heard the familiar heavy footsteps approaching down the hallway. Peggy had returned.

Peggy confirmed this by appearing in the doorway.

"Grace? You need anything before I put groceries away?"

"You do what you need to. I'm not going anywhere."

Peggy turned to go and then halted. "Grace. You're not going to believe this." Her eyes were shiny with excitement. "I bumped into my old friend Virginia Buckley and she's working for Mr. Atkins who lives in that white house at the bottom of this road. He had a stroke, you know. Whole left side paralyzed, poor thing." Peggy's voice erupted into a high-pitched giggle.

Grace was learning to ignore Peggy's inappropriate laughter, but sometimes it was all she could do to keep from snapping at her to stop it. She breathed in and then out, slowly, the way the therapist taught her, until she was ready to speak. "Eldon Atkins What a shame. He was always an active man."

"Virgie will take good care of him. But that's not what I want to tell you. See, My friend Virgie's husband's cousin twice-removed lives on Northside Road. And who do you think her neighbor is?"

Grace was still trying to work out the cousin's relationship to Peggy's friend. She shook her head. "Who?"

"Your AR. The Awkward Runner." Laughter.

"So she lives down there. What else did you find out? Did you get a name?"

"Well." Peggy walked over and sat down at the foot of the bed, leaning back against the bedframe. "Ariel Greenmountain, of all things. What were her parents thinking? Or maybe it's his parents?" Peggy shook her head. "No, I'm pretty sure it's a she. Ariel's a girl's name. But get this. She claims to be hiding out from the Mafia." Peggy's eyes widened. "Maybe it wasn't her parents. Maybe that's the name of the new identity."

"Maybe. Did you find out anything else?"

"Virgie said The A.R.'s from Indiana or Iowa or one of those I states."

"Idaho? Illinois? Grace offered, and felt pleased for remembering the names.

"No. I think it was Iowa, because that's why I thought it was a lie. I mean, no way would the Mafia be in Iowa. What would they want with all that corn? Anyway, the A.R. says she's a lawyer and the Mafia is after her for a case she prosecuted. Like some kind of TV show."

"My goodness. You don't think it's true?"

Peggy tilted her head and blinked her eyes, considering. "Well, maybe some of it. But not the Mafia part. That's too weird. Plus, if it was true, she wouldn't be telling nobody, would she?"

"I guess not." Even as she spoke the words, Grace wondered if she believed them. Perhaps being on the run from gangsters who want to kill you was like having a bad heart. You could die at any time. You could be walking down the street, standing in your yard, even sitting on the toilet, God forbid. Wouldn't the Awkward Runner be scared also? But the runner didn't act scared, going out every morning to run up the steep road, in defiance of death. Grace wondered if maybe she should try to be more like the Awkward Runner.

Peggy's voice interrupted her musing. "What are you thinking?"

"I think I'm exhausted," Grace said, unwilling to share her thoughts just yet. She laid against the pillows and sighed for effect. "And I shouldn't keep you from the groceries." She was getting worried about the bags of groceries sitting on the counter. She could imagine frozen food melting, soaking the paper grocery bag until it dissolved, spilling packages and cans onto the floor

"Oh good heavens," Peggy said, laughing. "I forgot I left them on the counter."

The next day, Peggy drove Grace to an appointment with the heart doctor. Grace could feel her heart beating quickly, but not in a bad way. She was nervous, a bit, and determined to say what she needed to, even if she didn't like having a serious conversation while the examining gown was slipping off her shoulders and coming undone in back. She had no choice.

"I want to get out of bed and live a normal life," Grace announced, as soon as the doctor walked into the room. "At my age, I'll either go sooner or a little bit later."

Usually, Dr. Bradshaw stared at the medical chart more than at her. This time he inspected her closely. He checked her heartbeat and examined her skin, her nails, her eyes. He asked if she got out of breath, and how often, and what was she doing when it happened.

"All right," he said, after Grace answered all his questions. "You've had OT? Occupational therapy?"

"Yes. For breathing. And exercises for my balance."

"The medication seems to be working. You can get out of bed, move around some more. Exercise could even be good for you, as long as you don't try to run up a mountain." Dr. Bradshaw's lips curved into a tight smile.

On the way home, Grace informed Peggy that the next day they would be up early and out on the road by 6:30.

In the morning, Grace slowly walked down the driveway, Peggy following behind with the wheel chair. When she reached the road, Grace was exhausted and grateful to collapse into the seat. Still, she insisted they wait until the Awkward Runner appeared around the curve, heading up Hillside.

"Good morning," Grace called out.

The runner turned and mumbled something that might have been a greeting, without a change in the ungainly stride.

11

In the afternoon, Grace's neighbors came to visit. The Custer sisters - thin-as-a-rail Christine Custer Schmidt and overlarge Maryann Custer Palmer - had grown up on their daddy's farm, a mile down the road. They'd married local boys and lived a block apart in the small town that was fifteen miles from the family farm. Now, the sisters were elderly widows, back living in the farm house with their ancient mother. They seemed to know everything about everybody in the county and they were never reluctant to share what they knew.

Although gossip made her uncomfortable, Grace decided to ask them about the Awkward Runner. "There's someone I'm wondering about. I see her every morning, early. You could set a clock by her. She lives somewhere on Northside Road." She went on to describe the runner's height and coloring the best she could.

The sisters turned to each other. A look passed between them, but Grace couldn't quite interpret it. She waited, leaning back against the pillow and breathing slowly. In, out, in, out.

Christine, the skinny, wrinkled sister, pursed her lips. "Well," she said, with a kind of huff. "We have heard a few things."

"Some very interesting things," Maryann said, winking.

"We have it on good authority that your runner is one of those women," said Christine. Maryann nodded her head, jiggling the folds of skin under her chin.

"One of which women?"

"Well," said Maryann. "You might say she's a manly-hearted woman."

Grace gave her a puzzled look. Whatever was Maryann going on about, she wondered. Why couldn't people just say what they meant?

Christine leaned so far forward, Grace worried the woman would fall off her chair. "A lesbian," Christine said, dropping her voice.

"Pooh." Grace snorted. "So what? I want to know her story. Why did she move here? What does she do?"

"That's just it. She's recovering from a broken heart."

"Had her heart broken by a woman," Maryann added, as if Grace couldn't figure that out for herself.

Enough, Grace thought.   She wanted the Custer sisters to leave. She was ready to fake sleepiness when Peggy thumped into the living room with a glass of water and the yellow pill dish.

"Sorry," Grace said. "You'll have to excuse me. I've got some pills to take and I'll bet Peggy is here to tell me it's my nap time." She stared at Peggy, willing her to agree, but it wasn't necessary. The sisters stood, said their goodbyes and scurried away, most probably to visit another neighbor and gossip about Grace, and how senile she'd become.

The next morning and the morning after that and every morning except Sunday when Peggy went to church, Grace would rise, and get dressed in a pair of Billy's sweat pants and an old Oregon Ducks sweatshirt that had belonged to Robert. She and Peggy would walk down the driveway to the gate, and wait to greet the Awkward Runner. "Good morning," Grace said every day and every day, the runner would give her a tight nod of acknowledgement.

The walk down the driveway became easier and easier, and after a few weeks, Grace convinced Peggy to leave the wheelchair behind. A week later, with Peggy nervously holding her arm, Grace ventured a short way down the road. That morning, when she encountered the AR, it was further down the road, but the runner didn't seem to care and only offered the same small nod of the head.

Despite a two-week forced time-out in late November, when a snowstorm was followed by an ice storm that made the road too treacherous for runners, walkers and most cars, Grace and Peggy continued to walk on the road in the morning. Robert, living across the country in New York, sent her a headlamp from Abercrombie & Fitch for Christmas and Grace loved it, but even that failed to elicit any kind of response from the AR beyond the quick nod.

In March, there was a stretch of mild weather. Grace and Peggy walked all the way down the road and around the corner, and another quarter-mile beyond that. "There," Peggy said, pointing to a large house perched up on the hill. "That's where she lives. All by herself in that big place."

"The Bartow place," Grace said. "Used to be a big family. They're all gone now."

By April, Grace was walking almost two miles every morning, alongside the watchful Peggy. The doctor was delighted and Grace couldn't recall when she'd felt so fit and healthy, despite her bum heart.

"You see," she told Peggy. "Walking is good for me." And for you, she wanted to add, because Peggy had lost a nice bit of weight. Grace was afraid she would embarrass Peggy, so she didn't say a word.

At 10:00 P.M. that night, Peggy got a phone call from home. "It's my dad," she said. "He has cancer. It's bad and he wants me to come visit. I might be gone a week or even two. I just don't know." For once, she didn't laugh.

"You go. I'll be fine. I'll call Jackie."

While Peggy scurried off to call for a plane ticket and to pack her suitcase, Grace called her oldest child, who lived just a few miles away.

"I can't be away right now. This is tax season," Jackie said, "and you know how Georgie gets."

Grace did not have a favorable opinion of her son-in-law George, who worked in the school district business office and moonlighted as a tax preparer. Even though Jackie denied it, Grace was convinced George was abusive, the same as Billy had been in the bad times. And I taught her to accept it, Grace thought ruefully, as she dialed Phillip's number.

He agreed to stay with her, without hesitation. "I'll catch a couple hours sleep and then head down. I can make it from Portland to you in four-and-a-half, five hours, easy."

"That's good news," Peggy said, when Grace told her. "You'll only be on your own for a few hours that way." Peggy's reservation was for the early flight to San Francisco and she planned to leave the house by 4:30 AM.

In the morning, Grace awakened to utter stillness. She was alone. There were none of the comforting Peggy sounds – the heavy footsteps, the clatter of kitchen utensils, the off-key humming. There were none of the Peggy constraints either, Grace realized. For the first time in a long time, she could do whatever she pleased. And so, despite her promise to Peggy, Grace climbed out of bed, pulled on Billy's sweats, a warm shirt and her tennis shoes. She left the medic alert necklace in its tray on the nightstand. Grabbing a fleece jacket from the coat-tree by the door, Grace set out on her morning walk.

She was surprised at how crisp the early morning air felt on her face. She didn't know that overnight the temperature had plunged. A late frost had coated the pasture white. In the orchard, the trees glittered with ice diamonds. When she came to the end of the driveway, she stepped onto a road was that was shiny and slick. Too late, Grace realized she shouldn't be out. She felt herself lose traction. She was falling, falling forever, it seemed. In the stretched-out moments while she fell, she had time to regret her choice to walk this morning, time to regret other choices, other times. As the ground came closer, she reached out to break her fall and then remembered the OT said not to.

She smashed onto the black asphalt with a force that shuddered through her body. The salty taste of blood filled her mouth.

As she sank into a dark sea of remorse, Grace was vaguely aware of voices, and she felt someone touching her head, her shoulders and arms, her hips and legs. The voice was soft and kind and the fingers were gentle. She drifted away. There were other sounds, and the sensation of being lifted and carried. She let herself sink back into the darkness.

When Grace finally roused herself, she was in her own bed. Sunshine streamed through the window. For a moment, Grace thought she'd overslept. Then she remembered the icy morning, and stepping onto the road, and falling. More hazily, she recalled the voices, the sense of movement. They'd laid her out on her bed. Did that mean she was mortally injured? With a rising sense of panic, Grace turned her head the other way.

The Awkward Runner was sitting on the Occasional Chair, next to the bed. "You're awake," the Awkward Runner said. "You fell." The voice was soft and comforting and for some reason, made Grace think of honey candy. "Lucky you were so bundled up in clothes. I think you bumped your head."

Grace touched the throbbing bump above her right ear. "It hurts a little. Not much. I bit my tongue though."

"You need to get checked out. I found your doctor's phone number and I called. I'm supposed to bring you there or get you a ride. They want to take x-rays."

"What time is it?"

"Almost 8:00."

"My son should be here any minute," Grace said.

The AR shrugged. "Should be okay to wait. I checked you over. No broken bones. You were too bundled up for that." There was a small pause and a muffled sound that could have been a chuckle.

A door slammed somewhere and moments later, Jackie rushed into the bedroom. "Mom," she said, bending down to look at Grace. "Are you okay?"

"I think so. But, why are you here? I thought Phillip…"

"Shh. Of course I'm here. Christine Schmidt called me, told me you fell. And you must be one of the nice people who found her," Jackie said, turning to the Awkward Runner.

"Hey," Phillip was standing in the doorway. "What's going on?" He was still carrying his suitcase.

"Mom fell. She could have broken bones or a head injury."

"Oh my god."

"Hold it," Grace said, struggling to sit up. Her children's hands reached out to help her, but she waved them away. "I want to show you I can do this myself." Once she was upright, and propped against her pillows, she announced that she didn't think she'd broken anything. "I'm sore and my head hurts. I'll let you take me to get x-rayed."

"I gotta go." The Awkward Runner stood.

"I'm sorry your run got interrupted," Grace said, with a broad smile. "Thank you so much for helping me." Jackie and Phillip echoed her, expressing their own gratitude.

"S'okay." The AR turned, bumped into the chair back, and stumbled from the room.

Late that afternoon, Grace and her two grown children returned to the house. The doctors and the staff at the medical center had repeatedly told her how lucky she was, and Grace didn't give them any argument. Jackie and

Phillip lectured her about forgetting the medic alert. She didn't argue with them either, shocked into silence by the reversal of roles. I'm not their child yet, she told herself.

It was more than two weeks until Grace felt steady enough to walk beyond the driveway. Peggy was back, overflowing at odd moments with teary-eyed memories of her father. "At least he didn't suffer long," Peggy would repeat throughout the day, and Grace understood she was comforting herself that way.

On a Monday morning, the two of them set out, Grace in Billy's sweats and Peggy in a hot pink athletic suit she'd bought at the airport on the way home. It was May now. The sun was already bright and the air was soft and sweet.

They were at the next driveway, an eighth of a mile from Grace's driveway, when the Awkward Runner came around the corner and started up the road. Grace slowed her pace, studying the approaching figure.

"It's funny. I still haven't figured out if that's a woman or a man," she said to Peggy in a low voice. "But I guess I don't really care that much anymore, one way or the other."

"I changed my mind. That's a guy. I'm sure of it. A really nerdy guy but a guy nevertheless. I mean, he'd have to be nerdy with a name like Ariel," Peggy laughed.

The Awkward Runner neared them.

"Good morning," said Grace.

Without breaking the ungainly pace, the Awkward Runner turned, gave Grace a little nod of the head and winked.

###

BLACK DOVE

FAYEGAIL MANDELL BISACCIA

Diana hurried toward the ballroom door and heard the last strains of a waltz. She stopped to compose her face. Her kid stiletto sandals perfectly complemented the sleek silk gown she had chosen, both black of course. The slit which allowed her to dance lay exactly below the point of the pelvic bone, and when she lunged, her black stockinged thigh would be exposed. Aunt Emily's pearls barely touched the broad vee of the bodice and glowed against her teak-colored bosom. She and Edwin had quarreled after dinner, and she was still irritated though she resigned herself to playing the gracious hostess. It was expected of her.

She drew the door open and stood stunned. Instead of the chatting, milling, highly affected crowd of dancers she expected, each person in the room stood smiling triumphantly in a semicircle facing the door, stood gazing with amusement at her and at a large, cellophane-wrapped object in the center of the floor. The lighted chandelier sent diamond droplets onto all the faces, and the cellophane caught the light and sent it into the corners of the room. There were too many layers of cellophane for her to see what was inside. Diana stepped past the footman into the room, and the guests shouted a belated "Surprise!"

Edwin came forward to meet her, smiling, no trace of irritation in his steel-gray eyes. "Darling. Happy Birthday." He drew her into the room and over to the cellophane package. Diana walked around it, found the place where the bow was tied. There was a card: "A Black Dove for my beloved." She pulled the end of the ribbon, and the cellophane dropped. Diana glanced at the double doors where she had entered and saw that the footman had thrown them open. With a cry and a leap, she landed on the seat of the classic Harley, kick-started it, and roared out of the room.

###

THE CASE OF THE SECRET SOCIETY OF THE GREEN FROG

SHARON SCHAEFER

"It began innocently enough, gentlemen, as a silly gift from one of the early members." Holmes was lounging in a rather shabby sidechair, his long legs stretched toward the grate where a small fire was burning fitfully. "This person had been traveling in darkest Africa, and brought home small hand-carved Malachite frogs for each of ten friends." He leaned forward, pulled a faggot from the blaze and relit his pipe. The overpowering smell of his custom-made tobacco soon filled the room. He inclined his head toward me; the light of the meager fire played upon the sharp planes of his face, giving him a rather sinister demeanor. "Be a good chap and pour the brandy around again."

I did as I was bid, and poured a healthy measure into the glasses held aloft by the Most Honorable Simon Foucalt, his father Joseph Foucalt, Earl of Totten-on-the Marsh and Sir Henry Wrightway. It was a bitter cold night and the fine brandy Sir Henry had brought with him fueled the internal warmth, which the small coal fire could not.

When the glasses were filled, the elder Foucalt coughed discreetly. His pale countenance gave no hint of the questions that must be churning within his fine aristocratic skull. "Ah hum, I say Holmes. This is highly entertaining to be brought to a cellar in the wilds of this God-forsaken country on this cold night." He paused and sipped from his glass. "But I am wondering where this discourse is going to take us."

"Oh do be quiet, Joseph." Sir Henry shifted his rotund torso in the wicker rocker placed by Holmes to the right of the fireplace. "You know as well as I do Holmes will tell the story in his own time. Your interjections will only postpone the inevitable." Sir Henry was known as a curmudgeon, and he obviously felt he must live up to his reputation, not-withstanding the fact that the younger Foucalt was to become his son-in-law the following week. Sir Henry was fond of his daughter's choice. Simon had graduated first in his class at Cambridge and was reputed to be an excellent Barrister.

It was well publicized in the press that both Sir Henry and the Earl were delighted with the coming marriage. Several large parties had been given by the bride's family and friends to celebrate. BethAnn Wrightway was an intelligent and beautiful young woman, who read Economics at Cambridge. She was the result of a late in life marriage between Sir Henry and a much younger fourth wife, and it was said that BethAnne, as the only child, was the logical heir apparent to the Wrightway business. The Foucalt family controlled commercial building construction, and the Wrightway family owned property on which these edifices could be placed. It would certainly be a fortuitous union of two highly successful family enterprises.

However, the elder Foucalt had some trepidation regarding the coming nuptials. Simon's father had heard rumors of a most disturbing nature. A former Kings College classmate of Simon's was observed in the crowded lobby of the Prince Albert Opera House during the intermission, talking about the upcoming wedding. The young gentleman stood in the midst of a certain class of young men and women who frequent these events, not for the cultural advantage, but in order to be seen and heard by the general populace, which they seemed to distain. But of course, in reality they seek approval from these very same people.

The former classmate was overheard by our reporter, talking loudly to a young woman whose clothes were of the latest fashion. That is to say, expensive and multi-layered. Her satin shoes matched exactly the color of her frock. She had a nervous habit of patting her hair as if to make sure it was still arranged in the newest style. The young woman occasionally glanced into the face of the young man, as if to show she was somewhat interested in what he was saying. The young man was also dressed in the manner of many ambitious males: an excellently tailored dark suit, a high-collared shirt, tie and expensive shoes. His blond hair was heavily oiled and slicked to his head.

The observer, an elderly compatriot of the senior Foucalt, was startled to hear BethAnne's name connected with a rather unfortunate word... Murder.

Edging closer-- the eavesdropper, while attempting to appear disinterested, heard the following discourse.

"Oh yes, BethAnne, and her cronies in their 'secret society' (the classmate flexed his fingers to emphasize the quote) frequently murder off their spouses, and various other people to whom they have an aversion." The young man smiled and barked a rather insincere laugh. "I do worry about the health of our friend Simon."

To which the soigné young woman replied, "But don't they get caught?"

"Oh no, they are deucedly clever. And, they make an enormous amount of money doing it."

Unfortunately, the lights dimmed to announce the end of intermission, and the listener lost sight of the young couple. The old gentleman, who admittedly had an active imagination coupled with a hearing deficiency, was upset enough by the conversation to inform the senior Foucalt, who immediately implored his old friend Holmes to investigate. Hence, the late night meeting of the five of us in the cold cellar of an ancient ramshackle mansion. Neither Simon nor Sir Henry was aware of the Opera House conversation; such was the secrecy demanded by Holmes.

Suddenly there came a fearful screech from the upper story. It took me a moment to recognize the sound of infrequently oiled hinges. "Hush, now." Holmes raised a finger to his lips. "The game is afoot."

The muffled sound of footsteps and laughter filtered through the floorboards. Holmes silently rose and with the efficiency of motion that is his trademark, slid open the cover to an unnoticed air duct. We heard the scraping of chairs and snatches of conversation from several female voices.

The sharp rap of a gavel on a hard surface brought the conversation to an abrupt close. "Good evening ladies. May the meeting of the Secret Society of the Green Frog come to order."

Startled, Sir Henry blustered "What the devil... that's BethAnne's voice"

Holmes leaned forward, his face lined with concentration. "Hush. It's a meeting."

"First on tonight's agenda is a report from member Jolene Smyth-Barkley."

The melodious voice of a young adult woman floated through the air duct. "Congratulate me sister members. Today I received notice that my most recent murder was accepted as complete and I was given ample compensation."

"Hear, hear" from the audience, followed by applause.

Although it was difficult to estimate accurately, I thought there were perhaps eight or nine separate voices, certainly no more than ten.

The disembodied voice, as identified by Sir Henry as BethAnne, spoke again. "I, too, have good news. I have been given a new assignment, which will involve newlyweds on a honeymoon. Of course only one of the newly wedded will return home." She laughed in what seemed to be a particularly cold manner.

Suddenly Simon Foucalt stood and waved his arms about in an agitated manner. "By Jove what are we doing here listening to this? Holmes, have you gone out of your mind?"

I quickly placed myself between Foucalt and Holmes, fearing bodily harm was forthcoming to my friend from this refined but angry young man.

Holmes seemed unafraid. "Sit down, young man. Your father has requested this manner of revealing to you the true nature of your beloved." He stood and leaned nonchalantly against the mantle of the small fireplace. "However, I can see by your demeanor that you are aware of the Society and its workings."

Sir Henry turned to Simon. "What the devil is going on upstairs in that room full of innocent women? And what is this 'Secret Society' bunk she is talking about?" He raised his glass to his lips and drained the last of the excellent brandy.

Holmes bowed low before young Foucalt. "I believe you can explain to your future Father-in-Law." He spread his arms wide. "Please, allay his fears."

"BethAnne told me about this Society several years ago. In spite of its name, there is only one secret...or perhaps I should say there are ten secrets." He started to pace, then turned to face Sir Henry. "Your daughter has a character trait you never dreamed of, sir. A trait she feared you would not condone. So as to spare your feelings, she has chosen to pursue her ambition to be a mystery writer under a nom-de-plume." Simon continued, "She and a group of like minded women meet once a week to critique their compositions. I believe most of the women are quite successful with their novels."

I couldn't help myself. I burst into laughter. The chatter above us ceased abruptly.

Holmes called up to the air duct. "Miss Wrightway, the farce has gone long enough. May we join you?"

To my surprise, she replied with a measure of hilarity in her voice. "Of course Holmes, please do come upstairs before you all freeze to death."

We men climbed a staircase hidden behind a curtain on the far wall of the cellar, groped our way along a dim corridor and entered a brightly lit, comfortably furnished parlor. Ten beautiful women of all ages were sitting around a large rectangular table. In front of each woman was a small Malachite frog, no more than an inch in diameter.

At the head of the table, with a gavel in her hand, posed a smiling BethAnne. She turned to the assembled women. "May I present my new friends to the Society?"

The women nodded their assent.

"This is the famous consulting detective Sherwin Holmes, and his companion Watson Crick." Holmes gave a small bow, and the ladies politely applauded. I admit I was too overcome by the preceding events to do more than mumble a thank you, and much to the amusement of Holmes, I blushed.

I heard Sir Henry gasp. On BethAnne's left, sat Lady Caroline Wrightway, the young wife of Sir Henry, and mother of the chairwoman of the Secret Society of the Green Frog.

"Caroline, please tell me what you have in common with these women," Sir Henry growled.

"Oh Henry, you would be surprised how many men I have murdered." She left her chair and threw her arms around her husband. "But never you, my darling, I love you too much."

Later, back in our rooms at Baker Street, I finally had the opportunity to question Holmes as to his reason for the secrecy, and the method by which he ascertained the identity of the Society.

Holmes packed his pipe with the foul-smelling tobacco he preferred. After a long ritual of lighting and puffing, his way of tormenting me, he began.

"When The Earl approached me with his suspicions, I immediately thought of the most recent New York Times literary find, a rather interesting but gruesome psychological thriller involving strict religious beliefs and some hocus pocus with certain landmarks." He paused and puffed his pipe to life, filling the room with blue smoke and causing me to cough.

I waved my hand to move the foul miasma away from my face. "Really Holmes, must you smoke that infernal thing?"

"I am addicted, my friend," he responded quietly. "Better this than my former habit, eh?" He drew in a frightful amount of nicotine and continued. "It was easy enough to purchase the aforementioned tome and read the copyright page. Few people realize the true name of the author is on this page, as is the name of the publisher." He stood and retrieved a pinch of tobacco from the Persian slipper on the mantle piece.

Holding the shag between thumb and forefinger, he resumed his musing. "On the page was the name B.Wrightway. The publisher was the Green Frog Press. I contacted Ms. Wrightway and the rest as they say, is history. To answer your second question, let us say that the future Mrs. Foucalt has a sense of humor." He laughed in a most sinister manner, and began refilling his pipe.

###

BUILDING BLOCKS

FAYEGAIL MANDELL BISACCIA

Devlin sat in the corner of the kindergarten and pushed the blocks around the tray. The three little girls at his table didn't notice. They were busy stringing big wooden beads.

Devlin heard a crash. He looked up. The girls were scrambling after the colorful beads which jumped and rolled across the floor. In their hurry to gather them, they were kicking beads in every direction.

Devlin pushed his blocks around the tray. He didn't try to pile them up. He'd tried that yesterday. Whenever he got to five or six high, the girls would bump the table. Crash. He knew they didn't do it on purpose. They were just clumsy. He didn't see the point of trying any more.

The teacher rang the bell. The other children ran to the closet for their boots and jackets. The little girls put on their fluffy hats and skipped out the door, laughing.

Devlin looked up. He noticed that one other little boy still sat at his table across the room. He didn't know the little boy's name. He didn't know the names of any of the other children. Devlin decided to see if he could stack more than six blocks while the girls were at recess.

He put one block on top of another. Another. Then another. He looked up. The other boy was still at his table. Yes. Good. Devlin put on a fifth block, then a sixth. He looked again at the other boy. Still there. He added a seventh.

He looked up. The boy looked back. Devlin saw admiration in his eyes. He added another block. He checked the other boy. Still watching. He felt exhilarated. He added another block, but it went on crooked, and the whole tower toppled.

Devlin looked up quickly. The other little boy dropped his eyes. He still sat in exactly the same place. He hadn't moved at all.

Devlin lined up all his blocks on the tray. Then, eyes down, he rolled his wheelchair over to the little boy's table. He saw the crutches, saw the little boy's leg brace and his twisted hand.

"Want to play with my blocks?"

The little boy smiled.

###

CAPTAIN FLASH AND THE MOON ILLUSION

ELLEN DAVIDSON LEVINE

Justin gets off the bus first, in front of his Mom and little brother Davy. He steps onto the sidewalk. *Whoosh*, a blast of wind grabs the breath right out of his mouth. Justin presses his lips together and wrinkles his nose. He wants to look fierce as Captain Flash, so the wind won't try to take away any more of his air.

"Davy. Give me your hand. You too, Justin."

His mother's voice is tight. He knows better than to ignore that voice but Davy doesn't. Davy is three and hasn't figured out that stuff yet, even if he can count to one hundred and say the whole alphabet.

"Davy." Mom makes a quick grab for Davy's hand just before they get to the crosswalk. But Justin's right hand is locked in his mother's grip. When she lunges for Davy, Justin is yanked sideways.

"I almost fell down," he says.

"I don't need any games from you either, mister," his mother says.

Justin looks up, ready to protest this unfairness. Mom's eyes are glittery, as if she is going to cry. Justin bends his head and says nothing.

They cross the street and walk to a small building made of purple glass. Mom gets tickets from a machine and steers Davy and Justin inside the glass building, where five or six grownups are standing and waiting. Two women have on white jackets, the kind Justin's doctor wears. Next to them, an old man with white grandpa hair reads a newspaper, holding it close to his face. Justin wonders if the man is looking at the comics. Maybe the man will read them aloud and show him the pictures the way Justin's grandpa does.

"Here it comes," shouts Davy. "Here comes the train."

"It's not a train," Justin tells him. "It's a tram."

"Tram," echoes Davy, eyeing the shiny metal and glass car as it descends smoothly to the platform.

"Come on, boys," Mom says. "Let's go."

Justin and Davy follow her into the tram car. Davy scoots to the front of the car and presses his face against the round glass. Justin follows, walking slowly, to stand next to his brother. He sneaks a quick look back at his mom to see if she noticed that he didn't run and Davy did, but she is staring out the window. Justin presses against Davy, nudging his brother just enough to gain a few more inches of window.

The doors slide closed. The tram car glides up the thick cable, rising quickly above houses and tall buildings and floating over the freeway on its way up the big hill.

"Look," Davy shrieks. "Look at how little the cars got."

"They didn't get little," Justin says. "They're down there and we're up here, so they look little."

"Uh uh," Davy says. He squishes a finger against the glass. "See?"

Justin rolls his eyes and turns away, frustrated with Davy's stubbornness and also with his own lack of words to explain to Davy what he is really seeing.

One of the doctors smiles and winks at Justin. A burst of warmth fills his chest. She knows he is right. She thinks he is smart and grown-up. He grins back at her and almost tries a wink but decides against it. He needs to practice winking in the bathroom mirror some more.

The other doctor leans forward. "Do you like the tram?" she asks Davy. "Is it fun?"

"Yes," he says, but the frown on his face says something else.

The doctor moves closer to Davy. "Your brother's right, sweetheart. The cars only look little because they're far away."

Davy doesn't care anymore. "We're going to see my daddy," he tells her. "He's sick."

"Oh." She darts a quick look at Justin's mom. "I bet your daddy's going to love seeing you. Are you going to give him a big kiss?"

"Yes."

"As big as the moon?"

"Yes."

The moon. Maybe that's the way to tell Davy about the cars not really getting small. He remembers how his dad explained it to him on their first camping trip together. It was last year, when he was only six. Just the two of them and he'd been so excited he couldn't sleep. Even after they were side-by-side in the big sleeping bag, Justin chattered on about school and friends and swim lessons. He was saying something about Captain Flash, his favorite TV cartoon hero, when he saw that the moon looked smaller as it moved up in the sky. He got quiet, working it out in his mind. He liked figuring out the answers to puzzles. After a while, he thought he knew.

"Dad?"

"Hmm?" His father's voice was muffled and sleepy.

"I figured something out. About the moon."

"What is it?"

"I think the moon changes sizes. When it's over there, over the mountains, it's really big. Then it gets smaller when it goes in the middle of the sky."

"That's what your eyes tell you, right?"

Justin nodded. He kept looking up at the moon and the zillions of stars in the sky.

"Our eyes sometimes trick us and we see things differently from how they are. Seeing the moon change size, that's called the 'Moon Illusion.' See, the moon is always the same size. Do you want to know how to see it correctly?"

"How?" This time, Justin turned to look at his dad, to see if he was being teased.

His dad propped his head on an elbow and smiled down at Justin. "I'll show you tomorrow night when the moon rises. I promise. Now go to sleep."

Justin didn't think he would be able to sleep. He was surprised when he woke up and it was daylight. All day, his curiosity about his father's promise was like an itch in his brain. At last, the sky began to darken and an almost-full moon was rising over the mountains.

"Now," said his dad. "Take a good long look at the moon. I want you to remember how big it looks."

Justin stared for a long time. "Okay," he said. "I looked long enough."

"Good. You're ready. First, turn around. Open your legs wider. Now, bend over and look at the moon upside-down, through your legs. Is it the same size?"

"It's smaller," Justin said. He turned and looked up at the moon. "Bigger." He tried again, looking at the moon upside down and then right-side up. He sat down on the ground next to his dad. They watched the moon together. As it moved higher in the sky, it didn't look so big. "How come?" he asked. "How come it looks so different?"

"I don't know why. I just know it happens." His dad smiled. "That's why it's good to look at things from more than one angle."

But now, as Justin thinks about it some more, the moon story isn't the right way to explain about the cars looking small. Justin's idea about near and far is the right way. That doctor said so. Maybe his dad is wrong about the moon and wrong about other stuff too. Maybe that's how come he's sick and has to stay in the hospital.

"We're here," Davy yells.

The tram has brought them to the hospital, which is a bunch of big buildings spread out on top of a hill. As the tram doors whoosh open, the man with the newspaper dashes out the door like Captain Flash on a mission. Justin watches the man disappear behind a sliding door. The other people are in a hurry too. The two doctor ladies wave goodbye to Davy and Justin and rush away.

Now it's Mom who is moving slowly, as if she's changing her mind about going to see his dad. Justin wants her to hurry, and at the same time, he doesn't. He hasn't seen his dad in a long time. What if he can't recognize his own dad? Or worse, what if his dad doesn't remember him?

Justin, Mom and Davy go through the sliding door and head down a long hallway. The floors are shiny, just like the gym at school. Justin recalls how some older kids made a noise on the gym floor with their tennis shoes. He scuffs the bottom of his shoe against the floor, savoring the high-pitched sound it produces.

Right away, Davy copycats him. "Listen to me," he says. His Thomas the Engine shoes rub against the floor, *pffft, pffft*.

"Your shoes are farting," Justin says, making Davy laugh. His mom doesn't turn around or tell them to stop so the two boys keep it up, squeaking and giggling down the hallway.

"All right, boys. That's enough." Mom stands in front of some closed elevator doors, hands on her hips.

Davy dashes forward. "I want to push the button." When he runs, his butt looks fat because Davy won't get potty-trained and he still wears diapers.

The doors part. They get into the elevator, which is like a little room. Mom points to number four and Davy pushes the button. The ride is over fast. The doors slide open and they are in a big room, with bright yellow walls and a bunch of red, purple and green couches and chairs. The side of the room across from where they are standing is really a huge window instead of a wall. Through the glass, Justin can see a tram car zipping up the cable and another going down.

TV noise grabs his attention, the sound of guns blasting and angry men shouting. In a dark corner, someone in a wheelchair is watching television.

"Ethan. We're here," calls Justin's mom.

The wheelchair spins around. There sits Justin's dad.

"Daddy," Davy shrieks. He runs the length of the room, almost crashing into a couple of chairs that are in his way, and climbs onto his father's lap. Davy and his father laugh and hug each other. Then Mom is standing next to them, smiling.

Justin walks slowly forward. Why is his dad sitting in a wheelchair? Is there something wrong with his legs? His dad looks tired. He looks small. And he is wearing pajamas. Justin's dad never wears pajamas at home. At home, he wears sweats and a tee-shirt. Most of them say *Ducks* or *Oregon* or *UO* on the front. Oregon is the college his dad went to and the one he and Davy will go to when they get old enough. That's what his dad says anyway.

"Hey, guys. I've got some news," Justin's dad settles Davy more comfortably on his lap. "The test results came back."

"And?" Mom puts her hand up to her lips.

"Negative."

"Oh, Ethan." Mom starts to cry. She leans down to wrap her arms around his dad's neck.

Davy wriggles off his father's lap and plops on the floor by the side of the wheelchair, facing the TV. On the screen, an orange car is escaping from a bunch of cop cars. The orange car gets further and further ahead but suddenly there are cop cars coming the other way. The orange car is trapped. At the last second, the car angles sideways, jumps off the road and speeds away through a field. The cop cars try to follow but they all get stuck or turned upside down.

Davy stares at the TV with unblinking eyes. His mouth hangs open and drool leaks down his chin. What a baby. Justin is careful to watch the TV out of the corner of his eye. He is sure if his mother realizes her sons are watching this show, she will make them stop.

"Justin."

Guiltily, Justin looks up his mom.

"Justin, you stay here with Davy and watch the TV. Don't go anywhere until I get back. I have to take Daddy to his room because the doctor is coming to talk with us. Do you hear me?"

Justin nods his head. He can't believe his mother actually told him to watch TV. Everything is upside down.

"Hey, son. You haven't said hello yet." His father stretches out his arms. They are pale and skinny. There are bruises on the inside of his arms. The bruises look like the black and blue ones Justin gets sometimes when he falls down. "Come give me a hug," his dad says.

All of a sudden, Justin can't breathe. His air is gone, like when he got off the bus and the wind sucked his breath away. Justin doesn't want to hug his dad. He doesn't want to touch him. His heart beats fast. He keeps his eyes down. He doesn't want to see his father's face.

"Ethan. The doctor."

"Okay." His father grasps the wheels of the chair and turns away. "Catch you later, guys."

Justin sits on the carpet next to Davy and stares at the TV, but the show is less interesting now. He thinks about the disappointed sound of his father's voice. He thinks about "Negative," and wonders what it means. It sounds hard and bad.

Across the room, the elevator doors swoop open. A man comes out of the elevator. It's the old man who was on the tram and he still has the newspaper under his arm. He stumbles to a chair, a purple one, and collapses into it. The newspaper slides to the floor, still folded.

Justin begins to worry. The man is slumped in the chair, eyes closed, not moving. If the man is dead, will he and Davy get in trouble? Maybe the man is sleeping. Probably, the man will be glad if Justin wakes him up before he falls out of the chair. The way he is leaning forward, he might fall pretty soon. Justin glances at his brother. Davy's eyes are fixed on the TV. Satisfied that he won't have to worry about Davy going anywhere, Justin gets up from the floor. He is Captain Flash stalking an alien on a strange planet. Cautiously, he tip-toes to the purple chair.

Two feet away, Justin halts. "Sir. Are you okay?"

The man jerks and sits back in the chair. "What?"

"I didn't want to scare you," Justin says.

"It's okay." The man smiles but his eyes look sad. He sighs. "I just got some bad news."

Justin nods. Is the bad news *negative*, he wonders.

"My mother is dying. And I can't bring myself to go in her room. What can I say to her? I can't do anything for her. I can't even cry. How can I go to her room?" The man shudders.

Justin is quite surprised someone this old can have a mother. He waits politely in case the man wants to say more. Finally he is sure it's his turn to talk. "Do you want me to go with you?" he asks. This is what his dad and mom usually say when Justin feels scared to do something.

"You would do that?" The man eyes him sharply, the way his mom does when she thinks he is telling a fib.

"Yes." Justin looks in his brother's direction. "But not until after my mom gets back. I've got to watch my brother."

The man chuckles, but not like he is really laughing. "You're a good boy," he says. Then he slumps into the seat with his eyes closed and his head bent down. Justin waits but after a while, he tip-toes away and sinks down to the floor next to Davy.

The show isn't on, just a bunch of ads, but Davy is stuck in the same spot, his eyes on the screen, his mouth open, drool on his chin. Justin hardly looks at the TV. He keeps turning around to watch the old man, even though there is nothing much to see. The old man hardly moves a muscle. Just like Davy. Maybe they are both under a curse and only Justin has escaped, like the time Captain Flash outwitted Freeze Man, the bad guy who turned everyone else into statues of ice.

"Justin, Davy." Mom walks towards them and sits on the red couch. "What good boys you are. You deserve a big treat for being so good."

"Ice cream," Davy shouts.

"What about you, Justin? Ice cream? We can go to Mr. Frosty's on the way home."

"Okay."

Mom raises her left eyebrow. Whenever she does that, she thinks he is sick and feels his forehead. Justin can tell she is getting ready to reach over to him when the side door opens and a man walks out.

The man is dressed in green pajamas. Maybe everybody wears pajamas in this place. The green is gross too, the color of cooked string beans. The man doesn't seem to mind wearing his pajamas. He is smiling as he comes up to them. "Mrs. Miller? If you want, I can take your boy in now."

Mom stands up. "Great." She smiles back at the man. "Justin. This nice man is Jose. He's going to take you to your daddy's room. Daddy didn't get a chance to hug you before and he wants to send you home with a big hug and a kiss."

Justin's ears fill with a rushing sound, as if the wind is blowing all around him. He sees his mother's lips moving so he knows she is talking. He just can't hear her. She leans down and wraps him in her arms. When Mom releases him from the hug, Justin looks where the old man had been sitting. The chair is empty. He looks across the room at the window and sees the tram cars moving up and down. Mom gives him a nudge. Reluctantly, Justin follows Jose through the door.

On the other side of the door, everything is different. Justin wrinkles his nose at the sharp smell. He is confused by the hustle and bustle taking place all around him. For a moment, he isn't sure where to focus his eyes.

Jose's pager buzzes. He unsnaps it from his belt and looks at it. "I got to make a call," he says. "You wait right here. Don't move." He clips the pager onto his belt, gives Justin an approving nod and moves to a phone on a nearby counter.

Justin looks around, studying this strange place. Instead of the cheerful colors of the waiting room, everything on this side of the door is white or the same green color as Jose's pajamas. Some of the people scurrying back and forth wear white or green pajamas, but other people wear regular clothes. All the way down the hallway, there are a bunch of doors. People go in and out of one door or another.

Justin tries really hard to stand still but he is curious about where the doors lead. He lets his feet inch down the hall, until he is standing in front of the closest doorway. The door is open a few inches. He gives the door a nudge. It swings open. A few steps more and he's inside the room.

At first, all he sees is a big bed. There are machines on the other side of the bed with tubes sticking out. With a shock, he realizes the tubes are hooked to someone's nose, someone who is lying on the bed. Justin lifts himself on his toes to get a better view. He sees an old, old woman. Her hair is gray and wispy. The tubes going into her nose give her the look of an alien monster, but she is so frail, Justin isn't frightened by her. He edges closer to the bed. The woman's eyes are closed. Her mouth hangs open, making her face look hollow and caved in.

The old woman moans softly and Justin freezes in place. His heart is beating so fast it hurts. The woman's eyelids flutter open. With great effort, she turns her head and stares at him with watery blue eyes.

"Stanley," she whispers. A small smile shows on her mouth. The old woman's eyes drift closed but the smile stays and her face looks softer. Justin takes a deep breath. This must be how Captain Flash feels after a narrow escape. And then he remembers the man in the green pajamas who is taking him to see his dad.

"Goodbye," he whispers to the old woman. "Good luck." He turns and walks fast, out of the room.

Lucky for him, Jose is just hanging up the telephone. "Sorry about that," the man says to Justin. "Now let's go see your dad." He puts a gentle hand on Justin's back, guiding him. "He's in the room at the end of the hall."

"Are you a doctor?" Justin asks, as they walk.

The man laughs. "No. I'm an aide. Where I come from, I used to be a doctor. Here, I have to go back to college and take some more classes."

Justin nods his head. "You can go to the U of O."

"Maybe." The man smiles and points his finger. "There's your dad, waiting for you."

His dad is sitting in the wheelchair at the end of the hallway, just two doors away. As Justin gets closer, his dad shifts forward in the wheelchair as if he wants to leap out of it. "Hey, bud," he says. Something about the way he says it, makes Justin think about the old woman in the room down the hall.

"Dad." Justin rushes forward. Dad's arms wrap around him, strong and safe as ever.

###

RATTLEBONES

KATHIE OLSEN

He is lounging next to me in the car, passenger seat pushed far away from the dashboard to accommodate his long legs and bare bony feet. We are quiet together. The car carries us smoothly along the interstate, early morning light illuminating the tops of the trees, catching the occasional floating hawk. We pass huge hulking trucks as they strain and pull themselves up the mountains.

I glance over at him, his skull resting easily against the neck rest, hands open on his knees, long fingernails curving gracefully as they make dents in his baggy trousers, faded red cravat hanging loose, suspenders on bone.

I'm used to him but surely tired of his being here. He has been with me for a long time. About fifteen years. When I first met him, I was scared, and frantically tried to make him leave. Back then, I knew that he had come for my father, a gentle humanist who deserved more time. Rattlebones ignored me then, just as he does now.

Daddy had been racked with an unquenchable fever and the inability to eat for several days. My sisters, my mother, my aunties, uncles and cousins and I took turns at his bedside, begging and pleading and bargaining for mercy, offering up whatever comfort we could to Daddy and to each other. We sang soothing lullabies to help him rest and heal, we massaged his legs, applied cooling cloths. But he just kept slipping farther and farther away, our hearts and songs straining to reach him as his ears heard less and less. I was watching carefully and so I saw the moment when Rattlebones hoisted Daddy up and took him away. Daddy's face, already ashen, suddenly transformed into something else – a husk, an empty satchel. He was gone. Rattlebones had simply taken him. All the force of our loving had been unable to stop it.

My Dad was the first of his generation. I assumed, with the naiveté of the young, that the next death would be the next oldest. That was not the case and thus I began to learn that Rattlebones doesn't pick and choose in that way.

The next death was that of a good friend, a woman my own age, the mother of two robust and just launched sons. She was worrying over her boys, still too young, still unmarried and not settled. She was not ready to leave and refused to even discuss the possibility of death. As she slipped farther and farther into her illness – legs swollen like balloons, less and less able to focus -- we brought her soup and flowers and our own desperate hope. In return, she smiled and greeted us with love. Every morning she woke up from a night of pain and fear and joyously greeted the new dawn with gratitude for getting another day. She fiercely held to every minute of life. But her courage, and our determination didn't alter the course. Rattlebones came anyway. For weeks he sat waiting in the corner of her bedroom, idly looking at the chintz and the flowers and the beautiful art on the walls, occasionally examining those long fingernails of his, ignoring our human wailings. Just waiting. And then, at 2:18 one afternoon, he just up and took her, leaving us with her husk and her house full of things, slipping away with her, without even a hiss.

I began to hate him and his arrogant taking. As I helped to pack up my friends household goods, I felt bitterness and confusion: What kind of rotten timing sense did he have, anyway? How did *he* know when it was or wasn't time? If he was going to take people, why not take them at the *beginning* of the suffering? And why didn't he leave the good people and take the bad? Or at least why couldn't he wait until those of us who were left felt ready to let go? There were no answers, of course. Rattlebones could care less about my angst. He answered to no one, remaining an independent, capricious, unfathomable creature.

Needless to say, we got to spend time with each other anyway. Over the next few years several of my beloveds died in rapid succession. First it was an uncle, then an aunt, then another aunt, then a young friend, another uncle, then the infant son of a neighbor. Rattlebones just kept showing up, picking and choosing at his ease. I stopped being surprised, stopped the theatrics, helped to tend to the dying before his taking-away, clearing up afterwards. I became a pillar of strength and efficiency.

One day, in the midst of all this dying, as I watched a good friend fight against a cancer that grew and flourished and ate away at her guts, I realized that Rattlebones had simply moved in. I began to fear for those who came near to me, personalizing his curse, thinking it was idiosyncratic. Thinking if you touched me too closely, you'd die. He had just been too present.

Standing in her kitchen one summer evening, I shared my fear with a wise friend of mine. She leaned her skinny eighty year old body against the counter as she poured our tea and told me calmly to brace myself, this would just get worse with time. It happens to everybody as they age, I should get used to it. "It's perfectly okay to grieve. Part of life, you know," she said. "But you grieve, and then you move on. Everything that lives, dies eventually. It's just how it is. Get used to it."

And so on this day, as the morning unfolds and the car moves up the highway, I look at him out of the corner of my eye and shrug. Of course he's here. His vacant sockets are pointed at me. He appears to be smiling. He is totally comfortable.

But I'm troubled. Right now, at this very minute there are two people that I love who want to live but who are dying, and there are two people I love who have lost themselves to dementia and who should be dying but aren't. This is horribly wrong. I think about it for about two seconds and then I will him to leave. I'm furious with him. My gorge rises. His sense of timing isn't just off, it's criminal. I feel grief and anger roaring up out of my soul.

He ignores my mounting rage, my human emotions, and enjoys the warmth of the early morning sun, looking at his fingernails or out the window of the car, languidly rolling his head from side to side, with that stupid toothy grin on his skull. He's not going away. He's always been here and always will be. I don't bother him at all.

I lose it. Pulling the car over to the side of the road, I feel my body wracked with all those repressed sobs. I scream at him to get the hell out of my car, finally burying my face in my arms on the steering wheel and wailing. My entire chest hurts. I cry until I'm all dried up.

Rattlebones has ignored me. I blow my nose and mop my eyes. I'm tired. I look around at the cars whizzing past. I pour tea from my thermos take a sip and then a deep shuddering breath.

Starting the car, I pull back onto the road and we continue on through the beautiful morning. I have a meeting to attend in a distant city and I begin to idly think about it as I sip my tea. The sun continues to rise. Rattlebones lolls, and suddenly turns his head towards his window, watching with interest as a squirrel runs across a telephone wire. Poor old squirrel.

###

HARD RAIN
ANNE BATZER

Vanessa noticed the reflection of her arm on the shiny surface of the attorney's desk as she reached across it to hand him the divorce papers. The quick glimpse gave her confidence. Her hand, with its neatly squared acrylic nails, her wrist, with the sterling silver watch just visible beneath the crisp white linen cuff and pearl button, created just the impression she wanted. *An accurate impression* she thought.

Before leaving for this appointment, Vanessa had carefully polished two bright copper pennies and pushed them into the slots on her chestnut loafers. Her burgundy sweater seemed just a bit large, so she belted it before slipping into her navy blazer. Finally, she plucked an errant eyebrow and smoothed her hair, tucking one unruly strand behind her ear.

She'd gathered the files she'd spent three months researching and preparing. Her first thought had been to simply find the do-it-yourself divorce forms on-line and submit them. She knew she was as capable as any lawyer. No detail would escape her.

And after her exhaustive research, filling out the forms had been easy. With her accurate financial records she could account for every dollar she and David had earned, spent and saved in their six years together. Of course she wanted to be fair, to split their money exactly in half, then sell the house and share the profit. She knew dividing the furniture would be the hard part. One activity she and David enjoyed together was antiquing. They had some special pieces, all from the Victorian era. The furniture placement had taken her a long time, but finally, after she carefully considered scale, each piece had found its ideal spot. She winced when she thought of moving any of it. She quickly comforted herself with the fact that they had two cars, compact Toyotas of equal value, so no problem there.

She'd chosen her lawyer from the yellow pages. She avoided calling those whose ads showed photographs of themselves leaning on their desks with shirtsleeves rolled-up or dressed in jeans and fleeces out on hiking trails. Instead, she felt immediately comfortable with a firm whose ad had information in elegant script and lots of white space.

"I think you will find everything is in order, Mr. Connors," Vanessa said to the attorney as he began to read the files she handed him. She waited patiently while he took his time perusing the material.

"This is the most professional and organized presentation I've ever seen," the lawyer said. He looked up and smiled at Vanessa. "I've never said this before to any client," he went on, "but truly, I don't think you need me."

"Oh, yes I do," Vanessa said.

"I understand," Mr. Connors said, "Your husband is contesting the divorce. You can't come to agreement."

"I don't know," Vanessa said.

"You mean you don't know which part of this agreement he's contesting?"

"I mean I don't know how he's going to feel about being divorced," Vanessa said.

"Well what has he said to you about it?"

Vanessa briefly bit her lower lip. She raised her eyes to meet Mr. Connors'.

"I've never mentioned it to him," she said. "I want you to tell him."

Mr. Connors leaned back in his desk chair and put his hands behind his head. He stretched and sighed. Vanessa thought his posture was highly unprofessional. She thought she may have made a wrong choice in attorneys, but her eye landed on his law school diploma in its expensive gold frame hanging above a huge, tastefully-lit globe and she relaxed.

"Have you thought about seeing a counselor? You know, someone who could help you talk about this?" Mr. Connors asked.

"That's not an option," Vanessa replied.

"Yeah, I know," Mr. Connors said, "a lot of men just aren't comfortable going to counselors."

Vanessa looked at him. "I mean it's not an option for me," she said.

"Oh. I'm just trying to understand here. This is just so unusual. You've obviously put a lot of time in getting your divorce information together. So…I assume you must be separated."

"Oh, no," Vanessa said. "Actually I'm meeting David for lunch after this appointment."

"So you've reached a truce, huh?" Mr. Connors leaned forward putting his hands on his desk. "You're getting along."

"Oh, we get along," Vanessa said. "We've always gotten along okay. I just don't want to be married to him anymore. I have standards."

"So he's broken his wedding vows," Mr. Connors stated.

Vanessa reddened. "It's nothing like that," she said.

Vanessa thought about the first time she met David. It was at a college friend's formal wedding. David was the best man. He'd looked impeccable in his tux, his hair cropped short, his skin acne-free. When Vanessa learned he was an accountant, she'd felt instantly attracted. Her former boyfriend was a graphic designer and it made her dizzy to go into his office. Papers everywhere, files in stacks on the floor, yellowing notes pinned to a huge corkboard. She tried to overlook it, and for a while she almost did, but finally she lost respect. She moved on.

The first time Vanessa and David made love it reminded her of the Christmas holiday when she'd finished a thousand-piece jigsaw puzzle. Everything fit. No awkward, extraneous parts. And when completed, the symmetrical scene stretching out before her perfectly matched the picture on the front of the puzzle's box. Promise fulfilled. Two weeks later she asked him to marry her.

"I have to tell you," Mr. Connors interrupted her thoughts, "I've had clients who surprised their spouses by serving them with divorce papers and I don't recommend it. When it gets down to negotiating a settlement the going gets tough, and the rancor often continues for years after the legalities are finalized. Why set yourself up for that?"

"I thought you could make an appointment with him and just tell him I want a divorce," Vanessa said.

"Unless he's a violent man, or you're afraid of him…is that it, are you?" Mr. Connors asked.

"Oh no, David's not violent," Vanessa said.

"Then I have to advise you to talk to him first, then come see me." Mr. Connors stood and held out his right hand to her. Vanessa's eyes fell on the perfect half-moons shining through his hygienic fingernails under carefully-clipped cuticles. She slowly shook his hand, then turned and walked out the door of his office.

After she left, Mr. Connors was surprised he had trouble concentrating on his work. Vanessa's prim tailoring and precise grooming reminded him of something. As a boy he'd spent hours sitting on the dusty floor of his mother's closet leafing through her Smith College yearbook. He loved examining the straight rows of photos in the heavy book, unaware of his oedipal impulses.

Hard rain was slanting down from the sky when Vanessa stepped outside. She pulled a pleated rain hat from her purse and molded it to the contours of her hairdo. She always thought briefly about her mother when she wore these. Vanessa had inherited the family crystal and the fine bone china when her mother died. While she enjoyed displaying the dishes, and felt great satisfaction during the hour-and-a-half she spent dusting them each Saturday morning, she most appreciated the seven plastic rain hats she'd found tucked into the satin divider in her mother's underwear drawer. It didn't bother Vanessa at all that the head coverings had been discontinued soon after her mother purchased them decades earlier on sale at Woolworth's.

When she walked into the restaurant where she was meeting David, she removed the rain hat and glanced in the mirror behind the bar. She was pleased that her hair looked exactly as it had when she'd left home, as if no time had passed. Vanessa was just as determined that no weather would alter her appearance as she was that no experience would change her perceptions.

When Vanessa was seated, David arrived. She watched with aversion as a raindrop slid off the bridge of his tortoise-shell glasses, trickled down the end of his nose and fell on his tie. David ignored it. He used a wrinkled handkerchief to mop the rest of the rainwater from his face and then blew his nose.

Vanessa ordered her usual: black tea with lemon, a raw spinach salad with low-fat thousand island dressing on the side and a whole-wheat roll without butter. She raised an eyebrow when David decided on the bacon cheeseburger with fries. *Fries* she thought.

She barely listened as David began telling her about a disagreement he was having with his boss. But Vanessa couldn't help but notice David was genuinely upset by his boss's tepid response to his attempts to work things out. This was evidence to her that David would be terribly upset by the news she wanted a divorce. She again promised herself she would not be the one to tell him. Messy, unpredictable conversations bored her. She returned her thoughts to Mr. Connors.

When David relaxed and leaned back in his chair, the four-and-a-half pounds he'd gained since their wedding were painfully obvious to Vanessa. A just-perceptible roll lay above his belt buckle. But worse, his chinos were now a bit too tight and when he sat down an unappetizing bulge emerged from his crotch. Divorce or no, Vanessa vowed to pick–up a couple pair of pleated khakis in a larger size for David's birthday gift. It was the least she could do.

After they ate, David leaned over and gave Vanessa's hand a quick pat before he hurriedly left to return to work. She didn't turn her head to watch him leave the restaurant.

Like a re-wind of an old family movie, Vanessa traced her steps back to Mr. Connors' office. His secretary was still at lunch, so she knocked on his office door and removed her pleated rain hat, confident her hair was in place. Because of the tight, tidy knock, Mr. Connors suspected it was Vanessa returning. He slipped his left hand into his sports coat pocket and slid his wedding ring off before reaching to open the door

As he greeted her she glanced past him, her eyes landing on the soft, auburn leather of his 9-foot sofa. *Perfect* she thought. Mr. Connors accepted Vanessa's wet trench coat and hung it on the hook behind his door. Vanessa strode over to the sofa and put her divorce files on the steel-and-glass coffee table. She sat down and turned to face him.

A wordless Mr. Connors joined her on the couch. Finally, he broke the silence.

"Have you had second thoughts?" he asked

Vanessa's cool gaze warmed slightly. She looked him in the eye.

"Not a single one," she said.

Mr. Connors slipped his fingers around Vanessa's belt and pulled her closer to him. She took her glasses off and put them on the coffee table next to her divorce files. When Mr. Connors had removed all of Vanessa's clothing--- and then, somewhat more urgently, his own---he lay down on the sofa, sliding smoothly over its plush surface.

He pulled Vanessa up on top of him. *Without even asking* she thought. Mr. Connors reached his left hand up and cupped Vanessa's rectangular, pointy breast. She felt something then. A rough callous at the base of his ring finger. *Married* she thought.

There was a little blip in Vanessa's narrow radar. She considered Mr. Connors' wife, wondered if he had children. Then, David's clean, fresh face came into her mind. But like so many other times in Vanessa's life, she sloughed these thoughts as easily as she had the rain.

She glanced down and the uneven zig-zagging of her breasts as she and Mr. Connors moved together distracted her. She moved her gaze to Mr. Connors' hands, now pushing into her thighs. Finally, her eyes rested on the symmetry of the bright half-moons shimmering beneath his fingernails.

When he had finished, Mr. Connors smiled broadly at her. He sat up and reached for her divorce files.

"Well," he said, "I'll be glad to call your husband and give him the news about his pending divorce."

Vanessa reached for her 100% cotton underpants and sighed with satisfaction.

###

HOT AS BLAZES

FAYEGAIL MANDELL BISACCIA

The Preacher

Elianne's stayin' in a shack out behin' the furthest shed on the Ainsley place. They don' mess with her. She hardly ever leaves. People bring her food and whatever else she needs. She don' like too many people knowin' where she is. Ever' once in a while she up and moves to another place. I don' like it that she's gotta hide out from the law. Don' seem right. But then she says she's gotta keep movin' to keep doin' God's work, and who am I to criticize her for that? She's a healer, awright.

And she does do God's work, that's apparent. I was preachin' at a revival one Sunday, and things got goin' real good. Sometimes somebody'll keel over and not get up. Most of 'em just find the Lord and walk on out of there, healed. Leave their crutches behin', leave their rashes behin', throw their glasses on the groun'. But then, there'll be one who just can't open his heart to the Lord. There they be, just lyin' on the groun' and nobody to help 'em up. So I get one a the brothers to help me load 'em into the back o' my pickup, and I carry 'em on over to Elianne, wherever she's stayin' at the time.

This one Sunday, there was an ol' man, skinny as anybody I ever seen. He wore a ragged shirt and pants from an old suit, but his boots were brand new. He was hangin' around the edge of that revival tent lookin' hungry. Wouldn't come in, though. I never seen him before that day.

I come out of the tent after the service, and there he was. Power of the Lord musta knocked him clean over.

I took him out to Elianne. God helps her in ways I don' understan'. Just reaches right in through her hands and heals 'em. Nobody ever leaves her the way they come in.

Got to Elianne's place and honked my horn. She called off 'er dogs and come out to the gate. Tol' me to help 'er get 'im inside. He was still out cold. By the time we got 'im onto 'er table, he were comin' aroun'. He opened 'is yaller eyes, and we could see he was wild. Crazy, like. Sat right up. Wanted to know where he was. I tol' 'im he was with a healer an' he lay back down. He was starin' straight ahead. Didn't say nothin' else. Shut his eyes after awhile.

Elianne put 'er hands out to work on 'im and snatched 'em right away agin. I looked at 'er.

"He's hot as blazes," she said.

"Sweet Jesus! Must have the Devil in 'im," I told her. "Better clear him out."

She got herself all ready, the way she does when somebody's real bad, an' reached out to try agin.

***

Elianne

Name's Elianne. I've done healing work for years. Energy work. People come. I never advertise. They just show up. "Alma sent me," they say, or Leroy or Lester or Mary Louise. Nobody in the Town Hall knows just what I do. Not officially. They wouldn't like it. I have no business license, no certificates on my wall proclaiming that I know what I'm doing.

But I do know. I do what my mother did, what my granny did, and her mother. We are a healing family.

One Sunday the preacher drove up to my gate and waited while I called off the dogs. He had a fellow with him in the back of the truck, passed out. We pulled him out, and the preacher helped me carry him into my back room and put him on the table.

He had on a tattered green shirt with ripped blue slacks, and brand new boots. White hair to the shoulders and lean as a hickory pole. He was an odd one. As we set him down, he awoke. He sat straight up and glanced around the room, anxious like. "Where am I?" he wanted to know. I saw his wild eyes. They were nearly yellow. I could see he was strung up tight as the skin on a tambourine.

"You're with a healer," the preacher told him.

He looked me in the eye and lay back down on the table. His arms were stiff at his sides, and his eyes stared straight ahead. I put on my smock, centered myself and stood at his side, ready to work. I reached out my arms, one hand above his face, the other above his belly, feeling for his energy. I jerked my hands away. They burned like fire.

He shifted his position and the buttonless cuff on his sleeve fell open. It was then I saw the numbers tattooed on his arm.

###

PATIENCE GOES TO THE VET

SHARON SCHAEFER

The smiling aide held the door and we passed into the freshly painted exam room. "Doesn't look like Dear Dr. Briskey's exam room back home." Mother sniffed in disapproval.

"You're right, this one is much cleaner," I replied, and gave the cat carrier to the aide. Mother hadn't lived "at home" in five years, but time had erased all bad memories and anything "back home" was always much better.

"Oh aren't you the fussy one." The aide trilled in the voice people use on animals, small children and dotty old ladies. I hoped she was talking to the cat. I glanced at her face, guilty as charged, but indeed she was speaking to Patience, Mother's overfed, spoiled and now very cranky cat.

Mother bent to examine a poster of kittens romping in some yarn as I sat down and began unwrapping the kitchen towel from my arm. "Be careful with my little darling," she cautioned the aide who was lifting the growling but unresisting Patience from the carrier.

Mother's little darling is a long-haired black and white tomcat with attitude. Patience spends his days leaving long globs of hair on the furniture, snubbing his food and his nights prowling the neighborhood looking for trouble. As near as I can tell the only patience around is what you need if you want to live with him.

I surreptitiously examined the scratches and tooth marks on my arm as the aide poked a thermometer into the furry nether regions under Patience's tail. Mother hovered over the two murmuring soothing noises.

The aide was a tall woman with wide shoulders and hips and a faint mustache. She was wearing what appeared to be pajamas made out of flowered sofa material. Large pink peonies on a pale blue background. Interesting combination.

A continuous low growl from the insulted cat distracted me from further examination of my ravaged arm. "Do you have to do that?" Mother asked the aide. "Patience isn't used to being mistreated."

The aide was leaning on the furry body with an arm the size of a fence post clutching the unhappy cat's tail. "Did you say something, dear? I'm afraid I can't hear a thing over this little darling's complaints."

Mother shook her head and sat beside me and began shedding her go-to-the-Vet outfit. She has seen the re-runs of the TV show featuring a Scots Veterinarian. She knows that a plaid wool cape, rubber boots and an ugly tweed suit from Goodwill constitute the proper attire. She was very sad not to find a Tam O'Shanter, but she had substituted a yellow sou'wester worn low and tilted over her brow. She actually looked quite jaunty, if a little off center fashion wise.

Mother reached over and poked at one of the puncture wounds on my arm. "My, my, he did get a nip in didn't he?" She tsked, "You should have been more careful when putting him in the carrier. You startled him, cats know when they are in danger." She sat back in her chair with a look of confirmed suspicion on her face. She crossed her legs and straightened her sou'wester. "He simply thought you were going to harm him."

"Of course I startled him. He was hiding behind the sofa after a chase through the house," I replied. "Remember when I finally caught him and I was ready to put him in the carrier, and you couldn't decide what color of blanket to keep him company?"

Mother pretended to examine the floral wall-paper, but I could tell she was listening by the way she was impatiently jiggling her upper most boot-clad foot. "Well, that's when he decided to use my arm as a chew toy."

She sighed. "Patience prefers blue, but sometimes yellow settles him down. I just couldn't decide with all that yelling and swearing you were doing."

The aide removed the thermometer, squinted at the numbers and dropped it into a basin by the sink. "No fever," she cheerfully reported. Lifting the surprised Patience by the scruff of the neck, she sat him gently in the tray of a baby scale. I waited in anticipation for him to leap to her throat, but the traitor just sat there glaring.

"Now let's see how heavy you are. My goodness, thirteen pounds. You are a big boy aren't you?"

"What do you mean by saying my 'goodness?'" Mother leapt up and asked in a voice verging on hysteria. "Is that bad?" She raised her hands to the ceiling in supplication. "Oh I knew I shouldn't have switched from the tuna to regular cat food."

Startled by the sudden outburst, the aide hastily explained that she was joking. "He is a little over weight, but carries it nicely." She petted Patience, who was living up to his name for a change. He seemed to like sitting in the tray of the baby scale. "Now you all just relax for a minute while I go and get Dr. McIntyre."

No one relaxed, feline nor human while the door slowly closed with an ominous click. That click was like a starting pistol for Patience. He shot off the baby scale with the precision of a downhill racer, and went directly to the baseboard of the cabinet. He obviously could see from his vantage point a space approximately the size of the eye of a needle. He squeezed his hairy body into it and disappeared. This activity took place in the blink of an eye. If it weren't for the tip of a tail peeking out we wouldn't have believed there had ever been a cat in the room. If there ever is an animal Olympics, I'm sure Patience will win in the escape cat-a-gory. Pun intended.

Mother and I sat stunned by the event. She recovered before I did. "How are you going to get him out of there?"

Before I could unlock my jaw for an appropriate reply, the door opened and a miniature woman popped in. "I'm Dr. McIntyre." A woman with a size two shoe, long shiny black hair surrounding beautiful almond shaped eyes, is not your stereotypical veterinarian. She had a tiny white doctor's coat on with her name carefully embroidered on the pocket, so I had to accept the evidence.

"Where is the patient?" she asked in a no-nonsense voice. Like a pair of mimes, we pointed in unison at the tail tip. The doctor reached down and with a quick thrust grabbed Patience's tail and pulled the very surprised cat out of his hiding place. She had that cat out and up on the exam table in even less time than he had taken to get into his refuge. What a team they would make in the animal Olympics.

Patience seemed bewildered and strangely docile. Dr. McIntyre rolled him around and felt him everywhere with her tiny deft hands. He made no protest until she found a sore spot on his left hip, and he yowled.

Not the ear-piercing yowls he had given when I attempted to put him in the carrier, but a dainty little that's-the-place yowl. "Ah, it seems that this big boy has been enjoying a love life. She glanced at us. "When cats are showing an interest in each other, the female often rebuffs the male with a bite in the butt." She turned back and continued to prod the cat, whispering sweet words to him.

I must say my eye brows shot up to my hairline when this porcelain face doll of a Veterinarian said the b-word. I slid a quick glance at Mother, the queen of euphemisms. Believe me she would never have tolerated that word out of my mouth. Butts were "fannies" or "behinds". In an extreme case, if you were a complete dolt, you might say "bottom". But Mother seemed completely bamboozled by this whole chain of events. In the sixty plus years I've been her daughter, I've never seen her speechless for such a long period of time. I tried to remember the symptoms of a stroke.

She shook herself and broke the spell. "But Patience has been fixed. He surely wouldn't be interested in" . . . She was at a loss for the correct word, "would he?" she floundered on.

Dr. McIntyre drew herself up to her full four- foot eleven self and cuddled Patience to her chest. "Who told you Patience had been neutered?" she asked in an imperious voice. Before Mother could answer, the Doctor held up Patience' tail and showed her the evidence.

I don't know who was the most insulted, Mother or the cat. I made a production of fishing in my pocket for a tissue so she couldn't see my face. It's hard not to laugh out loud when you need to.

The upshot of the whole affair resulted in Patience' incarceration for the night to attend to all of his problems.

Mother was quiet as we made our way to the car. "It's close to lunch time, want to go out?" she asked in a half-hearted way as she slung her cape around her shoulders.

I couldn't resist. "What's the matter? Did the doctor's language get to you, or are you upset that Dear Doctor Briskey charged you for something he didn't do?"

61

Mother stiffened and set her mouth into the now-you-have-done it moue. "How other people talk is none of our affair. We can only be responsible for our own behavior." She straightened her skirt and fastened her seat belt. "Just take me home. I need an aspirin and a nap. It's been a difficult morning."

We drove home in an eerie silence, and I was beginning to have second thoughts about teasing her. After all she loves that cat, even if I don't.

When we pulled up to her apartment, I stopped the car and touched her shoulder. "Mother, Patience will be OK. I don't think you need to worry."

She unfastened her seat belt and opened the door. "Oh don't be silly. I know Patience is in good hands. I was thinking about the letter I plan to write to that awful Dr. Briskey." She looked at me. "You better put some hydrogen peroxide on those scratches."

She got out and slammed the door. Setting her shoulders, she marched off. Head high and regal in her tweeds.

###

LEAVING

FAYEGAIL MANDELL BISACCIA

Lights flicker in their brass candlesticks. The blessings have been chanted, private prayers quietly spoken. The window catches light and bathes their faces in golden shadows. It is their last *Shabbos* together. On Sunday morning, Raisel will leave with her husband's family for America.

Sisters. Shayna's baby sister. Always, since Shayna watched her birth, watched her issue yowling from her mother's woman place, she has loved Raisel. The midwife gave Shayna the swaddled child to hold in her five-year-old arms, sweet smell of blood and dainty scent of baby skin fresh in her nostrils. Twenty-three years, and now they will be separate, they who have been inseparable.

Shayna watches the flickering candles. She shifts her glance, and from across the table Raisel catches her eye. Tears mirror her own, slip down the soft pink cheeks. Raisel shifts her attention to her daughter's dark curls, pats her head, twists a curl around her finger, as she sometimes does when she is deep in thought.

Memorize this scene, Shayna tells herself. *The curve of the neck, the tilt of the head, the pensive face as she fondles her daughter's hair. Remember her white* Shabbos *dress, pulled tight across her budding belly. Don't think that you will never know this child that grows within her.*

Shayna serves the dinner—cabbage borscht, roast chicken, kasha *varnishkas,* carrot *tsimmes.* All their favorite dishes. She has used her secret money for this meal, the money she has set aside. She wants Raisel to remember the abundance of her table, that Shayna has honored her family. It is a quiet meal. The children murmur and tease. The husbands speak of the impending voyage. The women sit silent.

Finally, the men arise and thank Shayna for the meal. Raisel and her children follow her husband across the courtyard to their rooms, as they will soon follow him to the other side of the sea.

Shayna clears away the meal. She tries to read, but has no patience, and she climbs into bed. She hears the hoot of an owl in the night. Her husband Reuven comes to her. Embraces her. Holds her gently. Kisses her tears, the secret place below her ear, the hollow of her shoulder. Making love on *Shabbos* is especially sweet, and she surrenders to his tenderness.

Saturday morning Raisel hurries across the courtyard. She carries, wrapped in her apron, one brass candlestick.

"Shaynaleh," she says. "Take this candlestick and give me one of yours. Think of me when you light candles. Remember me on *Shabbos*. Keep me close to you until we meet again."

***

Shayna twists an unruly gray curl around her finger. She leans against the sill to watch the sun set behind the New York skyline. She thinks of Raisel, as she always does at candle-lighting time. She turns from the window and smiles at her husband. She lights the candles, sings the blessing, says her private prayers in silence. Reuven chants the Sabbath blessing over wine. They sip and are grateful for the abundance of their life in America. Shayna watches Reuven lift the cover from the *challah*, sacred braided bread which weaves together God and Man and *Mitzvah.* They chant.

> *Blessed are you,*
> *O Source of Light,*
> *Who, with the effort of humankind,*
> *Brings forth bread from the earth.*

They have indeed made an effort. They labored in America, in the garment industry, saved when they could, invested, reaped the fruit of their commitment to their family. And now their children, Ruthie and David, both out in California, have all they need, and more. They are Americans, wear fancy clothes, walk out with friends, have children of their own.

Reuven looks at her and smiles.

"Shaynaleh," he says.

Shayna watches the candles flickering in the brass candlesticks, the ones she brought with her to America in the springtime of her life. One was hers, one was Raisel's. So many years ago. She has forgotten which was which. She has both sets now.

Raisel died of influenza six months after she arrived in New York, poor soul. Her whole family, gone. They never knew that Shayna and Reuven were already making plans to come to them the following year.

Shayna has both sets now, but she always uses one of each.

"Keep me close until we meet again," said Raisel.

###

The Woman Next Door

Anne Batzer

The woman who lived in the house next door is Syrian. Her name is beautiful and exotic, some syllables you glide over, like watercolors; others you pounce on, staccato dots on fine linen paper.

Every morning at 6:00 am she walked her dogs. Golden labs called Rose and Iris, they have the air of "animal companions" pampered as only the pets of childless couples are, sleek, well-behaved, confident. When I decided to join her one morning, my Aussie shep was a stark contrast. For years, my kids fed him scraps under the table. He was allowed to climb on furniture. There was never time enough to remove the burrs from his underbelly. He's shaggy and likes to rub his rump on your leg in hopes you'll pet his back. I pretend this isn't disgusting.

We walked together up the dirt country road that connects our homes. She's thirty years younger than me, just starting out. Emergency room doctors, she and her husband Jim met in medical school.

That first morning, I think it was two years ago, it was February and the sun had not risen above the ridge. Three owls, forming a wide triangle hidden in the high ponderosas, carried on a conversation, the sound seeming to come from the depths of the dank grey sky above us.

"Good morning," I said as our steps fell in sync. I yanked on my dog's leash to keep him from toppling her.

She smiled but said nothing, then nodded in the direction of the owl talk, as if she were afraid of interrupting their train of thought. We walked a mile-and-a-half in quiet witness to the exchange. When the sun's first rays pierced the blue expanse, the owls fell silent.

"What do you think they talk about?" I asked her.

"It seems like something important," she answered. "Pearls of wisdom we need to know. For weeks, I've been trying to figure it out." She paused and smiled at me, "But their secrets are safe, lost in translation."

I laughed, but I remember we finished that walk in silence.

***

Days passed; daylight came earlier and our conversations grew livelier. As we walked, her long black hair kept rhythm, swinging from side-to-side. In the way of women, we shared our stories. She'd grown up in the Middle East. A medical school scholarship brought her to this country, where she'd settled. About once a year she returned to the city of Homs to spend time with her mother and brother.

The first time she talked about her childhood, I confess I hurried home and Googled Syria, embarrassed that I couldn't place it on a map. I knew it was near Iraq, where the war raged on; and Egypt, where there were the first stirrings of what would later be called Arab Spring.

While she was gone visiting her Syrian family, I continued the morning walks, collecting Rose and Iris from their fenced yard. They kept a steady pace while my dog strained against the leash to pursue every random scent.

On his days off, her husband Jim would be out in the driveway hitching his riverboat to his truck or putting his hunting rifles in its gun rack. He had made a name for himself as the local head of Ducks Unlimited, often quoted in the outdoor column in the newspaper. Always busy.

"What do you hear from your wife?" I asked him one morning.

"Not much, brief emails," he said. I never could figure out how to get a conversation going with him.

When the woman returned from her visit she pulled a faded paper package tied with black string from her jacket pocket. "For you," she said.

My cold fingers unwrapped the gift and a glorious swath of silk unfurled. The long scarf was striped with rich shades of magenta and one simple gold streak. My dog became immediately alert, his knob of a tail perfectly still, he sniffed its musty, odd aroma. I pulled the scarf across my back and around my shoulders, out of canine range. Its colors clashed with the subtle greens and grays of the rural Oregon landscape.

"It must be so different there," I said.

"Yes and no," she answered. "It's ancient and poetic, a country full of beauty," she stopped walking, turned and looked at me, "but the people there are just like me.

"Educated. Strong. Exactly like me."

**

One June as we stopped to gaze at a field of wheat, catching its moment of transition from green to gold, she said, "I long to have a child." I smiled at her, delighted, imagining a tawny, black-eyed baby in a front pack on our morning walks. "But Jim says he's not ready."

"It's a big decision," I said.

"Friends tell me to just go ahead and get pregnant." She looked at me to check out my reaction. "That once the baby's here he'll adjust---he'll be a good father."

I tried not to look horrified.

"But I don't think I should do that to him," she continued.

"Good," I said. "A baby's a big responsibility. I think you're wise to wait until you're both ready."

"Yeah. Tell me, what's it really like to be a mother?"

I turned and looked at her. How do you answer this? How do you describe this alternate universe where everything, except yourself, takes on more meaning. Where heart and longing and fear expand? Where you see yourself barely apart, as if you lived in bas relief?

"It's not for everyone," I said, "but I think you would love it."

That June morphed into full-blown summer. We walked right through it and the following winter. She never mentioned wanting a child again. But that year brought a change in her. She walked more slowly, she gained weight. She cut her hair to shoulder length. Finally, I broached the subject with her.

"Have you and Jim thought more about having a baby?"

"He still says he's not ready. I don't know if he ever will be. It would interrupt his hunting and fishing."

***

And the news from Syria was bleak. Revolution, celebrated in Egypt, was not going well. People were dying. "What do you hear from your family?" I asked her. "Are they okay? What do they say?"

"They say they're fine," she said. There was a long pause. "But then what else can they say? It wouldn't be safe for them to send me any other message."

"What about you? What can I do to help?"

"Remember," she said, "I've told you I'm strong."

One morning when I went to meet her, she wasn't there. I walked to where Rose and Iris paced in their fenced yard. Jim came out of the house, carrying two fishing poles and a tackle box.

"Hi, where is she?"

"She went home," he said.

"What? To Syria? It's dangerous, right?"

"That's what I told her, but she wouldn't listen." He paused. "Now she doesn't answer my emails."

She's never answered my emails either.

###

Myrtle Gray

Fayegail Mandell Bisaccia

Myrtle heard the cat mewing at the baby gate. She couldn't stand it when the cat jumped on her in the middle of the night. She opened one eye and tried to focus on the bedside clock. Six-forty-five. No, it was still dark outside. Five-forty-five. Yes. Five-forty-five. That crazy cat. She never does well when the seasons change. "Well, neither do I," said Myrtle aloud. Didn't matter that she spoke aloud at five-forty-five a.m. Edgar had been gone for thirteen years, and she'd never invited anyone into her bed in all that time.

Myrtle shifted a little in the bed, testing. Stiffness in the lower spine, left hip achy. She reached out to turn on the lamp. Oh, dear. A twinge in the right shoulder. Funny, she thought. After all these years, I'm still sleeping on my own side of the bed. I know I ought to read with the light coming over my left shoulder.

She looked at her right hand, still resting on top of the comforter. People used to say her hands were beautiful. Long, tapered fingers, strong nails with perfect moons, smooth white skin.

Now look at them. Fingers twisted, knuckles thick. She had her wedding ring cut off last January. Thumb red and the base of it swollen. Myrtle stifled a yawn and resumed her examination. Look at the nails, all peeling and ridged. Zinc deficiency, someone told her last week at the book circle. She'd meant to buy some tablets last time she went to the pharmacy.

The cat was crying again. Myrtle supposed she'd dozed off. Oh, dear. Seven-thirty. "Well, Jezebel, you *are* entitled to some breakfast," she said, and eased herself over onto her right side. She bent her knees, just the way the physical therapist had taught her, and used her left hand to push herself up onto her right elbow. Another twinge in the shoulder.

Myrtle pushed herself up to sitting and let her legs down over the side of the bed. Her toes touched the tops of her slippers, and she wiggled them into the soft plush. Lean over, push against the bed with both hands, onto her feet and straighten up, as best she could. Good. Her knees held. That was always the question. She knew she should keep the walker near the bed, just in case they didn't hold, but she hated looking at it. Better to keep it in the closet for the really bad days than to have to look at it all the time.

Myrtle inched along the side of the bed and over to the door. She took down the baby gate and Jez dashed for her favorite spot next to the heater. Myrtle liked sleeping with the heat on. She wasn't quite so achy in the morning when the room stayed warm. She made her way to the bathroom and leaned against the counter. She eased herself down onto the toilet and relieved herself. She was grateful the bathroom was small.

Teeth next. She picked up her new toothbrush. Her caregiver Jenny had brought it over yesterday. It had one of those thick handles, and was easier to use than the old one. Myrtle squeezed the toothpaste onto the brush from the special dispenser. "Nice how many gadgets they've come up with lately," she said to the old woman in the mirror. "Mother didn't have such conveniences when she was my age."

Myrtle finished brushing her teeth and reached for the blue hand towel. Ouch! Pain sliced through her left knee and left her wilted over the sink and breathing hard. Damn! "Why can't you remember to lift up the foot before you turn," she chided herself. "You mustn't distract yourself with old-woman thoughts."

Myrtle heard a key turn in the front door lock. She straightened up and composed her face. She turned toward the bathroom door. This time she remembered to pick up her foot.

She smiled. "Good morning, Jenny."

"Hi, Mrs. Gray. Would you like a shower this morning?"

"Yes, I'd enjoy that. Would you mind feeding Jezzie first?"

###

THE FISHERMAN

KATHIE OLSEN

Every day, promptly at 6:00 in the morning, Jack woke up, swung his legs over the side of the bed and put his feet into a pair of worn leather slippers. With a stretch, he stumbled to the bathroom, washed and shaved, and got ready to go out.

In the kitchen, he'd pack himself either a can of sardines or a sandwich, two cans of V-8, a red onion, a tomato, and a piece of fruit, putting them into a lunch box, just as if he were going to a real job. He'd fix pancakes and coffee at the hotplate on the back porch, never using the 20 year old stove in the kitchen because he didn't like to get it dirty. He'd eat at the counter and listen to the radio, a morning talk-show that kept him company as background noise. After breakfast, he'd wash up, carefully covering the filled dish-rack with a clean towel. Putting on his jacket, he'd take his rod and his bucket and his lunch pail, and leave the apartment headed for the 7:00 AM bus, which took him to the pier.

It had been this way for 14 years. He hadn't missed a day.

At one time he had been an active fisherman, working on the boats of relatives and friends. A loner by nature, he was known for his reliability, his quiet, lack of fear, and knowledge of the sea. He was a short man, but strong and robust, a good guy to have on your crew.

On his 53rd birthday, he slipped on the deck of a blue boat called *The Nellie* and broke his hip. There wasn't even a good story to it. *The Nellie* was at dock in Newport when it happened. He had just slipped. He was never able to gain his sea legs again, and was put onto state disability.   It was lucky that he had no family to support.

Ostensibly he went to the pier to fish. In fact, he just came to the dock to have something to do. He would tell you that he was not unhappy. There was comfort in routine.

This particular morning was beautiful. When the bus wheezed to a stop at the foot of the pier, he got off and walked slowly to his usual spot, the bucket bumping softly against his thigh. Standing on the splintered boards of the old dock, he laid out his things, baited his hook, tossed it into the water, and then idly watched the few early-morning tourists who were marveling at the giant black shiny seals galumphing around below. One of the big yam shaped beasts rocked his head back and gave a mighty bark at no-one in particular, causing his neighbor to hump and bump to the side. The small crowd bending over the railing laughed and threw pieces of bread.

This particular pier was grayed and weathered. The benches that lined the sides were lopsided and splintery and stained with sea gull droppings. The center of the dock was covered with little buildings that had all seen better days. Most of the buildings were fish houses that bought fish from local fishermen every morning, cleaning the fish and selling them from counters covered with ice, or shipping them inland in refrigerated trucks. The seals beneath the dock got fatter and sleeker with the daily diet of fish bits tossed over the side by the fish mongers. A few of the buildings catered to tourists, selling items like shocking pink shells, or statuettes of Yankee fishermen or hula girls or sea gulls, all of them made in China.

On this morning, Jack noticed a young family – mother, father, three little kids – as they moved away from the others, wandering down to the end of the dock, looking at the sparkling bay. They stood in the midst of the fishy-smelling glorious blue sticky salt air, listening to the raucous seal chorus, seeming to be happy. The sea alternately sucked and slapped at the pilings below. The dock swayed a little.

The family wandered to the rickety stairs that led to the beach. Jack kept an eye on them. At the bottom of the stairs, the kids tore off their shoes and socks, and zoomed along the shoreline. They squealed at the jelly fish, and ran back and forth to show their parents found shells and worn glass. Pants legs rolled up to their knees, they played catch with the tide, arms flapping with joy in imitation of the sea gulls that flew up in alarm. Their parents slowly walked down the beach, hand in hand. As he watched, Jack could almost feel the cold water and grainy sand.

After about a quarter mile, the parents stopped near a big piece of driftwood and shifted their bags and packs off of their backs. Out came a red Mexican blanket, a thermos, a plastic cup, some paper towels, and waxed sandwich bags filled with snacks. The mother plopped herself down onto the blanket, pulled a paperback from her sweater pocket, and leaned luxuriously against the log. The father ran down to the shoreline to be with the children. Jack watched silently for most of the morning as he idly waited for fish to bite.

At noon, he sat down on one of the benches to eat his lunch, neatly putting a napkin over his lap before unwrapping his sandwich. When he was finished, he cleaned out the lunch box, carefully wrapped his leftover sandwich to eat later, and placed his empty juice can into a trash container. When he went back to his fishing spot, he glanced down at the beach and noticed that the family had gone.

At 2:30, he rinsed his bait box, stowed his hooks in his fishing bag, and put the bag and his lunch box into the bucket.

Thinking of the family on the beach, he realized that he hadn't felt sand under his toes for a long time. With surprise, Jack found himself, instead of limping down to the end of the dock and catching the bus as usual, going down the stairs onto the beach. Just as the children had done, he sat on the bottom step and took off his shoes and socks. He carefully put a sock into each shoe, firmly jamming the socks into the toes so they wouldn't fall out, tied the shoe laces together, and placed one shoe onto his back, the other hanging onto his front.

The sand was cold and damp under the shade of the dock, but hot and dry in the sun. He walked down to the shoreline, enjoying the cool of the water, and the sucking of the sand as the tide went out from under his feet.

Jack figured he would walk along the water line until he saw the tables at the *Old Salt Bar & Grill*, then he would walk away from the shore and through the alley next to the restaurant and catch the bus there. It was a walk of about half of a mile. His hip hurt, his lips felt chapped and salty, but he was proud that he could still enjoy this simple pleasure – this walking with his toes in the water.

He hoped that he wouldn't miss the bus.

As the *Old Salt* came into view he cut across, leaving the water, calf muscles straining, toes gripping the graininess of dry sand. He debated whether he should sit down and put his shoes and socks back on, but dreaded sand filled shoes and socks, and decided to wait for pavement. Finally, at the entrance to the alley, he sat down on a wooden box, put down his bucket, his rod and his lunch pail, and carefully brushed the sand from his left foot. It felt good to put on the warm dry sock, reassuring to put on the solid shoe.

It was as he was drying his right foot, getting ready to put on his sock, that he heard the sound. A miaow was coming from inside a sack lying by the dumpster at the kitchen door of the *Old Salt*. There was something urgent about the sound. Hobbling with only one shoe on, he approached the sack. Peering inside, he saw four very tiny kittens. Looking around in hope of human affirmation, and finding no-one, he gingerly reached inside. Three of the kittens were dead. The fourth was pitifully weak.

Jack felt sick to think that some person had done this to these little creatures. He didn't know what to do. It was about time for his bus to come. In haste, he picked up the living kitten, wrapped it carefully in the sock he still clutched in his hand, and gently put it into the bucket. He went back to the sack, and, muttering apologies to the lifeless bodies inside, carefully placed it inside the dumpster. Grabbing his gear and jamming his bare foot into his shoe, he hurried up the alley just as the bus came into view.

Sinking into his seat on the bus, Jack put his hand into the bucket to see if the kitten was still alive. He had a flush of gratitude at the rapid rhythm of a heart beat. Using his little finger, he began to stroke the kitty's stomach, and felt a vibrating purr of response. It was a shame that this little thing would probably die.

As the bus moved slowly through town, the old man thought and stroked the kitten. There was a convenience store near his bus stop. Jack figured that he should probably buy a can of evaporated milk and some cat food just in case the kitten survived. He could use the aluminum tin left over from last night's frozen meat pie as a cat dish. The cat was so little that maybe just a bed of newspapers would do for a bathroom. He wasn't sure. As the bus moved through the city, belching exhaust, Jack stroked the kitty's stomach.

He figured he might have to stay home with it tomorrow.

###

ONE MOMENT MORE

FAYEGAIL MANDELL BISACCIA

"One moment more," she demanded, gazing at the unlighted candle.

Elia had placed the blue candle there herself the day before, there on the trunk, on the white lace tablecloth her mother had crocheted for her trousseau, there next to the jade heart her beloved had given her fifty years ago, next to the photo of their sixtieth wedding anniversary. She had placed it there with instructions to her daughter: "At the moment of my passing, light this candle. You must watch carefully. There will be a sign. You will know. Watch carefully. Light the candle. Then, open the window."

And she turned her attention inward, to all that she had learned, and to the ovarian cancer which was claiming her.

"So," she said to the intruder. "You think I will submit to you in the end, you who have robbed me of so much?"

"You have no choice. I have carved a space for myself at the very center of your being. You have no control, now, of your body. You have no control of the pain. I'll soon triumph."

"It is true that I am no longer able to walk, to care for myself. But you cannot destroy me. What I see is not your triumph, but the face of my beloved. There, at the windowsill. There, beside the mirror. He watches me. He sustains me."

"He'll not sustain you long. I've squeezed the breath from your lungs, dried your lips. Your tongue is so parched *you can barely speak. You will writhe with the knowledge of my mastery."*

"No. He will not leave me wretched. It is the knowledge of our love that will transform me. You cannot."

"It is time," said the cancer.

Elia's breaths came shallow, far apart. Her daughter felt for the matchbox in the soft light. She held it tightly in her left hand, poised, watching. She wondered how she ever would recognize the moment. She yearned to ask, but her mother had been unconscious for hours. Yet Elia had been clear. She would know. "Watch carefully. You will know," Elia had said. And then she heard her mother's voice. Elia spoke, though she had not spoken for hours.

"One moment more," she demanded, gazing at the unlighted candle, the candle that would carry her spirit into the other world. Her daughter lit the match and Elia's breath whispered out as the candle ignited.

###

SORTING BEANS

FAYEGAIL MANDELL BISACCIA

Luisa looked up as I came into the sunny farm kitchen. She sat, elbows on the table and a cigarette dangling from her lips. She flicked an ash into an eggshell perched on a heap of cornmeal in front of her. Then she looked down at the red-topped chrome table that had been her mother's and took a deep drag on her cigarette.

"I was going to teach you how to make tortillas today, but I ran out of white flour. I made muffins instead."

"Not a problem," I said, wondering why she was going to teach me how to make tortillas. I've been making tortillas as long as I've known Luisa. "Where were you before? I tried to call you. I thought you might want me to pick up something from the market on my way out here. I could have brought you some flour."

"I was taking a nap."

That got my attention. I didn't say anything. Luisa doesn't like to be questioned. Luisa and I go way back. The reason we can be best friends is that I figured out right away that she'd tell me what she wanted me to know, and that icicles could grow on my nose before she'd tell me anything she wasn't ready to say. It wasn't long before I realized she'd want me to know just about everything about her, so it wasn't a problem. I just had to learn how to wait. I was not a patient person in my youth. I am infinitely patient after being Luisa's best friend for thirty-five years.

I took a Dos Equis out of the fridge and cut up a lime. I slid a slice of it around the top of the glass, dropped it in and poured out half a glass of beer. I raised the glass toward Luisa to see if she wanted some, but she shook her head.

"From the looks of the fridge, you need more than flour from the market."

"I know. I was going to go yesterday while I was in town."

"But . . .?"

"But, I didn't." She took another draw on her cigarette and stubbed it out in the eggshell. She let the smoke out slowly, and it curled up like a veil in front of her eyes. The muffins smelled heavenly.

"What kind of muffins are you making?"

"Green chili and corn with cheddar," she said. "Your favorites." She got up and cleared the cornmeal and eggshells off the table and dumped them into the chicken bucket. She brought the pink and green scrubby sponge back with her and swiped at the red Formica. Then she took a paring knife and meticulously scraped a lot of black guck out of the crack in the center of the table. This is not a thing Luisa normally does. Obviously. That's why there was a lot of black guck in the crack.

"Great. I'll stay for lunch."

"I figured you would. I made an extra dozen so you could take some home." Luisa is always sending me home with something delicious she's made. She worries about me, living in that tiny studio apartment downtown without a real kitchen. She's afraid I don't take care of myself.

Luisa went into the pantry and returned with a three-pound can of Maxwell House. She set it carefully on the table and opened it, and I could see it wasn't coffee. It was pinto beans. I should have known that.

Luisa switched to Café Azul six months ago. That's the fancy organic Peruvian coffee they sell in Café Azul on the Plaza. They have their own brand, and their customers are willing to pay a lot for it because the owners put a terrific picture of The Mountain at Dawn on the label, same as the painting that hangs behind the counter in the café. Besides, it's delicious.

Luisa drinks a lot of coffee. She's planning to paper the space between the kitchen counter and the dish cabinet with the labels and then paint it over with poly-something-or-other that will make it washable. She thinks it will look like tiles. I'm not so sure it will, but so what? It'll still look nice, probably.

"What a pal," I said with a smile. "Thanks for making the muffins. Guess I'm pretty predictable, aren't I?"

A hint of a grin crossed her face as she turned away. She took a cookie sheet out of the bottom of the hutch and put it on the table. Then she sat down and looked at me.

"I'm going to teach you how to cook frijoles," she said.

"Okay." Now I was sure something was up. Every time Luisa has something particularly important to tell me, she starts sorting beans. Once it was that her mother and father were thinking of getting a divorce. Once it was that her ex-husband Julio was diagnosed with a benign brain tumor. Once it was that her sixteen-year-old daughter Juanita was expecting a baby and was planning to leave school and get married to Ed, her childhood sweetheart. It could be something great, too, like the time she won a blue ribbon for one of her tapestry weavings at the State Fair, or the time her mom snuck off to Nevada for the weekend and won ten thousand dollars playing a dollar slot machine in a Reno gas station.

I waited. Luisa spilled about three cups of pintos onto one end of the cookie sheet and started moving them, a few at a time, across to the other end. Once in a while she would pick out a small rock or a piece of curled up bean skin and toss it into her empty coffee mug. She took out every bean with dirt on it, every bean that was split in half or discolored. Then she went back through them all again and started pulling out the deformed ones, too. This was going to be some serious bad news.

"I went into town yesterday." She stopped sorting beans and lit another cigarette. "I went to see Doc Jeffries. For a colonoscopy." She looked at me then.

My eyebrows must have shot up, because she shook her head and said, "I didn't want to worry you. 'Til I knew something."

"Luisa, I'm your best friend. We're supposed to worry about each other." Luisa's father died of colon cancer five years ago. Even though Doc Jeffries has been telling her she needs to have regular check-ups, she has refused to get them.

"What made you decide to see the doctor?"

"If you must know, I'm constipated a lot, and sometimes I get these terrible cramps. Lately, I've been seeing blood. That's the same stuff that happened to Dad. I finally decided."

"What did he say?"

"He found some polyps that he took out. But there was a growth in there that he couldn't see past, and he couldn't take it out with the scope. For sure I have to have surgery Monday. He said the bowel will close up pretty soon, otherwise."

"Oh, God. I am so sorry." I bent over to hug her and knocked my hand right into the tip of her cigarette. "Ouch!"

"Oh, God. I am so sorry." We looked at each other. The fact that we'd both said those words for such vastly different reasons startled us and made us chuckle, and then we were laughing hysterically.

"Nothing like a good laugh for stress relief," she gasped when we'd wound down. She sucked in a long breath and wiped the tears that were streaming down her cheeks. "I am so scared."

"Oh, I know you must be, Luisa. How can I help?"

"Just remind me to laugh."

***

I sat alone in the waiting room during Luisa's surgery. Juanita couldn't come because she was sick in bed with the flu. Julio was in Seattle helping his ninety-year-old mother through her latest crisis. Luisa said it was silly for me to be there by myself, but that's the way we do it in our family. Anyway, she sat with me during Mother's final surgery years ago, and last year, before my husband Lou died of lung cancer. Lots of memories in that room.

I heard my name called, and I saw a Pink Lady waving in my direction. A doctor in scrubs crossed the waiting area toward me, and I stood up to greet him. "I'm Dr. Ruiz. You're Mrs. Rivera's sister?"

"No, Doctor. I'm her best friend, Dena Felder. Luisa signed a paper so you can tell me about what you found."

"Oh, yes. Well, then. I removed the tumor Dr. Jeffries found during the colonoscopy. But there was a second tumor farther up that had already gone through the intestinal wall. I'm afraid it isn't colon cancer, after all, Mrs. Felder. We didn't know until we got in there. Your friend has ovarian cancer. I took out as much of it as I could, but I couldn't safely take all of it."

"You're sure?" I asked lamely. "Don't you need to wait for the pathology report?"

"I'm sure." He looked directly into my eyes. "I'm sorry," he said, and I knew he really was. My skin turned to ice, and I felt suddenly light-headed. The surgeon reached out a hand to steady me.

"I'm sorry," he said again. "The Pink Ladies will let you know when Mrs. Rivera comes out of recovery. I'll stop by to tell her what I found this afternoon before I leave the hospital. She should be alert enough by then." I watched him walk across the plush gray carpet of the waiting area. His shoulders sagged as he stepped back through the big double doors into the surgery wing.

* * *

I got to Luisa's room just as she was wheeled in from recovery. Two men dressed in scrubs moved her from the narrow gurney onto the bed with a royal blue transfer board that looked too cheery under the circumstances. Luisa was breathing oxygen from a tube under her nose, and three different-sized bags of fluid were suspended from a pole attached to the gurney. The man in blue transferred the bags to an IV pole with a machine in the middle that monitored Luisa's vital signs. I watched the blood-red graph trace Luisa's heartbeat. The man in green tucked Luisa into bed, took off her paper "shower cap," and checked to be sure everything was working properly. As they left the room, the first one said, "I'll let her nurse know she's back."

I sat on the arm of the vinyl visitor's chair and watched as the medications dripped slowly into the chamber in the tubing, then down the tube and into her arm. I found myself holding my breath as the drop of fluid got heavier and heavier in the chamber, then reached critical mass and plopped downward. Then I'd breathe.

Luisa stirred. She opened one eye and slammed it shut against the bright light over the bed. I turned it off.

"Hey, Luisa."

She opened both eyes and looked up at me. Her eyes were huge black almonds in her pale face, and a river of black and silver hair flowed across the pillow.

"Hi."

"Julio called while you were in surgery. They cancelled his flight back from Seattle. The storm is pretty bad up there. He'll come see you when he gets home."

She nodded and closed her eyes.

"Am I okay?" Her voice was fuzzy with sleep.

I stroked her forehead and wondered what to say. I decided to wait for the doctor. "Are you in pain, Luisa?"

She shook her head. "Sleepy," she mumbled.

"You rest, now. I'm here." I sat in the dimly-lit room and listened to Luisa's even breathing. How deceptively peaceful it was.

***

Luisa looked up as I came into the sunny farm kitchen. She sat, leaning her elbows on the table, with a line of white plastic bottles in front of her.

"What are those?"

"Supplements."

"You take supplements?" I still hadn't adjusted to the fact that Luisa had quit smoking. "Want a Dos Equis?"

"No. You have one. I just keep them here for you." That was a twist.

"So, Luisa. What's up?" I noticed my hand was shaking as I took a beer out of the fridge. Right around the time of her surgery, Luisa stopped being annoyed with me for asking questions. Actually, she stopped being annoyed about a lot of things. Like her relationship with Juanita. Like her cancer. After she declared she would not consider chemo or radiation, a lot of things changed.

"Dena, why does something have to be up?" she asked patiently.

"Luisa, you're taking *supplements*, for God's sake. Before your surgery, you were smoking a pack of Camels a day and drinking Dos Equis like it was lemonade."

"Cancer changes you."

"Your entire personality?" She wasn't my predictable Luisa anymore. I mean, *I'm* the one who takes supplements. I wondered why I felt so angry. Of course I wanted her to do everything she could to heal herself.

"Yes," she said, and dropped her eyes back to the line of bottles on the table. I could feel her pulling away from me.

"I'm sorry, Luisa. Of course supplements are a good idea." I sat down at the table and took her hand. "I'm so sorry." I smoothed the skin over her knuckles. "I'm afraid."

"So am I. But who knows? Miracles happen." She glanced at the picture of the Virgin de Guadalupe that now hung next to the pantry door.

"True," I said, and remembered what I'd read about the odds of somebody surviving ovarian cancer.

"I just read about one lady who had metastasized ovarian cancer. She went to a shaman, and she took a bunch of herbs and did a lot of exercises, and when she went back to the oncologist, there was no sign of cancer. The doctor had the nerve to tell her he must have mis-diagnosed it. Maybe that will happen to me. . . ."

I nodded. "Wouldn't that be something."

"Anyway, Julio drove me into town to see *my* oncologist yesterday, and he's a little more broad-minded than hers was. He said if supplements make me feel better, go ahead and take them."

"Hmmm. Sounds like the kind of doc to have."

"And another thing. His nurse told me about an Ojibwa herbal remedy that is known to help some cancer patients feel more comfortable, or even go into remission. You brew it up like tea. She said she knows several patients who swear by it. Could you pick some up for me at the Co-op next time you come out? I was too tired to stop yesterday.

It's called Essiac, and it comes in a little brown paper bag. And some ginger tablets, too, please. I'm almost out."

I nodded. "What else did the doctor say yesterday?"

"He said he'd like to see me get hooked up with the hospice program."

"Open-minded, but not particularly optimistic."

"That's what I thought. He said we're all going to die, and none of us knows when."

"Quite the philosopher."

"He said he has to go by the odds. The odds are that I won't be alive six months from now. Somehow, he managed to tell me that in a way that did leave room for miracles. He told me that hospice could help me live well until I die, and that they'd make sure I'd be well cared for at home. They'd help me be as comfortable as possible. They know what they're doing, he said. They're masters of pain control, and they're nice folks. That's what he said."

"Do you know Judy Bartleson? She's a hospice nurse. She's great."

"No, I don't think so. Not by name, anyway. How do you know her?"

"She came to visit us before Mom died. We were going to start hospice, but we never had a chance. Mom went too fast. Do you want me to call her for you?"

"Thanks, my oncologist already contacted them. They're coming out this afternoon."

"Do you want me to stay?"

"Thanks, Friend. I think I'd rather do this first one on my own."

"Anything I can do for you before I take off?"

"Would you mind feeding the chickens?"

"Nope." I grabbed the chicken bucket from under the sink and headed out to the chicken yard, where I was enthusiastically received. After I'd dumped the bucket and spread some grain, I went into the coop to check the egg boxes. One beautiful brown egg in each box, and a couple of them still warm to the touch. The hens' ovaries, it seemed, were doing fine.

***

Luisa was sitting at the kitchen table when I came in with her groceries, and she shifted uncomfortably in her chair. She was wearing her ruby-colored sweat pants with the draw-string waist and a purple over-sized cotton sweater.

"Well. Aren't you vivid!" I said, plopping into the chair opposite.

"Hi," she said and took a swig from her mug. "This Essiac doesn't taste all that bad."

"I bet that's a relief."

"Right. I decided to do visualizations when I drink it. I imagine the Essiac is like the Ajax in that old TV ad from when we were kids. Remember it? 'Use Ajax, ba-bum, the foaming cleanser. Ba-bum. Wash the dirt ba-bum right down the drain. Ba-da-ba-da-ba-di-bum.' Suds it up and wash away the cancer cells, just like little wads of chicken fat off the inside of a roaster."

The way she told it, I couldn't help but laugh. "That should do the trick. While we're on the subject of Ajax, want me to clean your bathroom?"

"Thanks, but Rosie came in from across the road and cleaned the whole house yesterday. The neighbors are great. People are coming out of the woodwork. I haven't seen some of these folks in months, and now they're stopping by with food or offers to help around the place. It makes me weep."

"Yeah, I know what you mean." I picked up a thick blue rubber band from the table, the kind they use to hold broccoli together at the grocery store, and I stretched it around my fingers. "What do you want for dinner?"

"Dena?" I looked up at the change in her voice.

"Luisa?"

"What are you going to do after . . . after the. . . after I die?" She looked at the cup of Essiac in her hand, then back at me.

I swallowed, and my eyes teared up. I didn't answer.

"Because, I want you to live here. Now, don't start protesting," she warned, when she saw me shake my head. "It's been hard for you since Lou died, and you living in that stupid little studio apartment. This is a thing we can do to thank you. If you hadn't been out here every day to check on me, it would have been a lot tougher on Juanita and Ed. They can't be here every minute, and we all know it."

"But, what about Juanita and Ed? What about their kids?"

"Juanita and Ed are happy in town, and so are their kids. None of them has any interest in living out here right now," she said, then anticipated my next objection. "And no desire to sell the place, either."

"Don't be silly, Luisa. I can't afford to pay rent on a place like this."

She wouldn't let me off the hook. "You could mind the chickens and look after the place instead of paying rent. They don't like the thought of renting it to strangers. They'd rather have the peace of mind than the money. Someday, they'll retire here. In the meantime, you'd be keeping an eye on it and letting them know if anything needed attention. It would be a favor to us. It would be like keeping it in the family. You *are* family, for God's sake."

"Well, I'll have to think about it."

"You think. There's no rush. I hope . . . ." she added, with a wry smile.

***

Judy Bartleson put her green bag into the trunk of her car and waved as I drove through Luisa's gate. I waved back at her and signaled with one finger for her to wait for me.

"Hi, Judy. How is she? Anything I should know?"

"About the same. I've upped her morphine. Rosie's with her now. She said she'd wait until you got back. I don't think she's in a hurry, if you want to take care of the chickens first."

"Thanks, I'll do that," I said, and stood there waving while Judy drove out of the gate. *So much kindness in this world*, I thought as I turned and went into the house.

I went into Luisa's room to tell her and Rosie I was back. Luisa smiled up at me from the bed. Her face was peaceful. She looked quiet inside.

"Rosie, if you can stay another minute, I'll feed the chickens before I settle."

"No problem."

I went into the kitchen and pulled the chicken bucket from under the sink. Not all that much in there. I rummaged around in the fridge and found some wilted chard that I added to the potato parings, egg shells and coffee grounds. I'd been eating all my meals out at the farm so I could look after Luisa, but I hadn't been too hungry lately, and she certainly wasn't eating much.

I headed out toward the chicken yard and caught my breath. In the moments since I'd gone into the house, the sky had become a delicate apricot. Each billowy cloud was lit from behind, molten edge after molten edge, waves and waves of liquid gold ready to spill off the end of the earth. I felt a timelessness in it, and I turned into the chicken yard, somehow comforted.

***

Luisa was sleeping when I went back into her room. I told Rosie she might as well go. I poured myself a cup of coffee and settled into the big chair by Luisa's bed. The reading lamp cast a peaceful glow over the room. I listened to Luisa's raspy, uneven breath and thought about all the funny, quirky things we'd done together, the family challenges we'd overcome with each other's help, the love and loyalty we'd shared.

She awoke and shifted in the bed with a sigh.

"Let me push that pillow closer, Luisa." She smiled and nodded, and I tucked it in to support her back.

"I dreamed of golden waves spilling off the end of the earth," she said, and fell back asleep.

I sat, listening, in the soft light. A nighthawk called nearby. After a while, I wandered out into the kitchen and poured myself another cup of coffee. I took the Maxwell House can out of the pantry, and the cookie sheet from the hutch, and I carried them into the bedroom. I spilled some beans out of the can, and moved them, a few at a time, across the pan.

###

POEMS

LOIS SCHLEGEL

ANNUNCIATION

it's a sensuous thing
to read a poem
out loud

to slip it around
on your tongue
just so

to feel the cool words
wet and slick
against your lips

the throbbing
hot words pulsing
in your throat

and the long still pauses
like a held breath
voluptuous pressure

pushing and shoving to get out
to annunciate one more
delicious phrase

SIMPLE WATER

on certain days
in a certain light
our boat glides
through the simple water
leaving a trail
where it has been
languid path
stretching to the shoreline
mapping out
before

my mates and I
dip our oars
just barely
just enough to
disturb the water
just enough
to measure
now

we focus our eyes
on the horizon
jagged Pilot Rock
standing several miles away
last remnant
of some great mountain
a survivor
looking out at
after

What We've Already Done

we row out across the lake
eight of us
digging oars into
dark, choppy water

the wind blows from the
west today
sending clouds skittering
across the morning sky

the scent of rain
and the heavy air
ride with us in
the narrow boat

we dig and pull
dig and pull

then glide for the
moment between

the moment when
we all slide back
and let what we've already done
push us forward

What The Womb Wants

the womb wants
wide open spaces
places so big the
crow cannot fly
far enough to not
still be there

the womb wants
elbow room, a
place to spread out
build fences, plant wheat
bring in horses
ride from sunset to sunset

the womb wants
sky so wide
and tall it hurts just to
think of it
cracks the brain
jars the senses
just to imagine

so much room

ALL THAT NOTHING

In the water there is nothing
but the rhythm of my breathing
and the flash of my arm
into the air, and then
cutting back through

In the water there is nothing
but the flutter of my feet
and the black line on
the bottom of the pool
and the splashes of sunlight
from the windows

In the water there is nothing
but the counting, the
one, two, three of it
the stroke, stroke, stroke
breathe of it
and then the quiet
at the end, when I near
the edge, and reach for
something solid in the midst
of all that nothing.

UNDONE

unwind me Ocean
untangle my threads
to flutter free in
Thy briny breeze

unmake me Ocean
as cliffs to sand
as waves to drops of spray
undo me

SPRING CLEANING

throw open the curtains
     the windows

let in the air
so the house can breathe
     so I can breathe

hang up sorrow on the line
     hang up despair

shake out doubt
plunge fear into soapy water
lay regret on the bushes
     to bleach in the sun

STORMS

the wind has changed
and trees bent for a
season with the force
of a gale, their
branches stroking the
ground, leaves
trembling
sigh and groan as
heartwood bends
nearly to breaking

then, a sturdy, familiar
breeze kicks up
from the ocean
and they sway and
dance, remembering
their old form, but
carrying always the
wind-whipped signs
of other wild, beautiful
storms

THIS HOUSE

Today, I slept through
the long hot afternoon

silent house below me
smoky air outside
a bandage of gauze
around my world

I slept fitfully in this house, where my
children ran barefoot down the
narrow hall
small feet pinging against oak
                    the first day we moved in

this house, where they splashed
so much water
over the edge of the tub upstairs
a brown spot the shape of California formed
                    on our bedroom ceiling

this house, where one son
snuck out the window onto the roof
first to smoke
cigarettes, later pot
                    much later, meth

this house, where the kitchen
door jamb is marked with heights
this tall when we moved in
this tall after sixth grade
                    this tall

this house
eaves stuffed with pictures
basement full of paint
we've yet to use
                    closets full of toys and books
this house
crawlspace full of spiders
                    dead rodents we poisoned

this house twice the size
we need
too many corners to keep clean
                    too much rattle and thump

this house, my house
where I slept for years
on the first floor
listening to muffled footsteps above me
                    drawers opening and closing
toilets flushing in the night

this house, three chimneys
two porches
one patio
a sandbox built from railroad ties

this house
we've begun to empty
boxes to Goodwill
                    to the dump
                    to be sold

this house, where now
I sleep upstairs
up where I can see the tops of trees
swinging in the smoky wind
                    up above the sound of anyone walking
                    or opening drawers

Spring Foreclosure

If it wasn't for the plum blossoms
I could leave this place
clear it out
lock the doors
walk away
without a backward glance

If it wasn't for the plum blossoms
lit up just now
by late afternoon sun
I could light a match
throw on gasoline
stand back and
watch it burn
see the walls crumble
and the paint peel
'til this house was
nothing but cinders
and pale ghost-chimneys
left behind in the
fading half-light

If it wasn't for the plum blossoms

LEFT BEHIND

there is nothing left at the old
home-place I love
save a water lily blooming
in the tired pond

yesterday, late afternoon, as we
loaded last remnants of
our wasted lives
it stretched its yellow blooms
toward the sun

A CONVERSATION BETWEEN MOTHER AND SON

We speak the language of the den
the language of the teat
of shared meat torn
warm and bloody from the bone.

We speak the language of the night
of bodies circling and pacing
then pressing into each other
against the biting chill – against fear.

We speak the language of
we against they
run and pounce
growl and bare teeth.

We speak the language of birth
of bits of you left behind
in the womb that still thrum
to my heartbeat.

We speak a singular language
of lineage and connection
so deep and so old
it is beyond words.

REPETITIVE WORK

Already, the grass around
the edges
has grown dry and brown

already, though you are not
yet dead, I have used a
sharp, flat-point shovel
to cut out a long rectangle

I have set aside the sod
piled it and sprayed it down
with the hose
covered it with a tarp

I have dug this hole
a thousand times
shovel after shovel
of heavy dirt

I have stood where your
body will lay and
thrown back my head to
see the teal blue sky
and the sun making
its predictable way across
and oak fringed above

I have looked down at
the chestnut red below
and wondered, how can
the sun still and
the dirt still
and my beloved son
soon to die

QUESTIONS ABOUT ALCHEMY

is there some secret incantation
some way to bow
before an altar
pressing my softened flesh
against the cold floor
in a thousand prostrations

some way to arrange candles
or spread incense smoke
through rooms

some prayer to speak
over and over
into the silence

a ritual forgotten
that once performed
will spin life in reverse
will undo these years
send them hurtling backwards
and me catapulting back too
dragging all this precious
emptiness with me
to its start
to begin it all again

TONIGHT THE MOON

Tonight the moon –
                    full
and closer to the earth than it will be again for a year
calls me out

clouds shift and pace across its bright face
then circle into the tell-tale ring –
                    prophesy of snow

a local flock of geese who've forgot
the nomad ways of their ancestors
honk across the horizon
their wings lit with moon-rays
their sharp voices –
                    cracking the stiff air

and I too, having forgotten the rituals for this moon-full
night
what sounds to utter
what dances to perform
what potions to set out under the –
                    streams of magic light

simply stand and watch as the moon –
                    slips behind another cloud

LAUNDRY

I still wash my son's clothes
twenty-two
not a boy anymore
my husband reminds me
perfectly capable

but there is something soothing
about stuffing my washer
full of his dirty sox
his boxers and undershirts
still smelling a bit like
they did when he was
ten
all freshly turned earth
wind in the hair
kinds of smells
mixed up with
his older self
locker room
cologne
skunky Mexican weed
occasionally, sex

I wash it all away in
my Maytag though
the water gurgles
through the fabric
with its familiar rumble and twist
then I pull gangly
wet clothes out
shove them in the dryer
hear the click, click, click
as it turns another
load dry

it's the folding
I like best though
hot clothes against
my lap
neat piles mounting
around me
T-shirts, pants, underwear
each in separate stacks
wrinkles smoothed
collars straightened
seams lined up
sox paired

ACCOUNTING

I've been burning days
like hundred dollar bills
pitching them into the flame
watching the small fire
flare and flash
then flicker high and
die down again

I choose another, this
one crisp and clean
edges sharp against my palm
the smell of bank vaults
and ink
of possibility
cling

no remnants of drug deals
coat this bill
this day
no cocaine resin
no tangy fragrance
of skunky weed
it hasn't lived
a crumpled life
in your pocket
shoved deeper as
your sweaty hand
kneads it

waiting
for the dealer
who circles the block
in his red Camaro
his hundred dollar bills
stacked, faces up
rolled and bound
with a rubber band

this one didn't buy
half a day sober
half a day for your
mind to clear, for
tissues to breathe
untainted air
it hasn't done
anything
been spent on nothing
still, I lay it on
the fire and watch
it burn
a perfectly good day
I burn it

AFTER THE MOVIE

thought I saw you
cross the street
same narrow bones
same physical arithmetic
posture
gait
angle
the ghost-white
car shot the intersection
upending you
body flicked away
like one of your cigarettes
the still-lit end burning through the night air

POTENTIAL

a summer
of unripe tomatoes
green ones
hanging
pale and hard
rain
sun behind surly clouds
thunderstorms moving through
lightning breaking the horizon
wind
    bending the vines
dropped fruit on the ground
from green to rotten in a week
the whole garden smelling of
tomato wine
while the seeds
drunk with regret
settle into the rimy earth
to wait
for another spring

IN SEPTEMBER

when blackberries hang rich and savory
against their desiccated leaves
and spew their fragrance out into the road
where I walk

why, oh why do I not stop to pick and eat
to feel the morsel dissolve on my tongue
to blacken my fingers and stain my lips

instead I walk further, pick a rose from
the edge of a farmer's pasture and tuck it
between my breasts, then
home to bed
alone

JANUARY FINCH

a dead bird on
the porch tonight
reminding me of the
stillness that awaits
yellow feathers
pale in the ebbing
light

after I carry it to
the edge of the yard
and toss it into the tall
grass

I throw back my head
and breathe in
night sky
drink in the darkness
the frightful, empty
space

NORTHERN EXPOSURE

the wind screamed
in a lick of snow
silver tongue
smacking the roof
glittery saliva left
along the gutter
up the chimney
gluing windows shut
and we inside with
hot tea and a fire burning
believe whole-heartedly
in the thin
wall separating us
from our soft-bodied
vulnerability

Relinquish

gravity is having her way with me
every morning as I ramble out of bed I feel her
pulling at my breasts
she covers my abdomen, my thighs, my chin with flutter-kisses
that burn my skin with the intensity of a relentless lover
come, come to me she seems to whisper to my fleshy places
come to the earth, come dwell in your weight and my force of will
come surrender to the inevitable decent, to what must be
though I rail against it
though I may dream of young firm buttocks and a jaw with
     sharp edges
still, as I melt into this body, that has borne the weight of her
part of me sighs and gives in with a shudder
a moments pleasure in letting go

PEACE POEM

if I never write
another poem
will you notice
you there, on the
nether-side of this page
feeling your way
along the words
will you feel
the silence too – the way
it oscillates
with the spinning
of the fan in
my quiet room, or
the way it is sliced
in two by the
car splashing through
the slick January outside

if I make silence
my art-form and
draw in my breath
will you follow me there
into that place
between
two draughts of air
where time and place and
thought and silence come
together, in a mad-dash
towards peace

###

EXCERPTS
FROM
WORKS IN PROGRESS

IN THE BEGINNING:
THE FIRST SECOND

JANET BOGGIA
Excerpt from a work in progress

CHAPTER 1

Once upon a time, a burst of energy gave birth to the cosmos. A mega-blast of heat like no other, a colossal singularity, thirteen billion, eight hundred million years ago (13.8 Bya) flashed into existence, a vanishingly small, unfathomably dense point of energy—this universe.

The turbulent cosmos,[1] less than one microsecond old, is crammed into space smaller than a pinprick and hotter than a trillion degrees. The universe enters in a gush of heat, creating time, space, energy and matter as it expands. It is hotter than the stars that will later form, hotter than anything on the planets it will create, hotter than a million simultaneous thermonuclear blasts. There is no existing space into which the infant universe flows. It creates and *is* the space, the forces, the energy and the matter that form within the first second of expansion. This chapter describes only one magnificent creative moment, the first second of creation. Four components are born completely intertwined: energy, matter, the great forces and space-time.

---

[1] The words *cosmos* and *universe* are used interchangeably.

ENERGY

Energy fills the turbulent maelstrom of the earliest part of the first microsecond. Energy expresses itself in many ways, including heat and radiant energy. Each form can be transformed into another. Nothing born into the universe is ever lost.

Radiant energy is light. Radiance expresses itself in two ways depending on how it is observed. Observed one way, light expresses itself as waves of radiation. Observed another way, light appears as *photons*. Photons are energetic bundles of light. Light *quanta*, photons, are the smallest possible particles of light. They collide and scatter, roiling, violent, dense. In this split second of a second, the miniscule universe *is* energy.

MATTER

In the billions of heat degrees of the cosmic fireball's first second, *matter* springs into being out of the sea of energy. The signature quality of matter that distinguishes it from energy is *mass*. The earliest matter in the form of quarks[1] and anti-quarks, electrons and anti-electrons (called positrons) move in and out of existence within the field of energy. These (and other) pairs of matter-antimatter collide, annihilating each other immediately. Because nothing can be lost, the annihilated matter and anti-matter become energy once more.

In this first second of time, most of the matter and anti-matter annihilate each other. In this cosmic frenzy, amazingly, there is a small percentage more matter than anti-matter. Consequently, a small amount of matter is left, and the bubble of energy and matter that is the infant universe is able to evolve beyond its natal moment. Had there been instead an equal amount of matter and anti-matter, the awesome cosmos would have been stillborn. Because there is an excess of matter, stars, planets and life will be born of this generative force. Physicists calculate that in the first second, the ratio of matter to anti-matter necessary to enable the cosmos to reach its 21st century state is miniscule. That ratio is: 10 billion anti-protons (10,000,000,000) to 10 billion and one protons (10,000,000,001).[2] It is because of the one proton not annihilated that the hidden potential can manifest.

Within this dance of a trillion furies, all potential is embedded. Future suns, galaxies, aardvarks, plagues, symphonies, acts of love and mathematical formulas are dormant, lying in wait, only possibilities. Each of these will be an outcome of conditions forming themselves at the heart of the universe in its first second. Like a game where multiple options exist at the beginning, as choices are made and the game continues, each path shapes what follows. The field narrows. Yet, in the cosmos, conditions both restrict and initiate. Unlike chess, it appears that initial conditions allow ever-new possibilities to emerge and change the game. Each new possibility weaves into a seamlessly evolving and endlessly creative universe.

THE FORCES

The large structure of the universe operates and is ordered through its four known majestic forces: the *strong force*, the *electromagnetic* force, the *weak nuclear force* and *gravity*. The forces are particles, too: *messenger* particles that hold matter particles together. The messenger particles (bosons) give matter specific characteristics. They are embedded in the matrix of space-time. In the first part of the first cosmic second, all the forces are united. Before the first second ends, the forces separate and become four.

Strong Force

The proton and the neutron, center of the atom—the *atomic nuclei*—are held together by the *strong force*, making atoms possible. The proton and neutron will become the nucleus of atoms when the first atoms come into existence in the future. In this sentence, "future" means in a few minutes. There are no atoms in the first cosmic second.

Prior to the 20th century, atoms were believed to be basic matter. *Basic* in this context means that they cannot be divided further. By the early 20th century, the proton and the neutron (atoms' nuclei) were believed to be basic matter. However, in the late 20th century, scientists recognized that the protons and neutrons interacted in ways that implied they were formed from an even more basic particle. When this basic particle was finally discovered, it was named the *quark*.[3] Subsequently, five more quarks were discovered, all subtly different. It is now the six quarks that are considered basic. Quarks compose the proton and the neutron. (The other basic elementary particle is the *electron*, composed only of itself.) The *strong force*, which binds quarks is the strongest of the four forces but operates only at a tiny range inside the nucleus of the atom.

Electromagnetic Force

The *electromagnetic force* binds the other basic elementary particle—the electron—to the nucleus. Together, these three particles—proton, neutron and electron—make atoms. Once there are atoms, worlds become possible, because everything is made of atoms. The atom, and therefore all matter, is possible only with the advent of the *strong* and the *electromagnetic* forces.

The electromagnetic force holds groups of atoms together to form molecules. Molecules are larger pieces of "stuff." In the future, atoms of helium and hydrogen will form great clouds of gases. Because of this, stars will result in about half a billion (500,000,000) years. Stars, in turn, will give birth to about 100 elements (such as lead, gold and carbon), all needed for planet-building. A molecule of water is composed of two atoms of hydrogen and one atom of oxygen (H_2O). The many molecules of water bound together by the electromagnetic force will make seas possible on at least one planet orbiting one star, making life possible in the far future of a yet undreamed time.

Weak Nuclear Force

The *weak nuclear force* acts in the nucleus of the atom to mediate radioactive decay. This means that protons transform into neutrons (and other particles). The atom loses energy and matter from its nucleus. For some functions the electromagnetic and weak nuclear force are described as one force, the *electroweak*.

Gravity and Space-Time

Despite its familiarity, gravity is the least understood force. The *gravitational force* attracts two bodies to each other. Isaac Newton believed that the bodies themselves (e.g. planets, billiard balls) generate the force, but Albert Einstein changed that view when he intuited his general theory of relativity. He deduced that gravity is a property of the curvature of *four-dimensional space-time*. The four dimensions are *time* plus the three dimensions of *space*. This view is now an integral part of the scientific model, known as the *standard model*.

It is difficult to visualize forces, but a word picture aids comprehension. Scientists often compare space-time to a stretched rubber sheet. When a heavy body (like a bowling ball) depresses the "sheet," anything smaller rolls towards it, although it too makes a depression in the fabric of space-time. The fabric is analogous to a *field*. The field is the area or space where the force acts. Princeton physicist John

128

Wheeler explained it this way: "Space tells matter how to move and matter tells space how to curve."[4]

In 2012, NASA's satellite, *Gravity Probe B*, confirmed that Earth's gravity bends space. It confirmed also that the Earth's rotation twists space, analogous to an apple rotating in a jar of syrup twisting the syrup.

The gravitational force is the weakest of the four great forces.

UNIFICATION

The forces that structure the universe seem mysterious. Einstein said of his relativity theory: "Scarcely anyone who has fully understood the theory can escape from its allure."[5] Einstein was entranced by the magnificence of the universe. He spent much of the latter part of his life attempting to find a unified theory. It eluded him and is still out of reach. His formula $E=mc^2$ describes the alchemical transformation of energy into matter and matter into energy. Nothing in the cosmos vanishes, it transmutes. All that unfolds during the next 13.8 billion years originates from the energy, matter and forces that come into existence in the first natal second.

Physicists continue the attempt to conceptually unite all the forces into a *Grand Unification Theory* (GUT). Although unsuccessful so far, they continue the search for a single fundamental force of which all the forces are each manifestations. The search involves reproducing, as much as possible, the conditions of the earliest fraction of the first second of the cosmic creation. The latest particle accelerator on the border between Switzerland and France, the Large Hadron Collider (LHC),[6] allows the model to be one step closer to success. The Higgs boson, discovered there in 2012 (confirmed in the following years), proves to scientists that the Higgs field pervades space. The field allows particles to gain mass, the signature of matter. When particles move through the field, they acquire mass much like swimmers swimming through water become wet. Discovery of the predicted Higgs boson confirms the Standard Model.

THE SINGULARITY OF THE BEGINNING

The first second of the cosmos is a jubilant *birth*-day party. This singular moment, the birth of space-time, matter, energy and the forces, is known by several names. The term *singularity* is used often to designate the creation moment. Physicist Alan Guth defines *singularity* as, "Point zero, an instant of infinite density, infinite pressure, and infinite temperature."[7] *Big Bang* was a derisive term used in 1948 by mathematician and astronomer Fred Hoyle at a time when he held an opposing origin view known as the *steady-state theory.* His original term, Big Bang, remains in popular use. The momentous and dramatic initial event calls for superlatives that communicate awe in the face of elegance and power difficult to capture. Other terms used by cosmologists include cosmic birth, creation event, origin, primeval fireball, flaring forth,[8] initial event, and cosmic fireball.

THE UNIVERSE EXPANDS: INFLATION

In 1995 physicist Alan Guth had an insight—later confirmed—that answers many questions about the initial second of time. He posits that separation of the great forces created an immense burst of energy that caused the universe's expansion to accelerate exceedingly rapidly. This rapid expansion, faster than the speed of light, is called *inflation.*[9] After inflation—possibly to the size of a galaxy— the universe continues to expand, but the great burst slows. At the end of this short but sped-up inflation period, cooling occurs because there is vastly more space. Only a millionth of a second has passed since the cosmic beginning, and at this point the universe has cooled to below a million degrees. The cosmos is no longer a miniscule, dense pinpoint.

EXOTIC PHYSICS AND COSMOLOGY

During the late 20th and early 21st centuries, several physicists and cosmologists moved in new directions to look for answers about the deepest problems of physics and cosmology: *How are the forces unified? How is quantum physics related to general relativity and gravity? Is there more than one universe?* The three examples below are theories not part of the standard model. However, building on accepted theories, leading edge exotic science could become the standard model of a new generation.

Vibrating Strings

One of the results of their search is known as *superstring theory*. Superstring theory posits that the basic structure of the universe is composed of numerous tiny vibrating dimensions. Superstrings with their multiple dimensions would replace the concept of particles such as quarks and electrons. In this theory, "the quantum of gravity, the graviton, is the simplest vibration mode of a superstring loop."[10] England's Astronomer Royal, Martin Rees, believes that the direction taken may lead to answers, but so far the work is theoretical and difficult to support with real-world evidence.

Exquisite Geometry

Another group of physicists attempting to achieve a unification theory view modern quantum physics through the lens of a stunningly beautiful geometry that creates striking patterns. James Owen Weatherall and A. Garrett Lisi present a theory of matter and the great forces as embedded in the twisting of a single geometric object, this universe. Their theory, called E8, posits the structure of the cosmos at the tiny scales of elementary particles as "248 sets of circles wrapping around one another in an exquisite pattern, twisting and dancing over space-time in all possible ways."[11]

Multiple Universes

Multiple universes is a theory presented by Stephen Hawking and others. In Hawking's 2010 book with Leonard Mlodinow, *The Grand Design*, they discuss how this universe could be one bubble in an infinite span of the multiverse.[12] This is part of their M-Theory, which they propose as the grand unifying theory and support with scientific principles. There is little or no experimental verification at this time, and Hawking and Mlodinow offer it as a matter of brilliant forward thinking.

THE NEW CREATION STORY

Behold the 21st Century creation story, which flows from the standard model of the scientific paradigm, a story less than a hundred years old. The drama is compelling.

At the beginning, a radiant burst of energy shatters non-existence and expands and cools. It is called Universe. Universe fights for its existence (matter vs. anti-matter) and succeeds. As Universe expands, it creates everything that is and ever will be. All the beauty and terror, creativity and imagination are born in a micro-instant flash of cosmic unfolding that has lasted 13.8 billion years, each moment unique.

132

ENDNOTES : CHAPTER 1

[1] Gell-Mann, Murray. *The Quark and the Jaguar: Adventures in the Simple and the Complex*. W. H. Freeman and Company, New York. 1994. See Chapter 13, "Quarks and All That: The Standard Model," especially pages 181–183.

[2] Ferreira, Pedro G. *The State of the Universe: A Primer in Modern Cosmology*. 2007. Weidenfeld and Nicolson, Phoenix Edition. p. 168

[3] The quark was proposed by Murray Gell-Mann in 1964 (and independently by George Zweig). In 1968 it was detected in scattering experiments at the Stanford Linear Accelerator (SLAC).

[4] John Archibald Wheeler. This famous quote is from a lecture at the University of Texas, March 2, 1979, where Wheeler taught from 1976 to 1986..

[5] Albert Einstein quoted in: Calaprice, Alice (Collected and Edited by) *The Ultimate Quotable Einstein*. 2011. Princeton University Press, Princeton and Oxford. He also said of his theory: "The theory is beautiful beyond comparison. However, only one colleague has really been able to understand it." 1915 letter to Hienrich Zangger,.

[6] *Colliders* and *accelerators* are instruments that are miles in length through which matter particles are accelerated to near light speed. Collisions among the particles create new particles and other effects.

[7] Guth. Alan H. *The Inflationary Universe: The Quest for a New Theory of Cosmic Origins*. 1997. Addison-Wesley Publishing Company, Inc. P. 341

[8] The phrase *flaring forth* is found in Brian Swimme and Thomas Berry, *The Universe Story*. 1992. Harper San Francisco.

[9] Ibid Guth

[10] Rees, Martin. *Before the Beginning: Our Universe and Others*. 1997. Perseus Books. p. 59

[11] Lisi, A. Garrett and James Owen Weatherall, "A Geometric Theory of Everything," *Scientific American*, December 2010, Vol. 303, No. 6. Pp. 55-61

[12] Hawking, Stephen and Leonard Mlodinow. *The Grand Design*. 2010. Bantsam Books, New York

COLOR, FLIGHT, SONG

JANET BOGGIA
Excerpt from a work in progress

Chapter 24

Change occurs when nature is solving a problem. Nature does not plan ahead. There is no scenario where she says: "We'll invent feathers now, then wings so that these creatures eventually will fly." Each evolutionary step must confer a present advantage. What is nature attempting to solve when she invents birds? What advantage comes with being a bird? This chapter traces the bird story, the saga of the avian dinosaurs.

WHY BIRDS?
HOW DINOSAURS BECOME BIRDS

Bird-like Dinosaurs

If birds are a solution, what is the problem? As in the old carrot-and-stick fable, evolution acts as a force that pulls and pushes. Creatures may be attracted *toward* (perhaps toward more food or mates) and *pushed away* (perhaps from cold or heat or enemies). By moving from dinosaur- to bird-mode, two problems are relieved. The first is a hot and cold dilemma. The second is a predator problem.

The Hot and Cold Problem for Reptiles

Early reptiles about 300 million years ago have difficulty with heat and cold. On a warm rock, the animals are warm. On a cold shore, the reptiles become cold. They have no internal mechanism for regulating body temperature. Dependence upon the environment for warming or cooling is called *ectothermy*, known as "cold-blooded." With each of these extremes, animals become sluggish and are easy prey. It is still an open question as to exactly how and when the temperature regulating systems of primitive reptiles becomes more sophisticated. Chapter 22 discusses *Dimetrodon*, a sail-backed 500-pound, eleven foot-long reptile that lived 280 million years ago, prior to dinosaurs. The large sail on its back may have been an early thermoregulator, a solar panel-like device.

By the Jurassic, 200 million years ago, theropod dinosaurs are on their way to dominance. For the next 135 million years they develop mechanisms that enhance their ability to find mates, bring down mega-ton prey, and survive in their environment. One adaptation is the development of internal body temperature regulation.

Fossil evidence indicates that small, feathered theropod dinosaurs, as they become more birdlike, have some ability to regulate their temperature, known as *endothermy*. The dinosaurs are probably not complete endotherms as are modern birds but somewhere in-between. Kevin Padian of the Museum of Paleontology at University of California, Berkeley, adds balance to the ongoing debate of endothermy vs. ectothermy in dinosaurs: "We should not think of warm/cold blooded as a dichotomy, but as a continuum."[1]

Bird Origins: Ancestors

Most scientists have narrowed bird origins to that group of small, feathered bird-like dinosaurs known as coelurosaurs. Feathered maniraptoran dinosaurs from this group are the top contenders, including turkey-sized troodontids, non-avian dinosaurs with large brains. (See *Troodon* image, Chapter 23). The ostrich-sized oviraptors— dinos that provide parental care and brood their eggs, sometimes with the fathers accomplishing this task (discussed in Chapter 23)—are also maniraptorans. All of these are theropod dinosaurs, the ones that walk on two legs. They are bipedal, both small and large. Most of them are omnivores.

A sister dino group, the dromaeosaurids, also bird-like theropod dinosaurs including *Velociraptor*, are ferocious carnivores. They are wolf-sized or larger with a stiffened tail, large grasping hands and agile bodies, and many are flamboyantly feathered.

In his book *Glorified Dinosaurs: The Origin and Early Evolution of Birds*, paleornithologist Luis Chiappe discusses features of birds that develop earlier in theropods, especially maniraptoran dinosaurs. These include skeletal changes as well as behaviors. For example, the way in which the wrists of these animals evolve and fold, the evolution of feathers, and aspects of microstructure are only a few of the changes from bird-like to bird. Bird behaviors such as laying egg clutches over many days and brooding their eggs are also dinosaur habits.

There are a multitude of physiological resemblances between coelurosaurs and modern birds. For example, the bones of theropod dinosaurs have hollow spaces similar to those of birds. There are correspondences in the pubis bone and in the large eye openings of the skull. The University of

California Museum of Paleontology lists 20 major similarities.[2]

Uncertain are the exact relationships of these groups to one another and questions about flight. Did the earliest birds start flying from the ground or did they glide and parachute from tree branches? Various species may have taken different paths as their various body parts strengthened and eventually enabled powered flight.

A few scientists maintain that birds and dinosaurs descend directly and separately from a common four-legged reptile ancestor. This minority opinion seems unsustainable in light of growing evidence to the contrary. The mainstream consensus derived from thousands of fossils and DNA analyses is that a theropod dinosaur is ancestor to birds.

Feathered Dinosaurs: Look at Me - I'm Available

Skin, that repository of sense receptors allowing the detection of sensation, pleasure and pain, also protects the inner organs of the body. Itself an organ system, skin includes additional structures, which together are called the *integumentary system*: nails, hooves, claws, beaks, horns, scales, shells, hair and feathers. The system serves to waterproof, insulate, cushion, protect, excrete waste and synthesize vitamin D from sunlight, among other functions. Invented by dinosaurs, feathers are considered the most complex of these skin structures found in vertebrates. Feathers evolve in multiple stages, beginning as hair-like structures, single filaments—a form of fuzz.

Feathered theropod dinosaurs covered in fuzz---or even feathers—do not fly. Simple fuzzy filaments cannot make a dinosaur airborne. To allow powered flight, the feathers have to become flatter with long hollow tubes, usually asymmetrical. Besides insulation, feathers help with camouflage, confusing enemies with color and pattern.

Having said that feathered theropod dinosaurs do not fly, Microraptor (*Cryptovolans*), 2 to 3 feet long, the size of a small turkey with a body thickly covered in glossy black feathers with long feathers on the tails and arms may have been able to remain aloft with some ability to glide. This animal has flight feathers on the upper foot bones of the legs giving it four wings. The feathers are far more developed than fuzz. These dinos climb trees, but their ability to fly is still in debate. The foot feathers become an obstacle to rapid running when they are on the ground. These animals are classified as non-avian dinosaurs.

Dinosaurs, first and foremost, use their long feathers for display. "These feathery fans only developed as the animal got older and was ready to mate," says Darla Zilenitsky, principal dinosaur researcher in the Department of Geoscience at the University of Calgary. She explains, "The same structures eventually evolve into flight-capable wings."[3]

Dinosaur-Like Birds

At a point in time, bird-like dinosaurs become dinosaur-like birds. Scientists do not yet know, nor may they ever know, which feathered theropod dinosaur was more bird than dinosaur and, therefore, "the first" bird (or *birds* if they emerged more than once).

The Concept of "Firsts"

The concept of "firsts" in evolution is an interesting one. What reptile-like amphibian is the first reptile? What dinosaur-like reptile is the first dinosaur? And, again, what bird-like dinosaur is the first bird?

In actuality, the modifications appear slowly and unevenly among species as one change glides into another. It is only in the human mind looking back, amassing fossils,

138

analyzing DNA, establishing relationships and grouping the fossils, does categorizing and naming take place. The sorting elicits a decision: This group of animals shares more qualities and characteristics with each other than with the former group, so they shall be classified as a new animal. In modern scientific language, these groupings are known as *clades*.[4] At the edges, it is difficult to say exactly where a transitional animal fits. In addition, scientists have only the found fossils, which is why so often the designation is "the earliest *known*" amphibian (or dinosaur or flowering plant). However, the new clade of animals is definitely a new emergence with its own set of qualities and new abilities.

The Emergence of Birds: Jurassic Period

The first birds arise in the afternoon of the dinosaurs, the mid- to late Jurassic, about 160 million years ago, from the same evolutionary line as feathered theropod dinosaurs. Jurassic bird fossils are scanty. By a stunning coincidence, the earliest discovered fossil of a reptile with feathers turns out to be the earliest bird known—*Archaeopteryx*—until the 21st century when some dispute its designation of "earliest bird." The story of *Archaeopteryx* is a perfect example of the problem described above of "firsts."

In 1861 when this new fossil is discovered in southern Germany, the concept of evolution is not well known and certainly not well understood. Two years earlier, Charles Darwin had published *On the Origin of Species by Means of Natural Selection* in which he introduced the theory, raising furious debate among philosophers, naturalists, church leaders and politicians. Fossils are not new, having been found in China and Europe for thousands of years, then often believed to have been the remains of dragons. Although many fossils were discovered in the 17th and 18th centuries, with this find for the first time a trace of feathers is evident on a reptilian-like fossil. A month later, a second 150 million year old specimen replete with feathers is discovered in the same limestone Jurassic formation. In 1863, the paleontologist Richard Owen names the specimen *Archaeopteryx*, "ancient wing."

Fifteen years later when a third skeleton is unearthed with its long reptilian tail and intact skull with teeth (dinosaur features), it plainly shows both primary and secondary flight feathers on the fully extended wings. Ornithologists can see that the feathers resemble those of modern birds. All the subsequent *Archaeopteryx* finds are dated to the same period, the late Jurassic with tropical climate, lagoons and palm-like trees.

A dozen *Archaeopteryx* skeletons have been found, the oldest transitional bird form yet discovered until a spectacular China discovery in the late 20th century. Two or three (the third is in dispute) recent fossil species are dated to the Jurassic but from ten million years earlier than *Archaeopteryx*. It is not certain if these species have the ability to fly, given features of their skeletons, even though they look somewhat like small modern birds with various colored feathers.[5] These transitional animals may be able to glide. Because of its skeletal and feather characteristics, it appears that *Archaeopteryx*, about the size of a raven, has the ability to glide and perhaps soar, even if not for long distances.

Even though they are feathered, what actually pushes or pulls the bird-like dinosaurs to inhabit air space? To become dinosaur-like birds? What forces produce an *Archaeopteryx*?

The Predator Problem

This question brings up the dire peril that all animals face, including feathered dinosaurs—the threat posed on an

Earth crowded with predators—to be caught and eaten. When possible, animals move into a niche with fewer dangers. During the fish-to-tetrapod transition, the land with its absence of predators acts as a magnet. The tetrapod leaves the sea little by little, becoming an amphibian in the process.

During the *Age of Dinosaurs*, Earth's surface teems with life. There is a competitive advantage to be farther away from land-bound predators. As birds begin to invent themselves, the skies are not completely empty. This is the era of dinosaurs on land and pterosaurs in the air (200 to 66 million years ago). Pterosaurs fly and glide in their own unique fashion. These toothed flying reptiles with long faces, "corrugated" skin flaps resembling corduroy, strong muscles and one elongated finger, swoop across the skies.[6] Early birds, too, have teeth inherited from their theropod dinosaur ancestors. The level of danger on land compared with risk higher up makes it worthwhile to enter this domain.

There are benefits to becoming strong fliers to evade, and perhaps prey upon, the mostly-fish-eating pterosaurs. Time spent away from Earth's surface, while enabling the animal to travel and have a clear view of the terrain below, is advantageous. The water hole may be crowded with predators—is there a secluded mountain lake above the throng? Is it safer to nest and breed higher in trees? As feathers differentiate, the more useful they become for gliding. The lighter the bones, the easier flight becomes. The stronger the breastbone and muscles, the more powerful is the flyer.

Birds and pterosaurs share the airspace, as do many modern animals. Even large beasts like leopards, giant pandas and Asiatic black bears share habitat because they occupy different niches in the same territory. Pterosaurs eat small dinosaurs and fish. Depending on the species, birds eat insects, fish, seeds and nectar. They may nest in various locales, hunt for food at different times and at various heights. Or, as modern Alaskan birds, all of which depend on salmon for their livelihood, they may share an abundant food source.

Birds of the Cretaceous

An exquisite 20th century fossil-find in Liaoning Province China is a treasure trove of Cretaceous birds, along with plumed dinosaurs, other vertebrates, invertebrates and plants. While Jurassic bird fossils are limited, multiple sites in China show a great diversification of avian dinosaurs (birds) from the Cretaceous Period with its warm climate and abundant lakes, 146 to 66 million years ago (evening and night of the dinosaurs). During this period, dinosaurs hold sway on land. However, huge pterosaurs are definitely sharing air space with the new emergence, birds. The fauna and flora found in Liaoning Province were alive approximately 125 to 120 million years ago and include insects, fishes and pterosaurs (one with her egg). Abundant also are turtles, lizards and other reptiles, plants, amphibians, small early mammals, dinosaurs—many of them feathered, and birds. Many many birds.

Most ancient birds—and Archaeopteryx is the exemplar—have teeth, claws on their feathered arms (wings), and often, long bony tails. *Confuciusornis*, a Cretaceous bird from 120 million years ago found in China, has a large claw on its hand but a shorter tail called a "pygostyle," a mark of modern birds. All six species, the size of pigeons or crows, have toothless beaks, the oldest known birds to have beaks even though *Confuciusornis* has a more primitive skull than *Archaeopteryx*. Almost one thousand specimens have been discovered.

Luis Chiappe believes this bird forages on the ground but some species may also perch in trees.[7] Some, like ospreys, eat fish (found in a skeleton's crop). *Confuciusornis* is brightly adorned with long wing feathers of red/brown, grey and black, possibly something like the modern Zebra Finch. The skeletons show it cannot do an upstroke and so it glides as opposed to flapping its wings. It has the ability to soar and glide over lake surfaces, and there is evidence that it moves in large flocks. A group of forty specimens were found together, appearing to have fallen from the sky into the riverbed below. Chiappe posits that gas from an active volcano asphyxiated the soaring birds, causing them to fall to their deaths.

Multiple species of toothed (and sometimes toothless) birds[8] from the size of finches and sparrows to that of turkey vultures with 4- to 6-foot wingspans from the Cretaceous display an array of adaptations: wading, mud-probing, swimming, perching, fish catching, seed-eating and sap drinking. They are good flyers but probably not migratory.

In Liaoning Province and other sites in China and Mongolia, hundreds of Cretaceous bird fossils have been found.[9] At the China sites, numerous volcanic eruptions "created a layer cake of fossil beds spanning millions of years,"[10] reported National Geographic in August 2005. Fine particles of mud and ash preserved soft body parts, and in some bird skeletons, even stomach contents including plant seeds.[11]

In the last decades of the 20th century, multiple fossilized Cretaceous bird species are found all over the world in addition to China and Mongolia. Madagascar, Australia, Spain, South America, North America, Germany and England, among others, yield more than 300 new fossil species of birds, all named since 2000.[12]

During the massive fifth global extinction at the end of the Cretaceous, which closes the Mesozoic Era 66 million years ago, pterosaurs become extinct. Perhaps they are too large—one species has a 40-foot wingspan. All large animals perish (Chapter 23). Birds, many species at least, survive the catastrophe. And so the avian story continues.

MODERN BIRDS: CENOZOIC ERA – 66 TO 0 MILLION YEARS AGO

As the fifth great extinction brings the Mesozoic (middle life) to an end, the Cenozoic opens with a warm, moist tropical climate. Cenozoic means *recent life* in Greek. The world is full of small animals, mostly weighing less than 50 pounds. The titans are gone. Plesiosaurs and their cousins no longer inhabit the seas, and dinosaurs have departed from the land. Now *avian* dinosaurs (birds) explore the air space in relative safety (except from each other) because pterosaurs no longer fly through the skies.

There is space now for all forms of remaining life to expand. And expand it does, into every niche. During the early part of the Cenozoic, ancient relatives of loons, ducks, albatrosses, shorebirds, geese and gulls are at home on a more familiar-looking Earth.[13] The continents continue to drift farther apart. Greenland and Scandinavia are breaking free. The Cenozoic Era is known as the *Age of Mammals* (Chapter 25), awarded that designation by a mammal, but it easily could have been called *The Age of Birds*. There are twice as many bird species as there are mammal species.

WHAT MAKES A BIRD?

There are several important characteristics that define modern birds. *Modern* in this case begins with the Cenozoic. These traits evolve over millions of years starting in the Jurassic when the last common ancestor gives birth to two lines: one line that remains more theropod dinosaur than bird, and a second that becomes more bird than dino. The second line produces a splendor of avian dinosaurs, one of which becomes modern birds (classed as Neornithes).

By the 21st century the approximately 10,000 bird species differ as much from one another through natural selection as dogs differ from one another through human intervention. The primary quality that places an animal into the clade of birds is flight. Most other characteristics of birds have developed to support this seemingly magical freedom from gravity.

Modern birds have skeletons that are strong and lightweight to enhance flight. Some aspects of the skeleton include air sacs in bones that take the place of marrow, known as "hollow bones." Birds have a wishbone (furcula), which helps downstrokes and upstrokes while flying. This furcula is a modified collarbone. The shoulder joint is adapted into a "pulley" arrangement for flight. Skeletal modifications in the sternum and wrist offer a degree of skeletal rigidity and help with maneuverability and flight control.

Birds' systems—respiratory, digestive, muscular and nervous (brain)—are highly adapted for flight. The eyes are in skulls on mobile necks with complex muscle control.

The most developed part of the brain controls flight functions. Their large eyes and brains (relative to body size) enable acute senses and excellent perception including the ability to detect atmospheric pressure and perceive ultraviolet light. On average, about one-fifth of a bird's body volume is devoted to the respiratory system compared to a mammal's one-twentieth. Their urinary tracts do not need a bladder; retained urine adds weight.

Modern birds lay hard-shelled eggs and have beaks with no teeth. They have a bipedal stance (they walk using two legs). Most birds have four toes with one turned to the back, which helps with hunting, perching and landing, as well as hanging and climbing. They have forelimbs (arms) modified as wings and differentiated feathers specialized for flight.

All birds have various degrees of endothermy (warm-blooded) with high metabolic rates and the ability to maintain and raise or lower temperature. They have four-chambered hearts necessary for endothermy. Becoming a bird is one answer to the reptile's problem of temperature regulation.

Avian dinosaurs (birds) inherit characteristics from the theropod dinosaur and, through time, modify them for powered flight. Not only does nature solve the problem of internal temperature regulation with birds, she must revel joyously in a vertebrate's ability to fly since there are so many birds, and they have been doing it for so long.

THE AIKIDO OF FLIGHT

Birds take to the sky and over a period of 150 million years, they own it. Extant birds are estimated at 300 billion individuals alive at one time from more than 10,000 species. In the Japanese martial art of Aikido, the practitioner uses the energy of the opposition to defend himself. *Rather than opposing that energy with force, help the opposition to do what he desires*, says the master. *When he runs toward you, move nimbly aside, turn and help him to continue moving in the direction of his momentum.*

Birds perfect the Aikido of flight. They use air currents for soaring higher, they glide and reach and drop in a dance like no other. Birds do not ignore gravity, they use it. A peregrine falcon, in complete control, plummets as fast as an arrow to capture its prey.

A 4-inch long broad-tailed hummingbird can migrate over 2000 miles from central Mexico to as far north as British Columbia, Canada, on wings that aren't quite two-and-a-half inches long—a five inch wingspan.[14] The hummingbird is able to hover in one location and fly forward or backwards. Other birds develop the ability to fly for thousands of miles and return to the precise location from which they started. Some birds, such as penguins and auks, "fly" through water.

Birds invent flight and become its unparalleled masters. It is more accurate to say they reinvent flight because pterosaurs, the first flying reptiles, were peerless in their time, but avian dinosaurs hone the skill to new heights and depths. It will never be known how magnificent pterosaurs may have been, but with their demise, birds—the flying dinosaurs—claim and control their domain.

BIRD INTELLIGENCE

Birds are among the most intelligent of animal groups, exhibiting many types of abilities. They use tools (e.g. rocks, sticks). Some species *make* tools by shaping sticks for various uses. They communicate through complex songs and calls. The brown thrasher has a vocabulary of up to 3000 vocalizations. Birds learn from each other as one generation teaches the next. Male parental care is rare in the animal world, but in birds it is common. Incubation, feeding, tutoring and defense are often shared roles, depending on the species.

Body Intelligence - Response to Conditions

By banding birds for research, avian scientists find that migrating birds fly enormous distances with a phenomenal sense of direction. One species, the sooty shearwater, migrates annually between breeding grounds in the Falkland Islands (off the coast of Argentina) and Norway's North Atlantic coast, a distance of 9000 miles. The Arctic tern is able to complete a 14,000-mile journey from islands off the east coast of England to Melbourne, Australia, in three months. Even when birds are caught, then released from places unfamiliar to them, they find their way home.[15]

While most birds fly in the range of 500 to 2000 feet above sea level, less than half a mile, some birds fly at elevations of three or more miles. Bar-headed geese fly over the highest peaks of the Himalayas above 29,000 feet—more than five miles above sea level—ignoring nearby passes of 10,000 feet.

Birds' worlds are opulent, blazing with color. Humans have evolved eyes and brains that perceive light from the middle part of the electromagnetic spectrum as light that is named red, yellow, blue, purple (and colors in between) known as *visible* light. Humans cannot see light from the powerful short-wave side of the spectrum (gamma rays, x-rays, and ultraviolet) nor can they see light from the long-wave side (infrared, microwaves and radio waves.) However, in addition to the visible spectrum, most birds have evolved to see ultraviolet light.[16] Their world is iridescent, useful in display and mating. Sometimes, the difference between a male and female is an iridescent ultraviolet patch that only the bird can detect (but not an ornithologist without special equipment).

Emotional Intelligence - Emotional Life of Birds

Birds are social and communicate through calls, song and visual signals. They participate in social behaviors including cooperative breeding (group care and feeding of hatchlings not their own), mobbing of predators and flocking (collective animal behavior used for movement, protection and foraging; many birds flock during flight). Some hunt cooperatively. Most birds have an extended period of parental care after hatching.[17] Birds bond with their mates, the vast majority of bird species being monogamous during one breeding season. Some birds bond for years.

Parrots and macaws bond also with their human companions. A famous contemporary example is Nelson, a macaw.[18] Nelson is attached to the woman in the home where he lives. He responds with affection when she holds and pets him. He likes to nuzzle and follows her everywhere he can. At bedtime he hops up a flight of stairs to the second floor, a long way with his short little macaw legs, one step at a time. Like humans' brains, Nelson's brain emits chemicals that result in the emotion of jealousy, and he exhibits jealous behavior when he perceives an emotional threat. If she forgets to hold on to the parrot when her husband comes to bed, the bird attacks him. Nelson flies at the "intruder," biting and scratching. Strong emotions underlie the social life and relationships of birds.

Magpies are observed to honor their dead. Sighting a dead magpie, a bird caws loudly and repeatedly until a flock assembles. The birds land, gathering around the dead magpie, calling at full volume. At one moment, they all become silent. A few probe or preen the dead bird. After a period of "contemplation," they fly away one by one. Some have been observed to return with blades of grass, which they place near the dead bird.[19]

149

Mental Intelligence - Cognitive Life of Birds

Not all bird species migrate. Some change location in response to local weather conditions as needed. Perhaps they move lower on a mountain or fly to a coast. For birds that are not dependent on only one source of food but have more diverse diet choices, this method is efficient. Many birds work hard to overwinter in their home area.

The nutcracker lark depends on pine nuts and will travel as far as twelve miles to forage. According to ornithologists, she buries them one at a time and marks each spot with a stone. For three weeks she gathers and buries 30,000 pine nuts in the site of the Grand Canyon, a hard dry dessert terrain. Even though the lark remembers trees and ridges, snow when it comes, transforms the landscape. Yet, for the next six months, the nutcracker lark relies on a mental map to find the nuts, and find them she does—90 percent of them.[20]

While studying how parrot parents teach language to their young, Timothy Wright, director of Wright Avian Laboratory at New Mexico State University, discovered that parrots speak in their own dialects. Groups of the same species living in different geographic locations have different cultures. When parrots are captured from the wild and placed in cages, they call out to wild parrots flying overhead in their own particular parrot dialect. They also speak and sing in their second language, the learned human language.[21]

Birds have a sense of humor. At least magpies do. These 7-ounce, black and white birds (related to crows and ravens) display pleasure by preening in a characteristic way. A skill native to magpies is the ability to imitate at least 35 other birds and animals. A PBS documentary shows a magpie as she observes a group of dogs that chase ducks as they land on a nearby pond. From time to time, the magpie imitates duck sounds and watches the dogs race around looking for non-existent ducks. An ornithologist reports that the magpie "preens itself with pleasure" when she fools the dogs. This demonstrates an example of planning—the bird looks forward to an event that it will cause to happen.[22]

Crows, ravens, jays, magpies and rooks (together known as corvids) have been studied extensively. These intelligent animals have brains (relative to body size) twice as large as a dog's brain. A raven named Bran is shown a puzzle box with three levels of intricacy to manage in order to release a tasty treat. Bran figures it out in under a minute and snaps up the bird treat. When poodles are introduced to the same puzzle box (containing a dog treat) they do not get beyond the first level of balls and string.[23] Corvids are considered among the most intelligent of all animals.

A cockatoo in an experiment removes a pin, a screw and a bolt that shifts a locking wheel, which then allows the bird to reach another bolt, enabling the bird to find and eat a nut. Can the cockatoo deduce how to open a lock where the elements are rearranged, with some being redundant? The bird studies the lock. Then, ignoring the redundant elements, it goes for the wheel, then the bolt and releases the lock. The bird is able to analyze the problem and carry out the correct sequence in less than 10 seconds without trial and error.[24] The bird can transfer knowledge—understand and apply knowledge to different problems.

Birds' brains are alight with planning and problem solving. Biologists Paul Ehrlich, David Dobkin and Darryl Wheye consider that birds make rapid decisions: "It is the combination of visual acuity, high-speed nerve transmission, and quick decision making… that permits a golden-crowned sparrow to weave rapidly among the branches of a thicket, escaping the clutches of a pursuing sharp-shinned hawk."[25]

EMBEDDED IN THE UNIVERSE

Genetic

Migration of birds reflects better than any other mechanism the embeddedness of a creature in the full evolutionary process. First, on the basic level of life, the level of the body, the urge to migrate and the migratory direction are genetically programmed. The genetic cues are released by changes in hormones and other physiological prompts. Even caged birds that have no orientation to changes in light or weather will alter their behaviors when they experience migratory genetic signals. When birds are prevented from flying, they hop in the migratory direction. They have been shown to display a preferential flight direction that corresponds with the migratory direction they would take in nature.[26] Thus, in genetic memory, migration is embedded.

Cognitive

A second level is the ability of birds to learn. In many species, baby birds must learn to fly and to recognize where they live to survive their bird world. They need to learn how to use and manage their acute senses. Many species use the sun as a compass. Using the sun for navigation means the bird has to compensate for the changing position of the sun. Night flyers learn to use the stars as a compass, observing the star patterns around the North Star. A team of ornithologists, led by Audrey Mukhim of the Max Planck Institute for Ornithology, asked: "How do songbirds develop a stellar compass if they sleep at night?"[27] The team attached miniature radio transmitters to each of several dozen juvenile songbirds, Eurasian reed warblers. They discovered that the birds *practice* the art of migration.

The birds have only a short time prior to departure because their journey begins, on average, fifty days after

152

hatching. For twelve days the fledglings take nocturnal forays over their own territory to learn about the subtleties of celestial navigation. They must learn to recognize how their territory looks from the air in order to find it again on their return. They are known to use a multitude of visual clues in the habitat over which they fly, changing flight patterns when necessary to avoid new barriers and dangers. The visual system of birds is one of their most developed senses. Successful long-range migration involves integrated visual acuity, cognitive ability and the making of mental maps.

Although female birds have vocalizations, the males are the ones who shine. They have the most variety, and they sing to attract females. Young male zebra finches are taught their songs either by their fathers or other male adult tutors. To learn a tune, recognize it and reproduce it accurately, birds need to rehearse endlessly. Rutgers University researchers have identified the area in the bird's brain where the "sound template" is stored.[28]

Cosmic

A third level of embeddedness is at the level of the cosmos. Multiple species of birds have evolved to sense the earth's geomagnetic field. Earth's geomagnetic field is created by the iron at the core and the mantle of fiery magma that makes up most of the planet. The surface is the crust, comparable to the skin of a grapefruit. The thin crust holds the mountains, forests, fields and oceans (Chapter 14). All life on the planet is continually penetrated by the magnetic field as it escapes through Earth's crust. The field reaches up for thousands of miles beyond the atmosphere. It protects life from harmful radiation. Birds sense this level of the cosmos through sensitive receptors and have the ability to use the field for navigation, some flying thousands of miles both day and night. The mechanism of this ability is not yet well understood by science; however, in 2012, scientists discovered neurons in pigeons' brains that record detailed information from Earth's magnetic field. Both the direction and the strength of the field are recorded.[29]

One Tapestry

The deeply dynamic evolutionary process keeps species changing. Each perpetually modifies in relation to other species, the geophysical world, and the cosmos. All are woven in one tapestry. The imagination of the universe—how else to express the wonder of the process—brings forth the chemical agents that produce the archaea that become fishes. One fish becomes a tetrapod and then an amphibian tied to the waters' edges. One amphibian in time becomes a reptile, the amniote that gives birth to all the other amniotes: beings as diverse and profoundly complex as the immense land-locked dinosaur and the feathered flying dinosaur—the resplendent birds. There is one more amniote. Among these animals runs and hides the meek little mammal. Will it have its day to bloom and shine?

ENDNOTES: CHAPTER 24

---

[1] Dunning,Hayley. "Dinos Not Necessarily Cold-Blooded." *The Scientist.* June 27, 2012
Original research published: M. Kohler et al., "Seasonal Bone Growth and Physiology in Endotherms Shed Light on Dinosaur Physiology," *Nature,* doi: 10.1038/nature 11264, 2012
[2] University of California. Dinosaur-Bird Relationships. "Are Birds Really Dinosaurs?" http://www.ucmp.berkeley.edu/diapsids/avians.html
[3] Yong, Ed. "'Bird-Mimic' Dinosaur Hints that Wings Evolved for Show, Not Flight." *National Geographic.* October 2012. Reference from: Zelenitsky, Darla (and six others). "Feathered Non-Avian Dinosaurs from North America Provide Insight into Wing Origins." *Science.* October 26, 2012, Vol. 338 no. 6106, pp. 510-514. DOI: 10.1126/science.1225376
[4] Modern Scientific Language: Clades. In modern paleontology (20th century and beyond) evolutionary relationships are shown in complex diagrams called *clades.* Groups more closely related to each other (than to other groups) are gathered together into a clade, a type of evolution-based ancestral tree or graph with the goal of showing relationships. This type of clade shows an evolutionary grouping that includes the last common ancestor and all of its descendents. Avialans (all birds extinct and living) are

the only theropod group (dinosaur lineage) to survive the 5th extinction, the Cretaceous-Paleogene extinction event. Because research in cladistics is intense and ongoing, position in a clade and membership can change every month. However, the clades are stable enough to have a generally accepted shape and definition.

[5] Three early potential avialans are *Aviornis*, *Xiaotingia*, and *Aurornis*.

[6] This description suggested by National Geographic article: "Pterosaurs— Lords of the Ancient Skies."

"Under the microscope the surface of the wing looked corrugated, almost like corduroy." http://science.nationalgeographic.com/science/prehistoric-world/pterosaurs/

[7] Chiappe, Luis M. *Glorified Dinosaurs: The Origin and Early Evolution of Birds.* 2007. John Wiley and Sons.

[8] From the clade *Enantiornithine* (which became extinct 66 million years ago) and the clade *Euornithes*, known also as *Ornithuromorpha* (from which modern birds evolved).

[9] Chiappe, Luis M. and Lawrence M. Vitner. 2002. *Mesozoic Birds: Above the Heads of Dinosaurs.* University of California Press. Chapter 7 by Zhou Zhonghe and Hou Lianhai. "The Discovery and Study of Mesozoic Birds in China." Pp. 160-163

[10] Tarpy, Cliff. "Jewels in the Ash." *National Geographic.* August 2005. http://science.nationalgeographic.com/print/2005/08/china-fossils/tarpy-text

[11] Brocklehurst, Neil, Upchurch, Paul, Mannion, Philip D. and O'Connor, Jingmal. 2012. "The Completeness of the Fossil Record of Mesozoic Birds: Implications for Early Avian Evolution." *PLOS One.* June 25, 2012. DOI: 10.1371/journal.pone.0039056

[12] Ksepka, Daniel T. "Flights of Fancy in Avian Evolution." *American Scientist.* January-February 2014. Volume 102. P. 34 (Pp. 34–41)

[13] University of California at Berkeley. http//www.ucmp.berkeley.edu/diapsids/birds.birdfr.

[14] Nature Conservancy letter. 2007. Arlington, Virginia.

[15] Matthews, G.V.T. "Navigation in the Manx Shearwater." *The Journal of Experimental Biology.* February 1953. Pp. 370–396. Online ISSN: 1477-9145; Print ISSN: 0022-0949

[16] Berger, Cynthia. "True Colors: How Birds See the World." *National Wildlife.* National Wildlife Federation. July 2012. http://www.nwf.org/news-and-magazines/national-wildlife/birds/archives/2012/bird-vision

[17] Wikipedia. http://en.wikipedia.org/wiki/Neornithes

[18] Animal Minds: Do Animals Have Emotions? Animal Consciousness. 2003. Nature PBS.

[19] Strycker, Noah. *The Thing With Feathers: The Surprising Lives of Birds and What They Reveal About Being Human.* 2014. Audubon Magazine 3/26/2014

[20] Animal Minds: Are Animals Intelligent? 2003. Nature PBS Documentary

[21] Guerra, J.E., J.Cruz-Nieto, S.G. Ortiz-Maciel and T.F. Wright. 2008. "Geographic Variation in the Contact Calls of the Thick-Billed Parrot." *Condor.* 110:639-647

[22] Animal Minds: Are Animals Intelligent? 2003. Nature PBS Documentary

[23] Public Broadcasting System NOVA. "Inside Animal Minds." PBS DVD series.

[24] Ibid PBS

[25] Ehrlich, Paul R., David S. Dobkin, and Darryl Wheye. "Adaptations for Flight." 1988. Stanford University on line.
https://www.stanford.edu/group/stanfordbirds/text/essays/Adaptations.html

[26] Bearhop, Stuart. "Change in the Air." *Natural History.* September 2006. Volume 115, Number 7. Pp. 36-42

[27] Atkinson, Nick W. "Secret Forays." *Natural History.* October 2005, Vol. 114, Issue 8, p. 13. Original work: Mukhin A., V. Kosarev and P. Ktitorov. "Nocturnal Life of Young Songbirds Well Before Migration. "*Proceedings of the Royal Society.* 2005. B, 272:1535-1539

[28] Flores, Graciela. "Sing It to Me." *Natural History.* April 2006. P. 32. Vol. 115, No. 3.
(Phan, Mimi L. and David S. Vicario. *PNAS* 103:1088-93, 2006)
The neuroscientists identified the song storage area as neurons in the area of the bird's brain known as the NCM, which plays a role in hearing.

[29] Gorman, James. "Study Sheds Light on How Birds Navigate by Magnetic Field." *New York Times, Science Section.* and Boyle, Rebecca. "Neurons in Bird Brains Encode Earth's Magnetic Field, Giving Pigeons Reliable Internal GPS." *Popular Science.* April 26, 2012. Original work: Le-Qing Wu and J. David Dickman. "Neural Correlates of a Magnetic Sense." *Science.* May 25, 2012. 336(6084) Pp. 1054-1057.

MORTAL ZIN

Diane Schaffer
Excerpts from a work in progress

Prologue

Santa Cruz County, California
September 27, 2009

Her dog had been restless all night. As dawn seeped through the fog, the girl unzipped a few inches of her sleeping bag, extricated an arm and caressed his damp fur.

"Hey, Joey. It's okay."

Ears cocked, nostrils twitching, the dog pointed his muzzle toward the south end of the cove. She peered into the fog, unable to see farther than she could throw a stone. Yesterday evening, all the sun-worshippers had shaken the sand from their towels and left. She'd made sure the parking lot was empty before she settled in for the night.

Nestled on dry sand beneath a stone ledge, they were cold but safe. Best hidey-hole she'd found in months. No bums. No drunks. Cruces Cove was her castle.

She listened. Surf *shooshed* on the boulders far out in the cove. Low tide—very low.

Good.

She crawled into the open. The stench of fish-garbage hung heavy in the damp air. Steeling herself against the cold, she shed her jeans, then rolled the hem of her T-shirt and tucked it under her bra. Her teeth chattered. She pulled her knit cap over her ears—that helped, a little.

She drew a leather-sheathed knife from her pack and clipped it to the neck of her T-shirt. Just in case. Then she extracted scissors and a small plastic garbage bag.

The dog whined, still focused on the south end of the cove. Like as not, the mist cloaked a dead animal, and he wanted at it. He'd rolled in a seal carcass last month, took her two weeks wash away the stink.

"Heel!"

Reluctantly, the dog obeyed.

She loped toward the surf-line. Before her lay the naked sea bed, a secret planet where she was the lone explorer. In the flat grey light, tide pools gleamed metallic. Boulders loomed black and spiky with mussels. The sand was cold and hard, barely dented by her feet.

Joey lagged behind now. He was pissed.

You and me both, fella. Last week Chef Antoine, the slimy snodge, had tried to pay her with a bag of mollies instead of cash. Didn't believe her when she said she didn't do that shit.

Rounding a whale-sized rock shelf, she knelt beside her meal ticket: a tiny forest of sea palms. *Postelsia palmaeformis,* she told the dog, proud of remembering the Latin name. She'd been good in biology. Mr. Billings had wanted her to go to college.

Like, that was happening.

All sea weed was algae, that's what Mr. Billings said. But you could see why these were called "palms." They gripped the stony sea floor with masses of tiny "roots." Their tubular trunks were about a foot tall, and leaf-like blades radiated from their tops.

With one knee braced in the damp sand, she began to harvest, clipping one palm stem at a time. While she worked, she let herself imagine Mr. Billings' classroom. When school started, had her absence worried him? Had he tried to phone her mother?

She yanked her attention back to the slippery little plants. *Snip, snip, snip.* When the sack was full, she slung it over her shoulder and looked for Joey.

Gone.

Inserting thumb and index finger between her lips, she whistled, the signal for "get your canine ass over here right now." She stared into the fog, waiting for him, running her tongue over the residue of sea weed on her lips.

Fish-flavored celery.

How did Chef Antoine turn sea palms into a gourmet delight? Unbelievable.

A minute passed. Too long. If Joey was into something rotten, she'd never get to town. No one would give a ride to a girl with a stinking dog.

Hoisting the bag over her shoulder, she ran back to the ledge and stowed it next to her sleeping bag. Then, with a scrap of towel, she brushed the sand from her feet and donned her jeans and hoody.

She whistled again.

The dog loped out of the fog, then backed away and whined.

"What is it, boy?"

He ran toward her. Swerved. Yipped, begging her to follow him as he backed away.

Resigned, she followed him into the fog. What if she'd been wrong? Someone could have stayed the night at the south end of the cove, and now he was . . . What? She drew the knife from its sheath, telling herself she was stupid. Joey wouldn't lead her into danger.

She leapt a pile of rotting kelp, scanning the cove, straining to catch the smallest movement. Nothing but driftwood, sand, boulders and kelp. Then the fog broke into wisps of light and shadow, pulling out to sea. At the the furthest end of the beach there was a white . . . something. A mass that shifted shape. She stopped, squinting, trying to name it. Too pale for a sea lion. A harbor seal, so sick it had lost its bearings?

The dog, far ahead of her, raced toward the pale mass, slid to a stop, crouched and attacked.

A flurry of white wings rose from the beach.

She laughed and re-sheathed her knife.

Nothing but a bunch of silly birds.

The churning flock of sea gulls screeched as they dove for the dog's muzzle. He backed away, shaking them off, then charged, snarling and biting.

She caught a glimpse of bright blue, something on the sand.

Grasping a branch of driftwood and whirling it above her head, she attacked the gulls, her stomach clenching with every sickening *thud*. Wounded birds wobbled away on the sand. The rest spread their wings and lifted off, hovering greedily just beyond her reach.

On the sand lay a man's body. Blue windbreaker, blue jeans, and gray tennis shoes. A bit of gray hair. A thick, reddish-gray beard. Where his eyes had been—

Bile rose, sour in her mouth. She knelt on the sand and retched the meager contents of her empty stomach. The dog leaned his warm body into hers, licked her ears, her cheek. She wrapped her arms around him, burying her face in his fur.

The gulls reclaimed their prize.

She struggled to her feet and scanned the cove. The air had cleared. Pale yellow light played across the sand. In a shallow tide pool, a wine-colored skiff swayed from side to side. On its bow, *Mortal Zin* was written in beige.

She recognized the skiff. She'd watched it enter the cove yesterday, expertly steered by the man now lying dead. Where was the boy who'd come with him?

CHAPTER ONE

Thursday, October 1, 2009
9:15 am

At the turn marked by a new Andolini Vineyard sign, Noli Cooper braked to a stop. Oncoming traffic rocketed past, commuters streaming out of the Santa Cruz Mountains to work in Silicon Valley.

The sign had so incensed her godfather, Peter Hanak, whose vineyard abutted the Andolini estate, that she studied it with interest while waiting. Approximately five feet tall, it was a wooden rectangle divided into quadrants. Each quadrant framed a picture or heraldic symbol. In the upper left, a castle on a hill. Upper right, a knight in armor. Lower left, a falcon gripping a writhing snake. Lower right, a cluster of dark purple grapes. A fake family crest.

At least they got it right with the grapes. But a castle? Marco Andolini, who had founded the estate in 1860, had been a Sicilian peasant.

Gunning the engine, she shot through a narrow gap between two BMWs and onto Andolini Road. To her left, a Victorian mansion gleamed with fresh beige paint, the gingerbread dressed in green, gold and mauve. The carriage house was surrounded by scaffolding. Four parked cement trucks churned in the parking lot. Surely they weren't pouring pavement? No one familiar with earthquake country would waste money on broad, smooth slabs that would rupture during the next tremblor.

Speculation on the intent of Andolini's new owners ended abruptly as Noli's rental car slammed into a pothole. The suspension heaved. With a tight grip on the steering wheel she focused on navigating Andolini Road, a pitted, one-lane track carved into the limestone flank of Loma Buena Mountain. Every spring, after the abuse of winter rains, fallen trees and tumbled boulders, Peter borrowed a tractor and graded the road. Only a handful of people used the road; even so, by October it was ruined again.

Stripped of its ancient redwoods in the 1850's, much of the mountainside was covered with forests of alder, laurel and madrone. The madrone trunks had already begun their seasonal striptease: delicate sections of last year's cinnamon bark were separating and curling, revealing the gentle gray, newborn skin beneath.

As she followed twists and turns, the morning sun ricocheted across her rear view mirror. What a beautiful morning.

If only her gut wasn't telling her that Peter was in trouble.

Half a mile along the road, she rounded a hairpin turn and eased-up on the accelerator. On her left the ground dropped steeply, no guard rail. Below lay a valley of grape vines, their ruby and golden leaves still moist from the early morning fog. It was a bird's eye view of the Andolini estate, from which Peter and Tina Hanak's vineyard had been severed in the 1970's. The vines appeared splendidly healthy, heavy with purple clusters, ready for harvest. Would the Hanaks' vines look as good?

Why this feeling of urgency? There was nothing she could do—at least, not until Peter and Tina returned. In her mind, she replayed her last conversation with Peter:

"I'm planning a surprise party for Tina's 60th birthday." A pause, and when he spoke again there was a catch in his voice. "Any chance you can come?"

A knife in her heart, his hesitancy—and the realization she'd been too wrapped up in work to remember Tina's birthday.

"I'll be there!" she'd said immediately, opening the calendar on her computer, confronting a solid block of

commitments that would place her in Rome all of September and October. "How's the '08 vintage coming?"

There'd been a long pause before Peter answered. "Having some trouble. Tell you all about it when you get here."

"What's wrong?"

"Nothing we can't beat. You know the wine business—good years and bad years."

"But—"

"Tina will be so glad to see you. We'll keep it a surprise, okay?"

The road crested and plunged into a grove of second-growth redwoods, trees so tall the morning sun was reduced to twilight. She slowed, knowing she was approaching the Hanaks' driveway.

Half the grove belonged to the Hanaks, but back in the day it had belonged to Marco Andolini. Legend had it, Marco's oxen had died from overwork before he'd reached this part of the mountain. Since the oxen had already cleared redwood stumps from the entire valley below, ample land for his prospective vineyards, he'd announced a new plan. Pointing to the tiny sprouts that already circled each mother-stump, he declared they would be allowed to grow. Homes for his grandchildren, great-grandchildren and all the generations to come would be built from the trees those sprouts would become.

He was a man of vision, old Marco. But more than vision is required to found a dynasty.

Gritting her teeth and holding a steady pace, she turned onto a rutted two-track that veered from the road, heading uphill. The sedan slipped, slid and inched forward. Next time, she'd rent a four-wheel drive. After a long ten minutes the car burst onto a level, graveled clearing.

She killed the engine, slid from the car, and stretched her travel-weary limbs. Here, nestled amongst tree trunks as stout as cathedral columns, stood the home of Peter and Tina Hanak, a place so different from her eastside Manhattan condo she might have landed on another planet. Two geodesic domes, large and yet dwarfed by the trees, resembled exotic mushrooms, one silver, the other rusty-brown. Each was girded by a broad deck, and an enclosed passageway connected them.

Her heart sank as she evaluated the new dome, the one whose redwood shingles had not yet silvered. A wheelchair ramp connected it with the parking lot, then branched off in the direction of the winery, a reminder that multiple sclerosis had now deadened Tina's legs. The money the Hanaks had saved for a badly-needed new winery had instead funded a wheelchair-accessible living space.

Remembering Peter's warning that the domes would be locked (another sign that something was wrong), she retrieved her briefcase from the back seat and opened it. A pair of low-profile running shoes sat atop her files. Hidden in a separate compartment were a change of underwear and a fresh blouse. Always assume your luggage will be lost, that was her motto, and on this trip—as on many before—the airlines had proven her right.

Exchanging her understated Prada pumps for the running shoes, she strode past the domes and up a well-worn footpath. The climb was steep, and she was grateful for the added traction.

In three minutes she emerged onto a rocky slope where an array of six solar panels were braced just beyond the redwoods' shadow. Further up the mountain spread a ridge with a gentle southern slope. There, in all its autumn glory, stood her godparents' prize zinfandel vineyard. Two hundred vines, all more than a century old.

Each vine stood alone and proud, its branches carefully pruned to resemble a five-foot-high goblet. Shoots carrying golden leaves and dark purple grape bunches cascaded from the goblet rims. Each gnarled trunk was unique, and as a child she'd named several for Disney characters (Sleepy, Grumpy and Sneezy). Later, she and her father had named the rest for more lofty entities: Plato, Socrates, and Aristotle; Greek gods (Athena was a favorite); and important stars, such as the guiding lights of Orion's belt: Alnitak, Alnilam, Mintaca.

One particular vine, in the center of the first row, had grown stouter and taller than the others; this vine her father had christened Bacchus. "Any day now," he'd said, "Bacchus will call to these old vines, command them to pull their roots from the ground, and lead them in an ecstatic dance." Smiling at the memory, she rolled the sleeve of her silk blouse up to her elbow, then plunged her arm through Bacchus' cascading leaves. Her fingers traced the gnarled trunk upwards. Where branches formed a deep "V," her index finger registered a cold, metallic edge. With thumb and index finger, she dislodged a key.

Rising to her feet, she surveyed the vines, her old friends, more beautiful in life than in memory. If any were drooping or turning brown, she'd know disease was attacking. Pierce's Disease, carried from place to place by the glassy-winged sharpshooter, had destroyed entire vineyards just a hundred miles southeast of here. It would be a death sentence for the Hanak's winery, not something Peter would have wanted to discuss over the phone.

But all the vines seemed magnificently healthy. Of course, early stages of vineyard disease could be difficult to spot, and she was no expert. West of the domes lay sixteen acres of younger but well established zinfandel vines, the vineyard which produced most of the Hanaks' wine. Perhaps it was there the problem had developed?

She should at least have a look before Peter and Tina returned, but first she needed to rest. Descending the path, she raised her eyes to the horizon, focusing upon a narrow strip of blue wedged between earth and sky: the Pacific Ocean. Only eleven miles to the west, but, as the locals said, jokingly, "You can't get there from here." No single road traversed the Santa Cruz Mountains, whose disordered topography resembled a badly rumpled quilt. Wild, beautiful, deceptively tranquil in appearance, at unpredictable intervals these mountains broke and reassembled, tossed by colliding tectonic plates deep below the earth's crust. In 1989, almost exactly twenty years ago, the Loma Prieta Earthquake had changed her life forever.

She climbed the short stairway to the deck of the older of the two domes. Many of the shingles were split and curled. Forest duff—the debris dropped by trees—had collected in mounds against the walls. Several decking planks had warped and pulled. They needed to be screwed down. So much deferred maintenance, so unlike Peter. Another sign that something was seriously wrong.

Duct-taped to the doorknob was a folded scrap of paper labeled "Noli." She peeled it off, unlocked the door and entered the dome. Inside, she removed her dust-coated running shoes and set them on a rack amongst Peter's dirt-caked boots and sneakers.

Three beams of morning light shot through the darkness inside, shafts from east-facing, triangular windows. Like spotlights on a stage, each focused her attention on a single object: an orange Pendleton blanket folded over a dusty blue couch; an obsolete computer battling stacks of paper for control of a wood-plank table; and Peter's favorite chair, a vaguely-plaid, overstuffed Salvation Army purchase that should have gone to landfill. She grinned, remembering how many times Tina had begged him to get rid of it.

The damp chill of night had not yet been chased from the deserted home. She wrapped the blanket around her shoulders. Raising the note into a beam of light, she recognized the left-sloping penmanship immediately.

Noli, call me. It's about your father. Top priority.
Fitz

The message made no sense. Her father had been dead for twenty years. And why, when Fitz had her cell number, would he drive up the mountain to stick a note on the Hanaks' door?

John Fitzgerald, aka "Fitz," legal champion of Santa Cruz County's poor and disenfranchised, had employed and inspired her all through college and law school. She considered him her friend and mentor. They planned to have dinner together that night. Why leave a note?

Then she remembered: among the twenty-three voice messages she'd listened to between 3 am and 5 am at the San Francisco airport—while United Airlines tried, unsuccessfully, to find her missing luggage—there had been one message from Fitz. "*Call me as soon as you get in.*" It had been too early to call him, and by the time she'd reached the Hanaks', she'd forgotten. He'd probably assumed her cell was dead and had driven up here expecting to find her.

There was no cell reception in the dome. On the Hanaks' desk, peeking out from a stack of paper, a dusty black phone offered access to a landline. She punched in Fitz's cell number and waited.

Six rings, then voice mail.

She left a message. "My flight was delayed, Fitz. I'm at the Hanaks' now. Call when you can—use the Hanaks' landline."

She lowered herself into Peter's chair. Fitz would call soon. Or not. Maybe he was with a client.

Weariness descended, and she felt content to watch dust motes swirl through the shafts of light. But discomfort grew. The scars on her back began to itch. The reek of smoke, embedded in the walls after years of wood stove heat, seemed to grow stronger, grating in her throat, rasping her lungs. Her hands began to tremble, and she could feel her heart pounding—not in a good way.

Damn. I thought I was over this.

Tossing Fitz's note onto the couch, she circled the room, opening windows. Then she wedged the front and back doors open.

No breeze. Not the slightest breath of fresh air.

Her hands were shaking violently. Her throat was closing. She raced outside and dropped into a cross-legged meditation pose on the deck. Closed her eyes and willed her lungs to open fully.

Slowly, her breathing deepened.

Slowly, her heart calmed.

The silence of the mountain enveloped her.

As her body relaxed, exhaustion claimed her. She'd traversed nine time zones in the last seventeen hours, reading and preparing legal documents all the way. She stretched out on the blanket, telling herself that, when the dome aired-out, she'd borrow a set of Peter's work clothes. Standing five-foot-eleven barefoot, she'd always shared jeans with Peter, not the delicate, barely five-foot-tall Tina.

Later, uncertain how long she had slept, she woke to the sound of a car engine climbing the Hanaks' driveway.

Fitz! She stood, ran her fingers through her hair, straightened her jacket, and watched for a glimpse of his restored Woody station wagon.

But the car that rolled onto the graveled parking area was a sedan, green-and-white, a squad car of the Santa Cruz County Sheriff.

In an instant, she was sixteen again, helpless in the face of disaster. She crossed her arms, hugging herself tightly, watching as two deputies emerged. One, a blond

Anglo, mid-twenties, was built like a line-backer. His pale blue eyes met hers, noncommittal.

At his side stood a solid young Latino with a broad Mayan face and sadness in his brown eyes.

The Anglo said, "I'm Deputy Naughton, and this is Deputy Villanueva. We'd like to speak with Eleanor Cooper."

"I am Eleanor Cooper."

CHAPTER FOUR

Pleasure Point, Santa Cruz
Thursday, 11:00 am

"She's only fifteen. This is how she looked six months ago, but she might have dyed her hair or cut it. She might have piercings or tattoos."

Luz Alvarado handed an enlarged photograph of Crystal Langley, a blond, eager-eyed girl, to the pot-bellied, greasy-haired manager of an apartment building on 32nd Avenue. The guy was on the far side of fifty, but he leered at the photo of Kirsten as if undressing her with his eyes.

Luz wanted to kick him in the *cojones*. Instead, she asked, "Have you seen her?"

The guy couldn't take his eyes off Crystal's picture. "No. This one, I'd remember."

Luz pulled the photo from his fingers. He'd left dirt smudges around the edges.

She handed him her business card:

Luz Alvarado
Investigative Associate
Fitzpatrick Legal Services

Her cheeks burned with pride. "My contact numbers are on the back of the card. Call me if you see her." She caught the manager's bloodshot eyes one last time. "There's a reward."

He licked his lips and chewed on his saliva.

She turned away. Silently praying to a god she didn't believe in, she said, *Don't make him the one who finds her.*

She checked her watch. Almost eleven. Time to change outfits and interview the *hombres* at Pleasure Point. A girl on the run could do worse than shack up with a surfer.

Her beat-up Corolla waited on the street, a yellow parking ticket hanging limply on its windshield. *No problema.* Fitz considered parking tickets a cost of doing business.

She drove along Portola Drive until she found a row of storefronts, pulled behind them and parked. No one around.

From a box of clothing on the back seat she chose a Forty-Niners cap, a denim jacket, ripped jeans, battered sunglasses and a faded brown T-shirt. She wound her long black hair into a bun, tucked it under the cap. Checked her appearance in the rearview mirror. Thus far, she hadn't used the cap or glasses, and she'd only worn the jacket once, five days ago. With any luck, the locals wouldn't realize they'd seen her before.

As she laced up a pair of black high-tops she'd scored for a quarter at Goodwill, she tried not to feel discouraged. Fitz had warned her to be patient.

"Kids hide better than adults—no job, no social security number, no car. If they use their phones, we can track them down in a day. But Crystal left hers at home. Not a good sign." Fitz spread a frayed map of Santa Cruz on the work table, then circled cheap housing near the amusement park, near the harbor, and near Pleasure Point. "Crystal's best friend says she bragged about 'going to live on the beach.' She's pretty, and as far as we know, not strung out on drugs. These are the places she's most likely find someone who'll take her in. The aunt says she's smart, so I doubt you'll find her panhandling on Pacific Ave. Then again, she might get desperate. It's worth checking once in a while. Our ace-in-the-hole is the German Shepard. It goes everywhere with her." He refolded the map and presented it

171

to Luz with a wink. "It's time you discover how boring this work usually is."

He pulled a cigarette from his shirt pocket and dug for the lighter that had Permanent Resident Status in his jeans. As he inhaled, his deeply creased cheeks grew concave for several seconds, then slid back into his trademark "I've seen it all" grin. Twinkly blue eyes, snub nose, rosy cheeks. Give him a big white beard and he'd be Santa Claus after a long stint with Weight Watchers. So jolly, so non-threatening. But if you watched his eyes—really watched them? Lasers stripping you down to the truth.

She tugged at the martial arts padding wrapped beneath her T-shirt, flattening her breasts and enlarging her small waist. She had honed some pretty good deceptions herself.

Had Fitz seen through her from the beginning? *No importa nada.* He'd given her a solo assignment. She'd find the girl, no matter how long it took. Mentors like John Fitzpatrick didn't come around more than once in a lifetime.

She slung her backpack over her shoulder and locked the car. As she strode through toward the beach, her cell vibrated. On the screen, a text from her youngest sister.

Elena's not at school

A blast of fog-chilled ocean air whirled up the street, cutting through her denim jacket. Shuddering, she returned the cell to her pocket and cursed Elena, picturing her getting stoned with her worthless boyfriend. She hadn't told Fitz about Elena. Would he have trusted her with this assignment if he had known?

She crossed Pleasure Point Drive, scanned the beach. Nearly empty. She checked the waves. Tall, but rolling into the north wind, tops crumbling. Bad conditions for surfers. Still, there were a couple of loners sitting on the sand, staring out at the bay. She walked up to one, a sunburnt blond wrapped in a blue-and-white beach towel. "Mind if I sit down?"

Shading his eyes, he looked up at her, then smoothed the sand to his left. "Be my guest. You bring a board?"

She sat beside him and mimicked his stare, watching the white caps. "Nope. Just watching."

"Not much to see. What's your name?"

"Kelly. Yours?"

"Bob. Haven't seen you around."

"I hitched from Fresno. Looking for a friend of mine. Crystal." She reached into her jeans pocket and pulled out a small photo of Crystal and herself, photoshopped to look like they'd been together in a photo booth. "I'm worried about her. Maybe you've seen her? She has a German Shepard named Trace. They're inseparable."

He squinted, stared at the photo for a long time. Maybe this was the break she'd been hoping for?

"I maybe saw a girl like this. Downtown. But her hair was short and black."

"She could have dyed and cut it, no problem."

"Yeah. Well, her dog was some king of mutt. Yellowish fur. Not a German Shepard."

"Where downtown?"

"Laurel Street, near Chez Antoine. Amazing green eyes, like these. I tried to chat her up, but she just kept walking."

"When was this?"

"Mmm. Last week. Wednesday, I think."

"And you haven't seen her since?"

"Nope."

"If you do, tell her that her aunt Julie is looking for her, okay? It's like, her home is a bad scene. But she can live with her aunt Julie now. She should call her."

Bob slid sideways and looked Luz in the face. Before she could stop him, he lifted the sunglasses off her face. "You're not really her friend, are you?"

"Yes, I am. She just doesn't know it yet."

Luz's cell vibrated. "Excuse me?" She stood and opened the cell. Its screen read "Office—Mrs. Moldonado." She walked to the road before answering.

"This is Luz."

There was silence, then the sound of a woman weeping.

"Hello?"

CHAPTER SEVENTEEN

Times like this, Peter always thought of his long dead Hungarian grandfather. "Born to love the vine?" his grandfather would ask. And before Peter could answer, his grandfather would thump Peter's chest with his fist, saying, "You give it your life!"

A horn blared, bringing Peter's attention back to the traffic on California's Highway 1. He checked his rearview mirror. A rusty Ford with four surfboards strapped to the roof had pulled onto the highway behind him and was now riding his bumper. The driver honked again. Peter floored the accelerator of his worn out truck, hoping the increased speed would be enough to satisfy. In truth, the beach traffic was crazy right now. The sun was poised to take its nightly plunge, and all the surfers and sun bathers had decided to head home to Santa Cruz.

His nerves were fried. Not only because of the traffic.

Tina, his wife, napped in the passenger seat. Ordinarily she loved to watch the coast between San Francisco and Santa Cruz: beautiful beaches, tan cliffs, showy surf, sometimes even whales. But two days at the Multiple Sclerosis Clinic had worn her out. As always, the doctors had emphasized the need for rest. And, as always, she had claimed she was careful not to wear herself out, sidestepping the fact that she held a full-time job.

Five days a week he drove her to work at Good Samaritan Hospital in Soquel. Five days a week he felt a leaden weight of guilt as he stopped at the staff entrance. When his wine had begun to win awards, he'd said, "Soon we'll be out of debt, and we'll have a big, new winery. I'll make enough to support us. Why don't you tell the hospital you're retiring?"

"Mmm," had been her answer.

He'd lifted her wheelchair from the back of the truck and positioned it beside the passenger door. She'd leaned toward him, wrapping her arms around his neck while he lowered her into the chair. She was light in his arms, lighter than she ought to be.

She'd held his face in both her hands and kissed his lips. "You keep forgetting. I like my job." With that, she'd pivoted her wheelchair and rolled toward the hospital door. He'd watched her go, silver hair streaming behind, delicate hands maneuvering her chair.

And it would be no different next Monday, of that he was certain. He pulled his eyes from the road and stole a glance at her. Cushioned by a neck pillow, her face relaxed in sleep, the pain-lines were eased. He would give anything—anything—to carry her pain for her, have her walk again. If she could retire, then maybe she'd get better.

She *used* to like her job, that he believed. She'd been a wonderful nurse. Who would know better than he? But after the last big MS flare-up, the one that put her in a wheelchair, she'd left nursing to become an administrator. A number-cruncher. A form-filler-outer.

She'd never spoken one word of regret. But hell, "like" her job? *She* worked so that *he* could pursue a dream. That was the truth.

Another horn screeched. A long line of cars had stacked up behind him. As soon as he could, he swerved off the road and onto a beach turnout, killed the ignition and waited for Tina to wake. She sighed, shifted position until her head rested against the truck's window. She snuffled like a kitten. Sound asleep.

Carefully, quietly, he opened the driver's door and stood, staring at the ocean. Even though it was early October, the breeze was soft and balmy. Wild fennel and sage perfumed the air. Soon the sun would nose-dive to oblivion. Maybe watching would bring him some peace.

Tomorrow he would prepare for the harvest. Tomorrow he would force himself to believe success was within reach.

For two years running they'd won gold medals in the San Francisco Chronicle's Wine Competition. Wine critics had been calling, wanting to visit the winery. Until two weeks ago, it had seemed that Hanak winery was ready for fame.

But then everything had changed. He'd been topping-off the barrels of '08 Zinfandel, adding wine to fill the space that evaporation created while the wine aged. Routine maintenance and an opportunity to taste the wine, to see how it was coming along. Routine.

But not this time.

The second he'd pulled the cork from the first barrel's bung hole, he'd known he was in trouble. The sharp stench of vinegar, the winemaker's nightmare, filled his nose even before he set the cork aside. And it wasn't just one barrel. The entire '08 vintage was lost, and he didn't know how it had happened.

He'd had to tell Tina, but he'd done his best to pretend he wasn't worried. He'd told her the new crop of grapes was extraordinary, maybe the best he'd ever grown. A cool summer had allowed the grape sugar to develop slowly, fostering the complexity of flavor his customers expected. If he was careful, if he could figure out what had gone wrong last year, he could save their reputation.

His customers. How many would he lose, now that the '08 vintage was ruined? The timing couldn't have been worse. He pictured the headline of the next Santa Cruz Wine Newsletter: "Was Hanak Wineries a flash-in-the-pan?"

As the sun dipped below the horizon, the rippling waves turned pale green, then gentle pink. The grapes of early summer. Then a short burst of flaming red resolving into purple-black. Ripeness. The moment of harvest.

As he steered the truck onto the pavement, his thoughts returned to his grandfather and a time when the ocean was, to him, nothing but a wash of blue ink on *A Child's Map of the World.* While they had huddled next to the only radiator in their frigid Chicago tenement, his grandfather, his *nagyapa,* had tried to warm him with stories of summer sunshine and fragrant vineyards, stories of their village in Hungary before the Communists had taken over, before they escaped in a hay wagon with nothing but their lives.

Nagyapa had told him of the Bukk Mountains, where early spring painted the vineyards with bright green shoots and tender pink flowers. As he spoke, the old man's hands wove through the air, tending remembered vines, counting buds, pruning branches. "Two buds only, you cut off the others. Not too much fruit, Pieter. Much fruit, no flavor." With a flat hand he contoured the air, showing Peter the mountainside in his memory. "Here the land slopes east, so I trim the leaves to welcome the sun. Over here, the vines are sick; I pull them out. The roots, Pieter, the roots! You know how long? Three meters, even four!"

When their lesson was over, Nagyapa grasped Peter's shoulder and confided, "Making wine is to love a beautiful woman. Waking up, you think, 'Today I will lose her.' Every harvest, I am crazy. Crazy for worry."

###

Meeting Elianne

Sharon Schaefer
Excerpt from a work in progress

Chapter One

Daddy works in a lumber mill down in town and comes home late on Saturday and stays till Sunday evening. Sometimes he don't make it home at all. Working his fingers to the bone, he says.

Mama is sickly since the last baby. So is the baby for all that. His name is Danny, and he's just short of two year old. Can't even sit up yet.

The boys are pretty useless in the house, but can do some hunting, work in the garden and help with the haying in the fall.

We girls are in charge of the house. When Mama isn't turned to the wall in her bed, she tells us what to cook. Other times we make taters and milk gravy for supper and oatmeal or eggs for breakfast. Sister is learning to make biscuits. I don't say she's good at it yet, just learning.

Dorthy has pretty much given up on going to school. She takes care of Mama and the baby, which takes up a lot of the day.

I go to school sometimes. I really like school, especially science. I love learning about plants and animals and why they are the way they are. But it makes more sense for me to stay home, take care of the chickens, clean up the house, and milk the cow. Daddy says "it ain't fair for Dorthy to do everthin'." I miss going though.

We make the boys go to school. As much to get them out from under foot as for the learning. Next fall Darin will be eleven and old enough to work at the dairy down the road. He'll milk in the morning before school, and again after school. That ought to keep him out of trouble is what Daddy says.

Then Davy will have to step up and do the hunting. All he does now is read books and daydream his way through life. Some times I have to shake him just to get him to bring in the wood for the cook stove. He reads out loud to Mama when she asks, and I will admit he does a good job of that. Of course we all listen, and his reading does make the chores a little easier sometimes. Davy brings me books from school, that our teacher sends. Daddy doesn't know about the books.

Well now that you know our family situation, I'll get down to telling you my story about our cousin Elianne. She isn't like anybody I ever saw before or after she done came to stay.

It had been raining all day and come dusk there is a knocking on our door. Mama cooked dinner for the first time in a long while, and we kids are sitting at the table waiting for Daddy to wash up for supper. Mama has just set Daddy's plate on the table when the knock come. Mama says, "Hush you kids, I think someone is knocking on our door." Daddy says, "What the hell?"

Daddy says, "Mother see who is at the door." Dorthy can tell Mama is weary, so she says "You sit down Mama, I'll go. It's just probably someone lost."

Dorthy opens the door, and standing in the dim light from the lantern on the table is a wet and be-draggled old crone. She is carrying a big carpet bag in one hand and a square leather bag in the other.

Daddy turns half way round and looks the crone up and down. He says to Dorthy, "Show her into the house and shut the damn door."

He says, "Move over Davy and let Elli sit down." Then he says, "Dorthy Jane, shut your mouth 'fore a fly gets in it, and get a plate for your kin."

We kids know better than to ask questions. We hunker down our heads toward our food while Dorthy Jane fetches up a plate. Then Daddy says grace. No sooner than we say "Amen" when Davy who hardly ever talks, turns to the woman and says, "Howdy. My name is Davy John Soder. Who are you?"

Daddy scowls at Davy, then the rest of us. When Daddy scowls we kids know to shut up. Not Davy, he looks at this woman with his open face. Daddy raises his eyebrows, but Mama touches his arm and he backs down.

The woman smiles, and pushes her hair away from her face. That smile changes her into a beautiful woman about our Mama's age. "My name is Ellianne Francis and I am your Daddy's oldest sister's oldest daughter. That makes me your cousin." Then she begins eating as if that explained everything.

###

POETRY

POEMS
KATHIE OLSEN

FOR CHARLEY: ONE

We fell in love with so much heat way back then
Stumbling holding on soaring
Lilacs and bread
Frozen noses and woolen warmth
We held on so tight we haven't let go for decades
That heat has become our very blood
Only now it mostly seeps warmth for weary bones
Not so much springing to life
As sneaking back with sweet slow power

FOR CHARLEY: TWO

At night our web becomes very small
We are tied to each other
You move   I move with you
I curl   You curl into me
You moan   I hug you
I wake   You softly query
Our smells are familiar
Our skin mutually alert
Our hair is known to our hands
After 40 years we are cocooned
In sweet loving slumber

FOR CHARLEY: THREE

We should be able to stay here
Always
We aren't bothering anybody
We're pretty quiet
We are kind to each other
Why can't we just stay this way
Always
I thought we were deeper than dust to dust
I thought we were warmer than death
I thought we were
I think we are
Always
We are

FOR CHARLEY: FOUR

Can you believe it's been 40 years?
I mean – Are we even that old?
Oh yes we are
We are that old

But when I look at you, I see you then
And when you look at me, you see me as I was
And we laugh at the illusion created by white hair and
wrinkles

FOR CHARLEY: FIVE

I love your hands and how they touch
Sometimes just giving comfort
Sometimes waking a wildness in me
Sometimes making bread

Long fingers, broad palm
The hands of a gentleman
A gentle man
An artist

I watch when you make pottery
Bent over the wheel,
Wet slurry coating your elegant hands
Clay rising into cup after cup bowl after bowl

Your face is concentrated, relaxed, intent
Your blue eyes flash at me
Your arms are strong
You are beautiful in your muddy world

FOR CHARLEY: SIX / AFTER THE APPOINTMENT

White hair
Big veins in your hands
Pale blue sheen on your face
Beloved face on the pillow.

I thought you were as unending as the earth
As solid as that tree outside the window
How did you get so fragile?
How would I survive without you?

In the morning I tell you my dreams
You stare at the wall listening softly
Patting my hand or my behind
Bringing me back to earth

Earth Solid   Warm Home
Earth Fragile   Tree Bent
Fear has crept into our bed

ON WISDOM: ONE

Like most people
Over the age of 70,
I believe time flies.
Except when it crawls.

I'm getting used to this.
The dialectic of life.
You know – if This is true,
That is also true.

I don't think it's senility.
I think it's wisdom,
This delight in the dialectic.
I like it.

I'm finding peace where I once found confusion.
I'm delighting in absurdity.
Finding joy in contradictions.
Settling into a cackling old age.

On Wisdom: Two

What's that bump on your face Ama?
Squeching humiliation, I say,
Oh, old people get bumps sweetheart.
It's because we have so much wisdom.
We just can't hold it all inside so,
Out it pops.

Now, when he's bored,
He places his small finger on my bump.
He says, I'm taking all your wisdom, Ama,
And you don't have any left.
I am now supposed to be simple.
He is now wise.

With great seriousness, he explains things.
This is where the snow comes from, Ama.
Those are stars up there, Ama. They are far.
You cannot run in the street, Ama.
And he is comforted by his wisdom,
While I admire.

When he tires of the game, or
He wants me to read to him,
He puts that finger back on my bump and
My wisdom comes back.
He is comforted by me being a grown-up again,
And I work on accepting my bump.

THE WAY OF THINGS

Coming home after too long away,
I cannot tell you the comfort of my things.
The exact kitchen knife for the job.
The book weight by the dining table so I can read while
eating.
Lamps softly lighting every appropriate place.
Mary's painting of fruit and blue glass.
The background tick of the pendulum clock.
Beloved faces gazing through frames, whispering memories.
The pillow that fits my neck.
Book spines announcing treasured contents.

This is a collection artfully, lovingly, built
Fork by fork, tea pot by tea pot, tablecloth by tablecloth.
In sum, they tell the story of who I am.
Where I've been. What I stand for.
My ancestors smile at me through their artifacts here.
The pillowcases have cradled beloved heads.
The table has hosted hundreds of meals.

This is my legacy.
My children have grown and they are marvelous,
But they are not of my making. They are themselves.
This house, this garden, and these things,
With their patina of use and age, they express my self.
I confess to adoration and a bit of preening.
This place is beautiful to me, and my stuff is my joy.

When I die, those who are left will have to plow through it,
Sorting out the treasures they want, tossing or giving away
the rest.
As soon as this begins, all but my essence will start to
disappear.
It is the way of things.

THE OLD MAN'S TABLE

Every Sunday morning
There they are
Bright eyed and watch capped
Grinning slyly
As they solve the problems of the world.

No topic is off-limits.
Israel, Congress, and Viagra
All fall before their quick wit
And infinite wisdom.
Laughing uproariously
They pontificate over their coffee.

Five guys. None less than 70.
Three cups of regular, one decaf,
One dry cappucino stirred with a tiny spoon.
Three heart guys, two hip replacements, one kidney
condition.
They compare the sins of aging.

They're a riot, and they know it,
These coffeehouse regulars.
They're proud that the barista knows their names.
They all think she's cute,
Worthy of a vaguely recalled hard-on.

I'm reading the paper
Drinking my soy latte and chewing my bagel
Occasionally trying to eavesdrop.
They could care less.
I'm not invited.

###

MEDITATIONS
FAYEGAIL MANDELL BISACCIA

BLISS

Source Within

Entice me with simplicity.
With You the worry slips aside

And in its place, a sweet serenity,
A roiling avalanche of Light,
A depth of Silence unbeknownst to me, 'til now.

All the days are filled with complications—
Things to solve and meds to try,
Broken hearts and broken dreams,
Distractions, all, from time with You, my Soul.

Clear away the clutter, Loving One.
When I but shift the focus from my thoughts
To You, all slides away, and I am left with

Sweet surrender into Bliss.
Away from time You carry me,

Dear Source Within.

from *Circles: Prayers for the End of Life,*
Fayegail Mandell Bisaccia

A DAILY MEDITATION

Source of Life, grant me grace and dignity to live
    this day.
Give me patience to notice a fleeting smile,
    a moment of tenderness.

Help me face today's challenges
with wisdom and with courage,
        courage to take a stand when I must,
        and to surrender when I have done all I can.

Forgive me the mistakes I make today,
        and help me to forgive myself.

Remind me to cherish a sunlit patch of grass,
        birdsong, a blossom in the yard.

Help me recognize the changes in my body,
        and the changes in those I love,
        as a part of Life.

And with all of that, Eternal One,
        help me to rest quietly in Your Love
        and to find peace in every breath.

from *Dancing in My Mother's Slippers: A Journey of Grief and Healing,*
Fayegail Mandell Bisaccia

###

TRAVEL
STORIES

FACE OFF

LOIS LANGLOIS

Several on-coming vehicles flicked their headlights at us, so we knew there was something up ahead. We just didn't know what it was. Thus, when we finally saw him, a frisson of excitement went through the van. He was headed straight toward us, in our lane of traffic, and he had no interest in getting out of our way. Step by inexorable step, he plodded toward us. He was large; he was dark; he was shaggy.

Yes, there he was, my very first bison. We stopped the van and sat there, transfixed, as the big creature shuffled toward us, ever so slowly. At the last minute, he veered slightly and ambled right past the driver's side. I could have rolled down my window and touched him. What an introduction to Yellowstone!

It was another annual outing of the Ladies' Backpack Group. We all agree we need a new name, now that we've aged into Travelodge Motels and day hikes. Still, we haven't come up with a catchy one yet, so I'll stay with the Ladies' Backpack Group until we do. Besides, the title provides a window into our history, starting with our yearly circumnavigations of the Mount Hood Timberline Trail back in the '80s; through our treks in Peru, the Dolomites, Switzerland and Eastern Europe in the 90's and 2000's; and now on to our explorations of various national parks closer to home the last several years. Not that we couldn't shoulder our packs and zip around the Timberline Trail, or into the North Cascades, any time we wanted to.   We just haven't done it lately.

Enough of that history, though.   This summer the Ladies did Yellowstone.   I had requested it, for I was the only one who had never been there.   The other four agreed. We chose our dates, made reservations, and started planning. Each of the others, Becky, Karen, Lu and Linda, has great skills in researching good hikes and trails, while I have the VW van that will carry all of us together.   So, we parceled out the tasks.   Soon we were set.

Of course, as anyone who has ever owned a VW van will know, a person could spend an entire vacation's-worth of writing just describing one's love-hate relationship with that particular vehicle.   On the plus side, five senior women in a VW van can drive as slowly or fast as they want, with impunity.   We come from the tie-dye and peace sign generation, so we motored along at whatever speed we chose, smiling benignly at any stares or glares we received. We had no grief from the Sturgis, South Dakota-bound Harley motorcycle set; they seemed to regard us as a separate but equal species.   Or maybe we were invisible to them.

We came in to Yellowstone from the north, through Gardiner, Montana, where we stayed for four nights.   After mingling with the crowds of people and elk at Mammoth Hot Springs and promenading along the board walks over the travertine-laced spewing springs, we started our hiking adventures with a loop around Beaver Ponds.   At the ponds, the beavers seemed to be long gone.   Even the dams were visible only in the imagination.   Still, it was a good warm-up hike, and we saw several animals, specifically, squirrels, birds, and a striped snake.   Becky went behind a bush for a bathroom break and found herself right next to an elk. Caught by surprise, she blew on her whistle, and the intruding giant left before the rest of us arrived.

The next day we ascended Bunsen Peak, 8,564 feet elevation, a vigorous hike up shale switchbacks. The view from the top was 360 degrees, with the vastness of the Yellowstone Canyon, Yellowstone River Valley, and Yellowstone Lake spread out to our east, while the Gallatin Mountains anchored the western horizon. It was my first chance to experience just how BIG Yellowstone is.

On the way down we took the back route, which was longer and more winding. Also, it was free of shale, which made it more appealing. We had seen a coyote, plump and healthy, sauntering by a pond at the start of the hike, as we were parking the van. Along the trail we were entertained by several grouse, including a gorgeous ruffed grouse. And at the end of the hike, I spotted a badger, my first ever sighting of one. He jumped off a log, ran down the embankment, jogged across the road, and skedaddled out of sight. I was thrilled. Lastly, though, we saw a worrisome sight. There was a momma duck – I don't know what kind – swimming with her babies on a pond near where we'd seen the coyote earlier. We went around a corner and saw a lone duckling cavorting in and out among the rushes. He was having a great time, I could tell, but he was way out of sight from his mom and siblings. Oh, no, I thought, this plucky little ducky is not going to last very long. Such is nature.

And so the trip went. We hiked along the Yellowstone River, made all the right stops along the Yellowstone Canyon, saw the Falls – Upper and Lower. We hiked to Lost Lake – is there only one in that vast territory? – and beyond to the Petrified Tree, a pre-glacial-period sequoia, of all things, near where we saw two bull moose on the hoof, browsing away in a meadow near the road. Bull moose have good-sized racks, and they are potentially dangerous, but these were oblivious to the rock-star attention they were receiving from the ogling humans. That was our first experience of a "moose jam," which is all about people

198

and cars, of course, and nothing you would want to spread on your toast.

It was on the day we moved from Gardiner to West Yellowstone that we had the face off with the bison. Our first steam vent sightings, the Roaring Mountain Vents, were along that road, and it was soon after that when we met up with Mr. Big. I was overwhelmed by his majesty and dignity. Little did I realize that, by the end of this day, I would see literally thousands of bison.

The Hayden Valley, where the Yellowstone River winds its serpentine way from Lake to Falls to Canyon, is the place to be if you love bison. They dominate the place, although they were hunted almost to extinction in the early 1900s. Now they number around 3,000, and I'll swear we saw most of them. We watched a large group down along the river from a perch up on the road. We saw families clumped together, bulls rolling in the dust to manage the insect bites, rusty-hued babies chasing after their moms, individuals eye-balling the lone coyote that sashayed among them. We saw them sharing the water's edge with pelicans, herons, and other water birds. We saw them chugging up the embankment and then moseying across the road, wreaking havoc on traffic flow and adding to the burgeoning "bison jams."

Farther down the road, as we stopped at a bubbling hillside aptly named Mud Volcano, we were entertained by a magnificent fellow up on the hillside. He seemed to be hemmed in by the trees, as he stood there for a long time, nibbling disinterestedly on the vegetation and looking down on the traffic. Then, to our surprise, he took a few steps backward and just walked away.

It was at Mud Volcano that we first noticed how much bison enjoy warm steam vents, pools, even geysers. All the scenic oozing and spewing spots have board walks with strict admonitions to visitors to stay on the walk, lest one break through the surrounding "crust" and sink into an over-heated death.   However, the bison clearly ignore these warnings. They bask in the warm dust and mud surrounding such places. Significant volumes of dried bison scat leave evidence that "inside the fence" is a perennial favorite hangout for the big creatures. In fact, the rangers told us, these places are bison spas as the autumn days become colder. I pictured dowagers at the mud baths.

At the end of the day, we moved on to West Yellowstone, with visions of large waterfalls, herds of bison, and steaming or mud-splopping hillsides dancing in our heads. To finish it off, we were treated to an elegant *pas de deux* by a pair of sand hill cranes in a meadow as we drove to our new lodging.

We had seen the dust-loving lowlands, and it was time to head back to the hills.   Linda suggested an exhilarating hike, to the peak of 10,243 foot Mount Washburn, topped by an actively staffed fire lookout station. It is part of the northern rim of the gigantic caldera which contains Yellowstone Lake, created by a volcanic eruption about 640,000 years ago. From parking lot to summit is a comfortable elevation gain of 1,405 feet. We geared up for a long day of good walking – water, food, hiking poles, clothing layers, band aids and various foot cushions. It took most of the day, and it was well worth the effort. Once again, we saw far-away peaks in every direction, the Yellowstone Canyon right below us, vegetation changes as we climbed up into an alpine zone. The only lack was a good animal sighting – we heard about a wolf one hiker had seen, but the wolf eluded us. However, we saw quite a variety of "plumage" on the some of the other hikers – flip-flops, tank-tops, all kinds of get-ups that seemed to ignore the rocky path and cool, windy conditions up on top.

The next day, we headed down the road to the geysers. I cannot adequately describe every pool or vent that we saw. I wish I could. Each was unique; each was exquisite. Some were muddy and viscous; others were clear and brightly colored. We learned all about thermophiles, little heat-loving organisms, and how the color of each pool was related to its temperature and the resulting specific thermophile which thrived in that heat range. A brilliantly clear aquamarine pool might be right next to a murky orange pool. Yellow, gold, lime, fuchsia, emerald green – it was, indeed, an artist's palette of colors. And we could feel that all of them were hot, very hot.

Of course we saw Old Faithful and all the fascinating geysers in its vicinity. The crowds there were rather daunting, but everyone was of good cheer. We chatted with folks from every corner of the world. All were enjoying the spectacle. As one can note from the names, the geysers in this area go out of their way to be individually amazing -- Castle Geyser, Turban Geyser, Grand Geyser, Spasmodic Geyser. And more.

So far we had managed a good balance between fine hikes and Yellowstone 'must-see' attractions. We spent our final morning in Yellowstone Park at West Thumb, admiring more thermal pools, with the usual array of amazing colors. West Thumb is a sub-part of Yellowstone Lake, a little lake within a big lake. It appears to be about the diameter of our own Crater Lake, here in Oregon. We learned that West Thumb is a mini-caldera, so-to-speak, at least in comparison to the larger caldera of Yellowstone. It is the result of a more recent eruption, only 140,000 years ago.

In the afternoon there was time for one more good hike, on a trail called Elephant's Back, near Yellowstone Lake. Perhaps it is not a '10' in the hike book, but it was definitely refreshing and with good views of the lake. We shook out our legs along the trail and were ready to drive to our next stop, Jackson Hole and the Grand Tetons.

Even though we'd had a long day, the drive to Jackson Hole was pure pleasure. We drove past Mount Sheridan, part of the remaining southern rim of the original large caldera, and on past the South Entrance of Yellowstone. The Tetons came into view – live, they are even more thrilling than as seen on a million natural scenery calendars. After pizza at a lakeside marina on Jackson Lake, we drove through sagebrush plains alongside the incipient Snake River. It was dusk. Sure enough, every pronghorn and deer in the area seemed determined to cross the road right in front of us. We drove slowly.

Safely ensconced in our new motel, we planned our attack on the Tetons. Let's see – front-range lake hikes, or canyon ones? We drooled over the high country routes, the loops between one canyon and the next. Now, we are in our 70s, not that age should stop us. But we had not brought gear for an overnight, which would be required for any canyon loops. Thus, we researched the lower elevations.

Next day, we started with a lake hike, to get a feel for the area. We walked briskly past shallow String Lake, where a dad paddle-boarded with his baby daughter swaddled to his chest. Then on to Leigh Lake, bigger, deeper, colder, with tempting views into the canyons on the other side. And, lastly, Lu and I hiked still further to Bearpaw Lake, a sweet little lake at the end of the chain. Along that stretch we had positive interactions with a flicker, a deer, and a German couple. No negative interactions, though I did manage to wear myself out, at long last, after so many days of hiking and admiring mud pots. Back at our motel room, I got the shivers, even though it was a hot day.

Thus, next day, when Lu, Karen, and Linda took off for the Cascade Canyon Trail, Becky and I decided to stay in town and check out the fabled village of Jackson. We rode the public shuttle downtown and spent the morning at the annual Arts Fair. Then we took in the book sale at the public library, where I picked up some fine travel books for $1 apiece. After that, we lounged around the motel pool, had a glass of wine, and got slightly silly. Oh, that was a much-needed day.

And, wouldn't you just know it – that was the day the others saw a little black bear, right on the trail in front of them. And a moose, way closer than the two we'd seen in Yellowstone. I realized I shouldn't whine about it when they told me, because I could not have survived another day of hiking right then. Besides, Becky and I had had a delightful day, ourselves.

The very next morning, we were all back at it. We scouted our maps, hike books and cell phone apps for options. The answer leapt out at us. Death Canyon. Let's do it, we unanimously agreed. The trail guide urged us not to drive to the end of the road, so we didn't. That added an extra half mile, which was fine – at the start of the day. We hiked to the trailhead, then up through the forest. Then back down again, toward Phelps Lake. You who are hikers know there is nothing more frustrating than giving up elevation gain along a trail. But, at last, we were beside Death Canyon, and up we went. It was a good trail, with long switchbacks and lots of white, shiny granite. It was hard work, and the day was very hot. Finally we reached some cascading water, then, around a corner, some pools in the river. Most welcome. Not much farther, we went back into the forest and came upon a log cabin. Oh! Hansel and Gretel, I thought. Sure enough, a man was living there, a Park Service employee, doing maintenance work on this lovely old Civilian Conservation Corps (CCC) cabin. He was eager to chat. After four hours of hiking, we surmised we had reached the outward terminus of our day. But, no, the Park man insisted, we really must hike still farther, just a little, down the trail, for that was where the views opened up.

Thank goodness for that. He was right. Another 200 yards along the trail, the vista appeared and we saw an entire Gaudi cathedral of mountain tops. There were pointy spires, large mounds, Holy Family groupings, everywhere we looked. It was truly magnificent. Now I really wished for a backpack and a sleeping bag.

But that was not to be. It was time to turn around and start back. We stopped for our lunch break at the stream.

And that was where I had my second face off. I was sitting on a rock, eating cheese and crackers. I had on a pink t-shirt and red sun shirt. Startled by a loud buzzing sound, I looked up to see a large creature flying straight toward my face. Mmm-mmm-mmm, gigantic bees around here, was my first thought as I flinched and ducked. But, no, it was a humming bird, who clearly took me for a colorful flower. I liked that. He – or she – came back for a second run at me, and this time I held my ground as the bird flew within just inches of me, helicopter-hovered right in front of my face, looked me in the eye, and then took off. What a gift.

That should be the end of the story – the exquisite book-end face offs with bison and humming bird at start and end of trip. And it is almost the end. But not quite.

We had to hike out of Death Canyon, and that turned out to be a challenge in its own right. The hike down seemed as long, hard, and hot as the hike up had been. Those white granite switchbacks certainly held the afternoon heat. Two of our group had a little trouble with heat exhaustion. I helped Becky work her way down, and then back up that one killer section toward the end. For a while we were setting goals of "let's make it to the next shady spot," where we would stop and regroup. Two gracious hikers provided succor – hydration tabs and water. Even though we had brought plenty of each, it was not enough. At last, we could see the trailhead in front of us, and there was a glorious sight. Linda, Lu, and Karen were driving up in the van. They'd finished the hike ahead of us and decided we'd appreciate not walking that final half mile. The VW van had never looked more beautiful.

On our final day in Jackson Hole, the others decided they'd had plenty of good hiking, so they took the ski tram ride at Teton Village. I, however, regretted that I'd missed the hike up Cascade Canyon, so I went there on my own. Boat ride across Jenny Lake, then hordes of people hiking up to Hidden Waterfall and on to Inspiration Point. I decided I'd go a little farther, maybe even find that bear the others had seen. I did not find the bear, but the hike was well worth the effort. I soon left almost all the other hikers behind. Cascade Canyon is a beautiful canyon, more open than Death Canyon, with a graceful waterfall cascading off the glacier of Tweewinot Mountain. The path stayed next to the creek, which sparkled in the sunlight and made joyous sounds. I felt ecstatic to be part of the vast expanse of nature. Once again, I looked up into the back country and longed to hike in there for a few days. Will the Ladies' Backpack Group ever do that again? I hope so. One more ridge beyond the day hikers – that is where I prefer to be.

***

Afterthought:

The lands of Yellowstone and the Grand Tetons are a rich blessing on our earth. I am grateful that people of power and influence – Ferdinand Hayden, U. S. Grant, Theodore Roosevelt, the Rockefellers, and others – had the foresight and wisdom to preserve them. At the same time I am sad to think that Native Americans, who preserved those lands even better for many years prior, must see them now with mixed sentiments of their own about what was once theirs to guard and enjoy. Yellowstone is incredibly BIG and diverse, while the Tetons are small in scope, with their incredible beauty packed into one tight range. I like that. I like knowing that the amazing properties of both are still changing, and that, geologically, anything might happen there in the future. Mostly, it pleases me that our earth is diverse, and that, given a chance, it will protect itself. I'm glad I finally got there, and that the Ladies Backpack Group had another fine outing.

###

ANOTHER SEASON IN JAMAICA

LOIS LANGLOIS

"Grandma, come and sit down. You need to rest." Oneal's smile is huge, full of gorgeous Jamaican teeth, as he comes bounding toward me across the large room. After nine years, I still have some resistance to that Jamaican honorific title, but it is a losing battle. I smile back, pull the pedometer out of my right scrubs pocket, and show it to him. "No, look, Oneal, I've only gone a little over 5,000 steps so far. I have to do 10,000 steps today. If I don't get my exercise, I'll grow old." Oneal laughs, takes hold of my elbow, and tries to steer me toward a chair. I dance away and keep moving.

I scan the room. All six dentists have patients in their chairs, but Doctor Richie is giving post-treatment care instructions to a man for whom he has just done an extraction – or maybe three or five. Clipboard in hand, I head outside, past the noisy compressors which keep our equipment running, and shout "Extraction # 23." A buxom mother in bright blue T-shirt and coral tights hands off her two little ones to another woman – her sister or neighbor, perhaps – and steps toward me.

Yanke materializes at my side, beaming his serene, four-toothed smile. He takes the woman's # 23 laminated ticket from her while I review her health history forms, and then he leads her over to our nurse, Chris, who will take her blood pressure before sending her to Richie's chair for her extraction. Yanke is the polar opposite of Oneal. Tall, grey haired, quiet in his smile and movement. Not just grey-haired, but magnificently Rasta in his coif. His long coils of hair stick out in amazing directions, and he wears something like chopsticks to keep them all in place atop his head. His smile is beatific as he reassures me, "You're doin' fine, Sistah. Ev'ryting Irie." His calmness washes over me.

It is Wednesday, our third day in this make-shift dental clinic in Priory. In my years of volunteering with Great Shape's 1000 Smiles dental project in Jamaica, this is the best space we've had – large and light, with plenty of room for each dentist and assistant to set up a "suitcase unit." It is the town's community hall, right next to the beach. Rumor has it that Bob Marley played a concert here once, before he was famous, if one can imagine such a time. With the help of Yanke, Oneal, and others on our local Jamaican support team, our own set-up group of Skip and the twins, Oshane and Roshane, has done a magnificent job of running hoses, cords and connectors so that each station has lights, water, and adequate power for the dental equipment. No need to worry about a power failure right in the midst of drilling on a tooth, as has happened more than occasionally in previous years.

Great Shape! Inc. is a non-profit organization started 25 years ago by three women from my community in Oregon, in response to the devastation they witnessed in Jamaica from Hurricane Gilbert in 1988. It is a wonderful example of how a small non-profit can grow into a successful service delivery system. With major sponsorship from the Sandals Foundation (the charitable arm of the Sandals and Beaches resort empire) and the support of Jamaica's Ministries of Health and Education, Great Shape! Inc. now annually provides eight weeks of dental clinics, two weeks of school-based literacy programs, two weeks of eye care services, plus computer systems set-up and training, teacher training, and other small projects throughout the island. All these programs are run by volunteers, and we work hard.

For years I have volunteered on the dental project, 1000 Smiles, and that is how I have ended up in this large room at this very minute.

I look around at our team. Doc Shinn, our clinical leader, freshly arrived from receiving the Humanitarian of the Year award at the American Dental Association conference in New Orleans, has a thirteen year old boy in his chair.   We planned to take only adults at this particular clinic, as children in Jamaica have some access to public health dental clinics, while adults have basically none. But this child's mom has brought him in, in pain. Doc Shinn sees that the situation is urgent. It goes to the heart of his values as a dentist to relieve suffering, so the boy is getting Doc's best and most attentive care. Doc's wife Faria, whom he met while working at his own volunteer dental clinic in Uganda, is assisting him. Her pregnant condition is evident to all, but she does not miss a beat in her chair-side duties. Each time I walk past I observe that the young boy is receiving extensive work, so I am surprised, eventually, to see him stand, with an anesthetized and lopsided smile on his face, to thank both Doc Shinn and Faria profusely.

Next to Doc Shinn is Doctor Jack, closing in on 70, still spry and full of energy. He is the jitter-bug dance champion of our group. Long ago one of the Jamaican dental nurses dubbed him "Jack-out-of-the-box," as he moved around her clinic at breathtaking speed. Jack also has received national and international awards and recognition. He and Doc Shinn met long ago while climbing and volunteering in Nepal. Jack is the clinical leader of our school-based Sealant project, which targets preventive care for children. He is involved in learning and training others how to provide the best possible dental care in developing countries, in less than ideal conditions. But here, other than

209

having each station's equipment and supplies laid out on packing boxes, this week's conditions are as close to ideal as I've seen in our clinics. Jack currently has Seymour, our dental student from U Tech, Jamaica's University of Technology, assisting him. They are engaged in an intense discussion about the treatment being provided to the patient in the chair. Even though serious, I see that Jack has a twinkle in his eye and a spring in his step as he works.

Seymour is clearly brilliant. He soaks up knowledge from each of our dentists and insists he's learned more in one week than in three years of dental school so far. Each dentist loves teaching him. Seymour has a few things to teach our dentists, also, about Jamaican culture, values, and teeth. It's a great exchange. Seymour is not sure whether he'll stay in Jamaica to practice, once he graduates. It's hard to start a private dental practice, and public health jobs are not so great. We hope to work in partnership with the Ministry of Health and the education system to make a positive change in that dynamic so that future dental practitioners can stay in Jamaica and have successful careers.

Doctor Peter has the next chair over. I worked as his assistant a couple of years ago. Jennie, who, like I, has a non-dental job back home, is his helper this year. Peter is a recognized specialist in cosmetic dentistry. I screen the patients awaiting fillings and organize the list in order to send him those who have chipped or broken front teeth, cavities in their front teeth, etc. I sidle over to watch at the end of each treatment, when he hands the patient the mirror and says, "What do you think?" All his patients are delighted with the results. Peter is a dental artist. Since Jamaica is moving inexorably from a sugar cane and bauxite-based economy to a tourism economy, all the best jobs require a brilliant and healthy smile. Peter's wizardry is much valued.

Doctor Ted comes from Philadelphia each year and brings along his entire staff, who are known as "Ted's Angels" because they are all gorgeous women. I'd never worked in a clinic with them before, and it turns out I'm in for a wonderful surprise. Ted is a great guy and a conscientious dentist. He is generous, too, to bring his staff to Jamaica for this volunteer project. Ted and I sit beside each other on the bus from hotel to clinic several times, and I learn interesting things about him. We share stories about where to travel and hike out West, like Yellowstone and Glacier. He's a solid family man. I'm impressed with his compassion and skill.

All the "Angels" are in this clinic, too. Leslie, assisting Doctor Richie and serving as our clinic manager. She's tough and sassy, with a great heart. Rene, one of the hygienists, knocking herself out cleaning teeth all day. She has 'complained' to me this morning that I've been giving her easy cases – folks who've had their teeth cleaned within the last year. So I am happy to learn that the next patient, a 30-something man, has never had his teeth cleaned. When he gets up from her chair well over an hour later, both of them are beaming – they've become great friends, and his mouth sparkles. Jessica, the other hygienist, with a radiant smile and welcoming attitude that encourages patients to relax and enjoy the cleaning. Roxie, Doctor Ted's assistant back home, making sure he takes good care of himself while working in these tropical conditions, and revealing her warmth and thoughtfulness to all the patients who sit in their chair. And Joyce, Ted's usual front-desk person, eagerly helping out as chair-side assistant to Doctor Donnie while here in Jamaica.

Thus, after years of assuming Ted's Angels were merely attractive window-dressing at an East Coast dental office, my preconceptions are blown away and I discover they are hard-working, intelligent, caring, competent women, plus loads of fun to know and work with. I like them all so much, I have to give up my jealousy forever.

Back to the dentists. Doctors Richie and Donnie, partners in a dental clinic in an upscale community near New York City, have been volunteers in this project since the beginning. Doctor Richie looks like a tall version of Sylvester Stallone. He works out. From participating in our various clinics with him over the years, I can vouch that he is one of the best dentists ever around kids. Doctor Donnie, who went to dental school with Jack in the 60's, is a personal favorite of mine – smart, sophisticated, occasionally crabby (I've worked as his assistant over the years, so I know), and he cares passionately about doing quality dentistry. He and Richie leave their lucrative practice near The City to come sweat and use our suitcase dental units along with everyone else for one or two weeks each year. In this year's clinic, they are our extractions specialists. Sadly, dental care is not affordable or readily available for most Jamaican adults, and extraction is the most frequent service needed and provided. We deliver this service with good anesthesia and skill, so folks prefer to come to us when we are in town.

There are more volunteer staff: another hygienist, Betty; our nurse Chris; local volunteer registration helper Amanda; Sandals Foundation intern Shantelle doing computer data entry; and our Sandals Foundation liaison Lindsay, working tirelessly to organize the crowd and keep them relatively happy. Oshane and his twin brother Roshane are two of about five Jamaicans working for several months on the eight-week series of the dental project. We are paying them to be our technical staff. Oshane is with us every day sterilizing all our dental instruments and maintaining our equipment. The day of the tropical deluge we have one little power outage. I enjoy the quiet for a few minutes, but I know it's not good. In less than ten minutes, though, the power – and the compressor noise – is back with us, and we hum right along. Having Oshane on-site to deal with equipment glitches is a god-send and keeps us productive throughout each day.

Besides Oneal and Yanke, we have additional volunteer help from the local community. Our clinic is very popular, and we cannot begin to meet the needs of all those waiting for service.   Thus, Paul is our crowd management expert. I can tell he's done this kind of work before, perhaps at some of the reggae concerts. A large and fit man, he adroitly helps keep the crowd calm and realistic in their expectations, even when we must tell people in pain that we cannot care for them today, and to please come back tomorrow – very early, to get in line and get a number. Paul keeps his eye out for me and makes sure I constantly have a bottle of water nearby, as he knows I'm not used to the humidity.

It is now Thursday, day four. I scan the crowd and check where we are on each of our three lists: Cleaning (green laminated and numbered cards – our goal is 27 patients per day); Filling (blue laminated cards – 22 patients per day); Extraction (yellow laminated cards – 35 patients). It is late morning. I see an older woman in the group waiting outside – definitely older than I. Since we are "first come, first served," I assume she has been here since early morning, like everyone else. "Let me see your card, please," I ask her. # 28 Extraction, she shows me. That will be mid-afternoon, I know, so I seek permission from the group to take her ahead of the others. "Of course," several respond immediately. A couple of the younger ones give me a little scowl, but not the middle-aged ones. They are closer to being in this woman's shoes. She is 84 years old.

We go inside, where she sits in the chair at nurse Chris' station to have her blood pressure checked. Doing fine. I review her health history, and then Richie is ready for her. "Hi there baby doll," he greets her, as he does all the women, patients and volunteers alike. He is so affable and good-looking, I've never heard one person complain. This patient, Annabelle, looks quite pleased as he leads her over to his chair to look in her mouth and see just which tooth or teeth he's going to pull.

Later, I notice Annabelle sitting over by Chris' station once again. Chris is keeping an eye on her for a while before we let her go on home. I sit down next to Annabelle. She looks thoughtfully at the linoleum-tiled floor. Then, around the gauze wadded into her mouth she tells me, "I used to dance on floors just like this." My heart gives a little lurch, and I take her hand. "I am sure you were a beautiful dancer." She smiles and nods.

Oneal comes over. I ask him where she lives and whether someone is with her. "No, she came on her own, and she lives alone in Bamboo Gardens, a little community up in the hills." "How will she get home?" "When she's ready, she'll walk out to the main road and then take a route taxi."

I dig into my scrubs pocket, around the pedometer, and pull out a couple of US dollar bills. "Here's for the taxi, and will you walk her to the main road?" Oneal gives me his eager-puppy grin and helps her pick up her parcel. I get a photo of her and me together – ageless dancers. Then they are gone.

I turn back to the room. Doc Shinn, Donnie, Jack and our student, Seymour, have their heads together, looking into a patient's mouth, trying to decide the best way to treat a complex situation. Roxie is just setting up Ted's station, ready for another patient. Jessica is almost ready for a cleaning. I dance back into action, check my clipboard, twirl out to the waiting crowd, and call out, "Cleaning # 17. Filling # 12."

###

Musings on Travel

Anne Batzer

Kenya

In 2006 when I first met Njoki, the African girl my family supports in school, she was the skinniest of third graders, so shy she would not even look me in the eye. When I asked her to show me around her campus in Nyahururu, Kenya, she said not a word but slipped her tiny hand in mine.

On the long walk to the soccer field, she finally spoke, "May I carry your bag for you?" she asked. I gratefully handed her my travel pack. Her shyness---and mine---evaporated.

I had traveled to Kenya to volunteer for the Makena Children's Foundation (MCF). Founded in 1997, MCF has American sponsors for the education of 52 deserving students. Many of the children are AIDS orphans, some have a single parent. All come from Maraigushu, a sprawling rural area of subsistence farmers who raise their families without the benefit of electricity or running water. The average educational level of the adults in Maraigushu is third grade. Unfortunately, even now, fewer than 40% of all eligible Kenyan students attend secondary school.

As President of the Foundation, every spring finds me in East Africa to join with our Kenyan colleagues and do the work of this small, personal organization.

A highlight for me is my annual reunion with Njoki. Last year, when I arrived at Njoki's secondary school, she saw me in the principal's office and ran to greet me. After a long hug, I turned to the principal and said, "Isn't she beautiful?" The principal looked a little shocked. I put my arm around Njoki, looked back at the principal, and said, "She's so smart." The principal looked somewhat less serious. Finally, getting the message, as I pulled Njoki toward me, I said, "And she works so hard." Then, the principal smiled, "Yes, she is a very hard worker."

These Kenyan students are in class from 6:00 am to 4:00 pm. Then, for two hours they play games: soccer, field hockey or basketball. Supper is the following hour. At the end of the day there are several hours of tutored homework. Some classes even meet on Saturdays. Any adult would have to agree these kids work hard.

In this part of Kenya---a country striving to deal with issues of blatant corruption, poverty, political unrest, violence and lack of education---children rarely receive compliments. There's concern the kids won't work hard if they get positive feedback. A couple schools even told us children are graded lower than their actual scores to motivate them to work harder. I don't question this stance. This is a country trying to bring its people into the developed world. I wouldn't dream of telling them how to raise their young. And yet, in private, I can't stop myself from reminding Njoki of her considerable strengths.

Letters from Njoki reflect her growing fluency with English. I treasure one I received from her about five years ago when she was obviously studying similies. She ended that letter saying: "I miss you just like roasted meat." Now, our letters are frequent and lively. We talk about current events, relationships, dreams, values, love. And yet I still marvel at the strength of our bond. We've spent maybe a total of 15 hours together. We're from different continents, different countries, different generations, different classes, different races. But from my most recent visit, I know she experiences our connection as deeply as I do.

Some of the "Makena kids" are understandably embarrassed to be seen on campus with a mzungu (white person) because it sets them apart as sponsored children, poor kids. So, at her new school, I asked Njoki if she wanted to sit in the principal's office for our visit, in order to be less conspicuous.   She responded by pulling me into her classroom to introduce me to her friends. Her growing self-confidence touches me deeply

***

FRANCE

Even in the July heat of Paris, the waiter bringing my morning espresso wears an impeccable white dress shirt, cuffs rolled in crisp bands just beneath his elbows. His perfect black vest dignifies the wide expanse of his mid-section. A poet could write about the way his huge hands cradle the tiny porcelain cup, with its tinier silver spoon. He carries the drink like a treasure, an elixir too strong and almost too hot to savor in any but the smallest of sips.

As the sunlight hits the street, it quickly dries the moisture from last night's wildly extravagant thunderstorm. The squall hit just as we walked out of a long day spent inside the Louvre.   We emerged feeling slightly, wonderfully drunk from the sensory overload of all that magnificent art. The gaudy lightning and raucous clamor of the thunder just left us giddy. But now---this morning---gentle waves of steam rise from the pavement, leaving behind a quiet air of civility in this breathtakingly beautiful city.

We're here for such a short time, just one week. In seven days we'll get only a small taste of the rich complexity of this lovely place—somewhat, I imagine, like that first seductive sip of morning espresso. But that's enough for now. We're visitors not only to Paris, but to our daughters' experience here, and we don't want to intrude. They seized this opportunity, almost too good to be true, to spend the summer studying at the Sorbonne with international students. And we accepted their invitation to stay with them in their little Latin Quarter apartment. It's a singular chance to share in an experience we know will alter them in ways they cannot yet imagine. Travel to a different culture, in their twenties, when their spirits are porous and their hearts wide open, is a wellspring they'll draw from for the rest of their lives.

Ernest Hemingway said it this way: "If you are lucky enough to have lived in Paris as a young man, then wherever you go for the rest of your life, it stays with you, for Paris is a moveable feast." We have fun trying to recall this famous passage one morning as we walk down Rue du Cardinal Lemoine, past Hemingway's former home with its bright blue door and globe-shaped clay vases filled with salmon-colored geraniums. Later, we realize he doesn't include young women in this observation---written in the 1920s---so we decide to edit it for him. (I'd also like to ask him about those flowers; he doesn't strike me as the geranium type.)

Of course we fill our time with visits to Paris highlights. And we wander for miles through her delectable neighborhoods. But each morning we share what will be my most lasting Paris impression---grocery shopping. Writer Bill Bryson says travels' most vivid experiences and lifelong lessons come from discovering that "there are so many interesting ways to do fundamentally mundane things." Visiting a different culture is re-visiting the wonder of childhood: a chance to experience what is now familiar as if for the first time.

With supermarkets and shopping centers located only outside city limits, Parisians still frequent the series of tiny cheese shops, bakeries, meat stores and wine shops that enliven every neighborhood.   57 open-air markets or *marches decouverts* (perhaps the finest spots to mingle with a cross-section of locals) sprout every morning throughout the city. Each day we visit the lively market on Rue Mouffetard where museum quality displays of the produce celebrate *l'art de la gastronomie.* We find beautifully constructed pyramids of white asparagus, long pink-and-white radishes in impressionist arrangements, bouquets of fresh cucumbers with the fragrance of spicy lilacs and vine-ripened tomatoes redolent of bright red roses.

We join militant cheese shoppers at the *fromagerie* where---in this country that makes over 500 different cheeses---we can choose from cubist displays of ten different Chevres, a whole bevy of Camemberts, Bries and more Bries, cheeses with blue molds, cheeses covered in ash, cheeses wrapped in grape leaves, cheeses dotted with rows of multicolored raisins, cheeses...At the wine store we remember that we're on a student budget (and recall the Toulouse-Lautrec paintings from our visit to Musee D'Orsay) and chance a two-dollar bottle of Beaujolais. Uncorked later in the noonday sun, it tastes...bright purple. Saving the best for last, we follow our noses to the tiny *boulangerie* that offers 23 kinds of bread. We sample many, but it's hard to resist the simple baguette (so fresh it breaks your heart!) for just a quarter.

Our last day in Paris, we pack our groceries *du jour* and head for a picnic in the Jardin du Luxembourg, where each of the reportedly 350,000 flowers planted each spring seems to be blooming just for us. We've heard about the grand noontime concerts here. As we approach the gazebo, an enthusiastic French crowd is applauding an orchestra and chorus of young people. A little closer and we see a banner that says the performing group is "the young Ambassadors of Oregon." We explore the paths through this park that inspired a famous Van Gogh painting to the strains of "America the Beautiful." Must be time to go home.

We end each day the way we start it, lingering in a sidewalk café. My daughters are eager to share the discussion from the day's classes. They're excited by the European feminist thinkers they've learned from and intrigued by a whole new paradigm of race they've explored. To us, their faces are the most beautiful sight in France. I look at them sitting just across the little table, but---for a moment---I see us separated by the canyon of my life experience. I don't want to go. But it's time to leave them in their tiny little apartment, six floors above the streets of Paris.

***

C<small>UBA</small>

It had been a long day of talking politics.

There had been a morning lecture on the Revolution, the visit to the American Interest Office in Havana and then the bus ride back through the streets, some lined with billboards of a handsome, much younger Che and a smiling Fidel.

At one point along the route, a sign said, "The U.S. embargo: the longest genocide in history." And every public bus had a poster with a raised hand, "Obama, give me five" referring to the five Cubans arrested and jailed as terrorists in Miami. The Cuban version of the story being that they are heroes who had traveled to the U.S. to stop suspected terrorists from entering Cuba.

I parted from my traveling companions and went to sit in the hotel lobby with a cup of coffee. I was tired but I wanted to stay awake for the evening's Jazz performance.

I collapsed unceremoniously in a heap in a comfy chair, and gulped the coffee without even tasting it.

An old Cuban man sitting at a small table nearby looked at me and clucked, "You must be American." Embarrassed by my slightly uncouth behavior, I looked at him and said, "How can you tell?"

"In Cuba," he said, "all food is ritual. It's a big deal. There is no "to go" food. Even a cup of coffee is a ceremony."

I sat up straight. "I'm sorry," I said, "I guess I'm just really tired and a little overwhelmed."

"It must be overwhelming," he said "for you to be here in my country where there are so many contradictions."

"Contradictions to be sure," I said. "Our guide refers to Cuba, her own country, as a third world country. Yet nearly every home has electricity and everyone can read and write, one of the highest literacy rates in the world---and the health care is excellent. There is so much beauty---the art, the dance, the music, it's exquisite---and, yet, decades of misunderstanding between our two countries."

"Ah-h-h," he said, "intelligence has its limits, ignorance does not."

While I laughed, he cut off a piece of the pastry on the little table in front of him, put it on a beautiful little blue plate and handed it to me.

I carefully picked up a napkin, put it on my lap, thanked him, then took a knife and fork and cut a delicate little bite. I chewed carefully, my mouth fully closed.

He smiled. "I see I cannot apply one of my favorite Cuban sayings to you," he said.

"Which is…?" I asked.

"The human being is the only animal that stumbles twice on the same stone."

"You're right about that," I said, "after humiliating myself in front of you with my lousy manners, I'll definitely be more careful. You know 'the ugly American' and all that."

"Yes, but Cubans know that if we want to be modern, we must turn to the U.S."

"Tell me more about Cuba," I said, pulling a copy of a newspaper, the *Granma International*, out of my bag.

"Oh," he said, barely glancing at the paper, here's another Cuban saying, "Nothing is as shining as reported in the *Granma*, but nothing is as dark as it looks in the *Miami Herald.*"

"So how do I discover the truth?"

"The truth?" he said, waving his hand as if batting at a gnat. "You'll find it in the art, the dance, the music," he paused and looked at me, "not in the politics." He stood up and stretched, gathered his things to leave, "just enjoy, don't take it all so seriously and remember, we Cubans have a tendency to exaggerate everything."

###

SANDBAR

FAYEGAIL MANDELL BISACCIA

I awaken to a slanted ceiling and three little beds with lamps on bedside tables. A breeze touches my cheek in the green and white and yellow room, and reminds me to be grateful for the windows at each end which will later provide blessed cross-vent relief from hundred-degree heat.

Four women from my writers' group are staying in a little house by the Sprague River at Sharon's ranch in Eastern Oregon. We're on retreat, taking quiet time for writing, reflection and friendship.

Anne and I follow the ranch road to a sturdy gate, green metal. We lift it off a wooden block to open it, then close it carefully behind us. Past the gate, the grass and yarrow creep into the roadway until there are two narrow tracks, and eventually even those give way to riverside reeds and soggy ground.

We make our way out to a sandbar, where our conversation rouses a worried drake. His dash across the river alerts a languid duck with seven ducklings swimming in her wake. In an instant the ducklings disappear, and the two adults head upstream with apparent nonchalance while we settle onto the sandy soil.

The still light transforms my senses, makes me see without thought. I watch, transfixed, as tiny fishlings dart before us, dark against the sandy riverbed. Black and white checked dragonflies flit about the backwater, while strands of spiders' webs bob and sparkle among the water plants in the morning sunlight. Golden breasted barn swallows swoop and dive after invisible insects.

An island of algae floats slowly by on the glassy surface of the river, seemingly suspended between the sky and mud and grasses on the far bank and the deeper hues of sky and mud and grasses in their reflections. In this moment I sense no substance above or below—only that moving island projected upon illusion. Still air, still water, still grass: nature holding her breath and making me hold mine.

Suddenly a dozen tiny beetles, black, with pin-point dots of white upon their wings and red epaulets, hurry across the sandy beach and stop short at the water's edge. A few take flight, but most dash back again. One stops, abruptly, before the toe of my black sandal. It stays a while, and gives me a better look at its elegant markings.

Red-winged blackbirds, three of them, call out and swoop across the water. They perch, sway precariously on slender grass stalks, then disappear into the thicket.

A tiny butterfly, yellow with a blue spot on each wing, alights a yard away, lifts off, alights again. I will it closer, but it doesn't come.

###

THE SCRUM

LOIS LANGLOIS

Rung by rung, I have been climbing the chronological ladder of time. It is apparent in my egret-hued hair and my increasingly bruisable skin. A few wrinkles have crept in around the edges, too. However, unless I look in a mirror, I don't notice these accelerating attributes, and I tend to forget that others are likely to consider me "older."

Thus, while on my recent trip to Jamaica as part of a volunteer dental group, I was regularly taken aback by such remarks as, "You are how I want to be when I am a senior," or "You remind me so much of my grandmother." Or even, "It's so amazing to me that you choose to be here, doing this hard work." Certainly, the comments are meant as compliments, and I try to remind myself of that.

To me, I am just part of the gang, a diverse lot to be sure, and I don't perceive myself as being different from my younger counterparts. I expect to work and play along with the rest of them. Of course I'll go for the early morning swim. And, yes, you betcha, that's me on the elliptical machine in the gym at the end of the day. It's true, I don't go out to the reggae concerts and the nightclubs in the evenings, because I like my eight hours of zzzz's prior to a full day's work in hot, humid, non-air-conditioned circumstances. But several others of various ages are in the 'early-to-bed/early-to-rise' group along with me, so a sensible night's sleep does not stigmatize me as old.

One evening the large vacation resort that hosts our hardy volunteer group had its regular dinner party on the beach, followed by entertainment. Actually, the Activities Director explained, 24 of the guests would be selected to provide the entertainment. Two teams of twelve persons each were to be established. Our dental group, named 1000 Smiles, had more than enough members present to field one team, and twelve other guests formed the Rest of the World team. I agreed to be on the 1000 Smiles team. It was the usual assortment of humorous relay races on the beach and scavenger hunts in which one member of each team had to go find an article of clothing or some specific item.

Eventually, the Activities Director called for the teams to collect as many shoes as possible and pile them in the chair that was provided for each team. The team that collected the most shoes would win one point. Off we flew, grabbing sandals from our supporters. Some people even tossed their shoes to us, to help out. The piles of shoes were growing. But in one of my forays out into the crowd, I saw that a member of the other team, Rest of the World, was taking shoes from 1000 Smiles' chair and moving them to Rest of the World's chair. 'Unfair,' I thought. Oh, my next thought wasn't the best one I've ever had, for it was, 'If they can filch our shoes, we can steal theirs.' I dove toward their chair and started grabbing shoes, tucking several of them under my arms before making a mad dash back to our chair. I was completely energized and feeling clever about my strategy to help our team get the most shoes. It was quite exhilarating.

Just as I started back with my armload of shoes, someone from Rest of the World team tackled me and I sprawled, face-first, into the sand. I could hear a gasp of concern from the crowd, but I found it amusing that I had thrown myself so heedlessly into the contest. I felt youthful and reckless as I discreetly spit sand out of my mouth. I was fully in the moment, with no thought to creaky bones or wrinkly skin. I felt totally alive.

Of course, the shoe-counting part of the contest had to be abandoned, as both sides had cheated, so another event was added to break a tie, and eventually 1000 Smiles won out over Rest of the World by one point.

The next morning I saw several members of the Rest of the World team eating breakfast, and I went over to apologize to them for my thieving behavior of the night before.

"It was wrong of me to steal your shoes, and I'm sorry I did that -- but I'm not sorry for the fun I had doing it," I explained, trying to sound contrite.

One of the young Rest of the World women responded that she, too, was sorry.

"Why?" I asked. "I'm the one who did wrong."

"I'm the one who tackled you," she said, "and I'm so ashamed that I tackled a grandma."

###

CREEK CROSSING
LOIS LANGLOIS

Rumble, tumble, sounds from afar.
Drawing nearer, louder, clearer.
Water spilling, splashing, sprudeling over rocks and under logs.
Ever nearer, ever clearer.

'Round the bend now I see it.
Sunlight sparkling on silvery, slippery water.

Creek crossing ahead.

Looks dicey, dangerous; could be deadly.
I'm full of dread.

No rock-hopper I. No log scootcher.
No wobbling, toddling, trembling across a tiny, laid-down tree for
me.

Be brave; be bold.
You can do it; you can get through it.
You can reach the other side.

Yes. I can. I know a way.
Careful, cautious. I can make it.
Fellow hikers standing by. there to help me, hold me steady.
They can guide me, coax, cajole me.

Daring, dangling, one foot forward.
Icy water licks my legs. Laps and lingers 'round my toes.

Slish, slosh. I slog on through it. Swish in boots and silt in socks.
Tumbling water rushes by, tries to take me, knock me down.

Purposeful, I plunge across, reach the shore and
Laugh out loud!

###

LIFE
EXPERIENCES

A Patchwork Quilt
Dolores Holmes Scheelen

Green Street

It was a grand old house. I visit it often in my memory. The house was not just the place I lived. It was another character in my growing up, a presence that enfolded, protected, and encouraged me.

Built in 1900 it was quickly occupied by my Grandma and Grandpa Shine and their seven children. My mom moved into the house when she was a toddler and lived there until she married. When I was a toddler, in 1943, my family moved into what had been the upstairs bedrooms of the family home. With the addition of a kitchen, plus a wall and archway to separate living room and dining room, it made a cozy apartment for our family of four: Mommy, Daddy, my brother Tom (age 8), and me (age 2). Aunt Mary, my mother's sister, lived downstairs, as did Grandma Shine until she died when I was five. My friends and I had the run of the place, upstairs and down except for the grown-ups' bedrooms.

High ceilings and wide mahogany moldings provided spaciousness and solidity. In the entry hall the wooden boot bench and carved coat stand exuded comfort and welcome. In the living room the huge wall mirror, five feet square and bordered left and right with wooden pillars, added a sense of spaciousness, the leaded glass windows a touch of medieval elegance. The glass-fronted bookcase offered an array of adventures, and the easy chair a cozy place to read by the light of the marble-based lamp.

The Monk's Cloth drape between the hall and the front parlor became the curtains for our stage plays. The columns on either side of the arch between front and back parlors were our launching pads as ballet dancer, airplane pilot, or mountain climber. The swinging door from dining room to kitchen was castle entrance and corral gate. The dining room table was ping-pong table or play house and, for my quiet hours, sewing table and craft bench. The back parlor was my music domain, with the piano bench adjusted just for me with a block of wood to let my feet rest rather than dangle.

I loved the deep porch across the front of the house and its wide wooden steps. When Dad replaced the bottom step with concrete, he also put in a new pad of smooth concrete, ideal for roller skating and jumping rope. Sometimes, when I was alone, the post at the foot of the banister stood in for a playmate to handle one end of the jump rope. Other times it was a silent witness as my friends and I mastered the intricate steps of Double Dutch jump roping.

The porch was a stage for imaginative escapades. It was a ship and my playmates and I were the pirates, climbing up the rails over the flowers and shrubs that Dad selected for their pirate-hardiness. It was the home and I was the homemaker, sending my husband off to work on his tricycle while I stole a few minutes to read my current library book. Sometimes the porch became Rusnak City (our own town named after the neighborhood furniture store) where my friend and I worked out in ongoing detail the triumphs of the imaginary heroines, Barbara (her) and Jeannie (me). It was here that I lounged on the green wood-slatted bench or bounced on the metal chair that always stuck to my legs in the sweaty heat of summer. Here that the adults sat after a summer dinner as I wandered on my own, at first just the five feet to the sidewalk, then to the street light in front of the house next door, and later all the way to the corner, two houses to the north where Mary and Carole lived in the front apartment on the second floor.

I saw my very first television show, *Howdy Doody*, at Mary and Carole's house. Carole was one month older than I was to the day and Mary a year and a half younger, and they had that most marvelous of all beings, a baby brother. Even though they were not Catholic, I prayed their bedtime prayer with them when I spent the night: "Now I lay me down to sleep and pray the Lord my soul to keep." Mommy didn't like the next part about "If I should die before I wake" but I was undisturbed.

Two houses in the other direction lived the twins, Joan and Janet, also in the front apartment on the second floor. Joan and Janet told me about the day my family moved into the big house on Green Street. When they heard my mother's voice call out, "Dolores, come here," they looked for a pudgy four-year-old like themselves. Instead they saw a little two-year-old toddling across the walk, holding a blue teddy bear. Soon enough we were good friends.

As we grew older, they came to my back door, all the way to the high second floor porch, calling me, as I called when I went to theirs. I yodeled, "Yo, Joan and Janet," but it was a melody drawn out more like, "Yo – oh, Joan and Jan – neh – ette." If they were available, they answered. If not, no one came to the door and I went away. Front doorbells were for grownups, back doors for kids.

It was in the twins' apartment that the neighbors from our street (Green Street between 77th and 78th) met to say the Block Rosary, an endeavor to take the oopmh out of the Communist Menace. Adults and children, we knelt on the worn carpet in the twins' living room and took turns leading the 10 Hail Mary's of each part of the rosary. Even we children took our turn to lead but I often lost count. Wanting to make certain that I got in the full ten Hail Mary's, I often started conscientiously on number twelve or thirteen (as my mother told me later) at which point my father cut me off with a loud "Glory be to the Father," indicating the end of that set of ten.

Since my family did not have a television set until my teen years, it was in the twins' living room that I regularly watched *Kukla Fran and Ollie* and *The Morris B. Sachs Amateur Hour, sometimes with them and sometimes alone while they played in the bedroom.* It was there that I stood alone, caught by an emotional charge I didn't understand, and watched the ticker tape parade for General Douglas MacArthur when he said his famous line, "Old soldiers never die. They just fade away."

In addition to the front porch, the back porches were also a center of childhood discovery. Aunt Mary's porch downstairs had a removable shelf. It was laid across the corner where the railings came together and held a potted plant. Often my troupe removed the shelf and transformed it into a tent for an Arabian princess or a bedroom for a baby doll. We also commandeered Aunt Mary's back door mat, a piece of linoleum with a Persian rug pattern which became a magic carpet, similar to the one in *The Little Lame Prince* book.

On sticky hot Chicago evenings, my family sat first on the front porch and then, after putting on pajamas, on our tiny second floor back porch, just big enough for two folding chairs. Mom and I made popcorn on the gas stove in a deep pot and turned the red wooden handle to keep the kernels from sticking. I loved the sound of the first single pop, followed by a few more and then by a cascade of pop-pop-pops. We served the popcorn in bright clear plastic dishes, shaped like half of a cut apple. We sat in the dark stillness, each with a different colored bowl balanced on our knees.

When adults sat in the chairs, I sat on the top step. Usually the air was so still that not a leaf moved on the big catalpa trees in our back yard. Dad pointed out the constellations and told me about the space exploration that would happen in my lifetime. We held great rambling conversations that set my curiosity on fire and aroused deep respect for my father's knowledge. Other times Mom and I sat and talked about people and the ways of life.

It was on this back porch that the daytime life of the city came to us. Occasionally a man alone with his hat in his hand knocked on our back door. I heard a quiet exchange of words and watched as Mommy fixed a sandwich and a cup of tea and handed them out the door. The man ate as he sat on the top step, my customary place, then rapped lightly on the door to return the plate and cup.

It was also on this back porch that our milk was delivered. Each day the milkman stopped his cart in our alley, walked up the backyard sidewalk through the gate, and deposited a pair of quart bottles of milk by the door. It was non-homogenized milk so the cream sat rich and yellowish on top of the milk. Mommy poured some off into another jar for Daddy to use for his coffee. Then she shook the cream and milk together. In the winter the milk expanded in the cold and pushed up to form a column of frozen cream with the paper lid perched like a cap on top.

A heavy wooden door led from the back porch to the upstairs dining room. Above it was the transom, a window above the door that was opened by a metal rod that lay alongside the door frame. In summer it gave extra air and in winter the wind whistled an eerie tune through tiny gaps.

Beneath this window Mom set up the ironing board every Monday. On Sunday night she laid out each item that needed ironing, sprinkled it with water and rolled it up like a jelly roll. She then wrapped the pile of items in a towel and put them in the refrigerator overnight. I loved the smell of the steam when the hot iron hit the damp cotton sheets and shirts.

My brother Tom and I shared the upstairs bedroom until Grandma died. He then moved downstairs and slept in the alcove made by the bay window in Aunt Mary's back parlor until he left home to get married eight years later.

Tom saved money from his paper route and bought a record player which sat under the leaded windows in the living room and filled the downstairs with a mix of sounds from *Victory at Sea* to Stan Getz jazz. He sat at the dining room table and assembled intricate models: World War II airplanes and cars of all kinds. My favorite was his scale model version of the Green Street house itself, complete with patterned wallpaper in the bedrooms and cellophane windows throughout. One day our cousin's little boy stood in front of the model house and put his finger through every window. My brother lost heart and never fixed it, but he continued with increasingly more challenging model kits, some with small engines.

I too used the dining room table – to create not models but clothes. I laid out material and patterns and cut things to sew on Grandma Shine's Singer, a treadle machine that I was thrilled to use and able to repair when needed. Every Saturday for two years starting at age thirteen, I walked a mile or so with my friends Kathleen and Pat to the home of Miss Eschbach. In her basement she had cutting tables and sewing machines and we worked our way through an increasingly complex set of sewing tasks, all neatly documented in our own black paper notebook. Everyone started with a hand-sewn apron with a cross-stitched embroidery pattern and a machine-sewn cotton slip and pair of pajamas. The first project of my own choosing was a flowered print dress with a Peter Pan collar and circle skirt which I actually wore quite a bit. My last project with Miss Eschbach was a wool jacket, lined with satin.

In my teen years Green Street was a welcoming haven, a comfortable place for my friends to hang out. Aunt Mary's downstairs space became ours as she retreated to her tiny bedroom and we entertained ourselves in her living room and back parlor. We gave little thought to the fact that the adults had to sleep so they could rise early for work or early morning Mass. Mom, Dad, and Aunt Mary never complained and seemed relieved to have a houseful of noisy teenagers – "When they're here, we know where they are and what they're doing."

My friends and I gathered around the upright piano and sang show tunes (*Oklahoma, Carousel, Student Prince*) and the songs of the previous generation (*My Wild Irish Rose, Ave Maria, Danny Boy, The Sunshine of Your Smile*). I was the accompanist, using my dad's music, much of it repaired with scotch tape, all of it neatly dated when it was bought. The music was all written in the key of tenor – suited to my dad and also to the soprano voices among us, so we did okay.

After school dances I often called home and said, "Is it okay if I bring my friends home?" The answer was always, "Of course," and in we piled, the girls in our tulle-petticoated dance dresses, the boys in suits and ties. We took off shoes and made ourselves comfortable, eating whatever was available, usually popcorn and lemonade.

Summer found my friends and me in the back yard. We played croquet or softball, using the sewer clean-out cover as home plate. Dad covered his zinnias, "liveforevers" (sedum) and marigolds with little wire cages to protect them from the balls, but never suggested we play elsewhere. Often we had a cook-out. Dad started the charcoal grill and supervised the cooking of hamburgers and hot dogs, his only area of cooking experience. Mom made potato salad and sliced the lettuce, tomatoes, and dill pickles.

As I began dating, Mom always encouraged me to bring my date into the house after our evening out rather than sit out in the car to talk. Often the boy and I would come in for a cup of tea and whatever sweet thing was around – maybe Mom's apple pie or potato chip cookies.

Any ongoing beau was eventually invited for Sunday dinner. My shy father had one topic of conversation that connected him with young men: military service. Dad started by asking," What is your draft status?" and eventually got around to the gas masks and troop ships of World War I. I groaned inwardly with embarrassment, too young to have compassion for the sensitive young soldier my father had been. Although he had witnessed so much death and suffering, the only parts he could talk about were the superficial discomforts. Nonetheless the awkwardness for the younger generation was more than balanced by the friendly welcome and good food.

My growing up years were filled with happy meal times and comforting foods. Sunday dinner was meat, potatoes, vegetable, salad, and dessert, often beef pot roast with mashed potatoes (no skins), frozen peas, a square of orange jello with fruit cocktail on a leaf of iceberg lettuce, and home-made tapioca pudding. Other supper favorites were chop suey, meat loaf (with cracker crumbs, not bread), and Swiss steak. Mom was the cook and when it came to clean-up time, Aunt Mary always said, "I'll give your mom a hand; you have schoolwork to do." They enjoyed standing together at the kitchen sink, getting caught up on the day.

Although rich in love, knowledge and food, we were poor in some aspects. Other than a Model-T Ford long before my birth, my family never owned a car. For special outings an uncle came to drive us. But for most occasions we walked one street over to Halsted and got a streetcar, replaced later by the bus. It took us to various transfer points, often the elevated/subway at 63rd Street which carried us downtown or to the other end of Chicago.

My friends and I got around by walking, roller skating, or riding our bikes. When friends came over, Dad and I often walked them home, especially Kathleen (to Sangamon Street, west of Green) and Margie (to Eggleston, several blocks east of Green by the lagoon). Their widowed mothers worked all day. Dad felt better if he knew Kathleen and Margie got home safely – and we both enjoyed the quiet time together on the walk back home.

Home – the wonderful sense of arriving in a place of love and warmth whether from a two mile walk or a two thousand mile journey. Green Street gave me a high standard for the sense of Home and instilled the desire and the capacity to make any residence – for a week or a decade – into a welcoming and comfortable nest.

* * *

MY FAVORITE THINGS - CHILD

Flannel bed sheets
Old Spice bubble bath
A hot water bottle in the bottom of my bed on cold winter
nights
Ski pajamas with crew neck top and band at the cuffs and
bottom to keep out the cold
Running through the whirligig on the end of the hose to cool
off on hot summer days
Baby doll pajamas to keep cool on warm humid nights
Clamp-on roller skates and double-bladed ice skates
Single speed white-wall-tired girl's bike
The smell of fresh sheets

MY FAVORITE THINGS - TEEN

Pajama parties
Shoe skates – roller and ice
Midnight Mass on Christmas Eve
Shoe boots to replace galoshes that go over shoes
Eye glasses so I can see the black board
Hot baths in the claw foot tub
Brush hair rollers
78 rpm records

EMPATHY

Carole, Mary, and I were playing on the sidewalk in front of their apartment house on the day after Carole's fifth birthday party. We watched as the little red-haired girl from the other end of the block came closer to us. She was by herself, dressed up in party clothes, and carrying a nicely wrapped present.

She looked questioningly at us in our play clothes, as if wondering why we weren't ready. Perhaps I was remembering my deep distress the year before when Carole's party was cancelled by chicken pox. I stepped forward and said as kindly as I knew how, "The birthday party was yesterday." A look of horror came over her face before she turned and ran the long block back to her house by the big tree.

I felt helpless.

I never saw her again.

* * *

THINGS THAT GO BUMP IN THE NIGHT

In the carefree light of day I loved our house on Green Street, my personal playland. But alone in the darkness of my bedroom, I felt the grip of fear. Fear absorbed from overheard adult conversations about crime and violence. Fear of the dreadful creatures that scurried through the walls. Fear of the menacing shadows that hovered in the living room. Fear of the strange noises that echoed from outside.

Who was there? Would they get me? What to do?

I shut my eyes and put fingers in my ears. I hummed quietly to cover the din. I hunkered down silently in my bed, trying to be invisible. Terror fought with desperation. Desperation won. "Mommy, Daddy," I cried out in terror.

"What's wrong?" Daddy asked one night.

"I'm afraid of the rats in the walls. I'm afraid they'll come and eat me. I hear them running around."

"There are no rats in the walls," explained my patient father. He turned the light on. "This is an old house, you know. The walls are made of plaster. When the house cools at night, the plaster cools too and pulls apart a little bit. What you hear is tiny cracks forming in the plaster. No rats."

"What's wrong?" Daddy asked another night.

"There are shadows moving in the living room. It's robbers."

"There are no robbers making the shadows move," explained my still patient father. "At night I bank the coal furnace but heat still comes out of the radiator. It warms the air and makes it move. So the shadows of the furniture in the light from the nightlight just seem to move. No robbers."

"What's wrong?" asked my mother when it was her turn.

"I hear bangy, bumpy noises. Someone is breaking into our house."

"No one would want to break in here," said my mother also patiently. "Sometimes I was afraid too when I was a little girl. My mother told me that no one would break into our house because there was nothing here they wanted. Only kids and old newspapers."

Each time their confidence quelled my fear and I fell asleep cradled in my parents' calm wisdom.

* * *

A DIRTY HAND PRINT

Daddy was soft-hearted and kind in many ways. He allowed my friends to play in both the back and front yards. He helped me with my arithmetic homework and fixed anything that got broken.

Daddy was also strict about some rules: return his scissors to the middle drawer of the desk, put back a nickel for the phone if you borrowed one from the spare change dish, don't go barefooted even in the house, and always wash your hands before eating.

One summer day my friends and I were playing outside in the dirt. On the stairs going down to the basement was a hose connection, one that had to be turned off carefully so it wouldn't drip on the wooden steps below. I wasn't forbidden to use it, but was cautioned to be careful.

We were thirsty so I offered drinks from the faucet. Bending down to the faucet, I cupped my fingers, filled them and drank.

My friend, Mary, a year younger than me and an inch or two shorter, looked at the dirt on my hands and said, "You should wash your hands before you drink with them." I straightened up, reached out, and slapped her right across the face.

I was stunned to see my dirty handprint.

I was more stunned at my passionate reaction. When she told me not to do something I knew I shouldn't do, I punished her for being right.

* * *

MY FAVORITE THINGS EARLY ADULTHOOD

Watching the ice floes break up on the shore of Lake Michigan in
spring
Chicago Vocational High School football games as faculty
member
Grocery shopping list on the refrigerator
Easter sunrise service outdoors
Sterno stove for camping
Car with a gas gauge
Baby car bed
Car safety harness for toddler

Towels soft from the dryer not stiff from the clothesline
Being in a 4-person Folk Group at church
Yellow drop-leaf table for tiny kitchen
Low waist pants, bell-bottom jeans
Star Wars in the movie theater
Crater Lake National Park
Ten-speed bicycle
Mini-skirts
Huaraches
Electric blanket
Hot showers to replace baths

Canvas carrier for wood for the Orly woodstove
Cutting the Christmas tree in snowy woods
Real candles on the Xmas tree
To-do lists to check off
Long telephone cord
Fleece robe with a hood
Playing Spoons with high schoolers
Lightweight nylon tent with rainguard
View of Mount McLoughlin from my workspace

SAME SAME: CHICAGO 1964

I grew up with intense racial prejudice all around me in my part of Southside Chicago, resulting in "changing neighborhoods." In summer, 1964, as one black person bought a house, many of the white-owned houses on the block went up for sale. Fear was rampant. My usually tolerant family grew more and more worried that they would be the only white people left in a sea of black people. Neighbors stopped talking to each other, afraid that someone would find out they were selling. The family who lived next door to us for over twenty years moved out overnight without saying goodbye rather than face my parents. Many people sold at a considerable loss rather than live in a "mixed neighborhood."

The folks near us were relatively poor and could not afford to move out quickly. Although my childhood haunts did shift gradually from all white to all black, the process was slower than in some areas. As a result newcomers lived with old-timers for a period of time.

My Aunt Mary stood at the corner of Halsted Street every day as she had for years, to catch the northbound bus on her way to work at the Chicago Stock Yards. Our new neighbor, a black woman two doors down in the twins' building, waited for the same bus. Eventually Aunt Mary and the woman spoke to each other, starting with comments about the weather and moving to talk about their families. The neighbor expressed concern about a rumor of a man shot while walking down the street. She asked Aunt Mary about it and shared her fear: "Where we used to live a lot of crime was coming in. I work hard to pay for this new place because I want my little girl to have a good place to grow up. I want her to be able to play outside on the sidewalk without worrying about wild cars and shootings. I thought we were moving to a quiet place and now I'm not so sure." At dinner Aunt Mary said that she had never really talked with a black person in this way. "Isn't it amazing?" she said. "That woman is worried about the same kinds of things we are. I wonder how safe this neighborhood is going to be for them."

* * *

TORN JEANS

Someone said: *Show up, listen, respect differences, and you can change the world.* I'm pretty good at getting two of those steps at a time. Once in a while I get all of them right. I did with Jacquie.

In the early seventies I was a teacher of homebound high school students who were barred from school for reasons that ranged from mononucleosis to pregnancy to "psychological problems." The school district gave me no history, no information about background, no Individualized Education Plan, just a name, address, and phone number, plus an English textbook for the appropriate grade. What I did in my hour a week with the student was totally up to me.

Jacquie was bright and energetic. I met her business executive father only once, on my first visit. He stood over Jacquie and announced that she would attend my classes or "face the consequences."

Mostly Jacquie did come to class. She was silent and sullen, she exuded anger and resistance, but she was present. Her mother was usually home when I arrived. Appearing distressed and tired, she'd say, "I think Jacquie is upstairs."

Jacquie's mother fretted about the clothes Jacquie wore to our classes. "I don't know why she wears those jeans with all the holes in them, holes in such awful places. I buy her new ones but she insists on wearing the ripped ones. I hope you aren't offended." I assured her that I was delighted to see Jacquie regardless of what she was wearing.

One of the first assignments I gave Jacquie was to write about her jeans. She wrote her essay in pencil on a piece of wrinkled paper, an articulate life history of the jeans, the exploits she'd shared with them, and the values they represented. Each rip, tear, or hole had its own story.

A few weeks later she was not there for our session. "I had to run away," she explained apologetically at our next meeting. "But I'm here now." In some mysterious way in our time together we smoothed the bumpiness of her life path.

Even when Jacquie refused to see the math teacher, she came to English class. When she said she couldn't find pencil or paper, I agreed to have them with me. When she said she had no time for assignments, I offered an arrangement. "Since I'm the one being paid to do this, I am willing to make two preparations. One based on the assumption that you have done the reading or writing assignment, the other that you haven't. Will that work for you?" She agreed.

We spent many enjoyable hours together discussing short stories, essays, poetry – and her completed assignments. I was young and in transition myself. Her need prodded my creativity. I was sad when our time together ended with her family's move.

Years later I received a well-written letter, in ink, on nice paper – with no return address. Jacquie thanked me for our time together. She recalled some of the things we had discussed. She mentioned specifically *The Little Prince* by St. Exupery and *By the Waters of Babylon* by Steven Vincent Benet. She said the reading and talking had helped her grow into herself. I wished I had been able to tell her she had changed my world too.

* * *

SPIRAL OF LIFE

One

Enwombed

Birthed

Cherished
Nurtured

Launched

Sea legged

Joined together

Wrenched   apart
All   Alone

Amidst

Lonely

On my own
Alone

Soulmated
Sharing
Cherishing

Treasured

Lost

Tossed

Threads

Fragments

Stripped

Adrift

Present   Beyond aloneness

Grounded
Deep-rooted

All one   All one

ONE

My Favorite Things – Middle Adulthood

Playing CDs
20-speed bicycle
Key fob to open car door
No-smoking airline flights
Automatic garage door opener
3 prints-for-the-price-of-one film developing
Cordless phone

DVDs
Burning CDs
Converting VHS tapes to DVDs
Nightguard to eliminate jaw pain and tooth pain
The Green Flash at sunset on the Pacific Ocean in San Diego
Towel roll inside the pillow case to relieve neck pain
Smoke-free restaurants in Oregon
Down comforter
Digital camera

Unacknowledged Acknowledgement

Smoking was a source of irritation for many staff in our mental health center. The air in meeting rooms was thick with smoke from staff cigarettes. The air elsewhere in the building was invaded by smoke from the waiting room.

Some took the point of view of non-smoking staff who were being subjected to unpleasant odor and unwanted carcinogens. Some took the clients' point of view, pointing out that people who sought help at our agency were often anxious and relied on smoking to calm them.

At our monthly all-staff meeting I made a request that smoking in the building be limited. The director cut in before I had the chance to lay out my carefully developed rationale or elicit input from other people. "A topic that needs further study," she said. "I'm appointing you chair of a study committee. Please report back at our meeting next month."

At a break in the meeting I went into the restroom, furious at the director. I banged my papers down on the sink counter and exhaled sharply a few times. A mental health therapist was washing her hands, someone I knew but was not close to – she struck me as a bit aloof. "You seem angry," she said.

"She didn't even let me finish what I wanted to say," I fumed. "I can't believe how she cut me off."

The therapist dried her hands and looked calmly at me. "The boss put you in charge." As she walked out the door, she added, "Which is better – three more minutes at the meeting or the power to bring about change?"

* * *

SIDEWINDING

Sometimes I hit a task straight on and work my way right through it – but not always.

Last night I returned from a long driving trip after a lovely quiet week of retreat. I dumped one bag in the office, another in the bedroom, the dirty laundry in the hall. I put the books, briefcase, and mail on the dining room table. The food bags and soft-sided coolers went in the kitchen.

Every room was strewn with shoulds. I should unpack my clothes. I should put away the suitcases. I should put away the food remnants.

"Too much," said one voice inside me. "I'm too tired," said another. "I don't wanna," this time right out loud. "Looking at all this stuff tires me out even more. I'll NEVER be able to get it all done."

Should, Should, Should.

Enter the sidewinder.

"Well, you have to take out the trash for tomorrow's pick up so you might as well go thru the food."

"ALL right," with a big sigh and shuffling of feet.

"Just wash out the two little coolers too." More shuffling but it's done.

"You could just clear off the dining room table so at least one room is restful." A few trips into other rooms.

"Oh, that is much better to look at, welllllll, except for that pile of dishes. Maybe just one sinkful." Water running, soap swishing.

"Seems kinda silly to leave the other few dishes, don't you think?"

"And let's move the two suitcases onto the bed for tomorrow. And stack the mail in this pile, the books in that one. That's much better."

"Can I eat now?"

"Of course," as she slithered away until next time.

* * *

SAME SAME: CHINA 1993

In 1993 our older daughter invited us (my husband, younger daughter, and myself) to join her in traveling through China after her year of volunteer work in Taiwan. Traveling on our own as backpackers was eased by her ability to speak Mandarin Chinese. Nonetheless I was bombarded daily with things I couldn't understand or communicate.

The population density in the cities, the crowds at train stations, the bicyclists knee to knee were all strange and new. The overheard bits of conversation had a distinctive lilt, the breeze had whiffs of coal smoke and unknown spices, and the faces had a different look. I was thousands of miles from home, more than half way around the globe from the familiar sensory occurrences of my own life.

Yet I was surprised every day by scenes that were familiar.

Around dinner time each day, I'd find a quiet inconspicuous place on the sidewalk, by a tree, or in a doorway. I'd stand quietly and watch life unfold around me just like at home.

A child running toward her father as she saw him come down the street. A man carrying a loaf of bread under his arm. A car waiting for children to cross the sidewalk before turning into an apartment building. A woman talking to a toddler in her arms, pointing out a bird on a nearby tree.

Sometimes messages from my childhood would put themselves into words: "These are Communists, the Red Menace, the Enemy."

"No," countered my grown-up self. "These are people like me, going home from work, going to work, going out for their evening exercise."

Different but so much the same.

* * *

MY FAVORITE THINGS – LATER ADULTHOOD

Tai chi
Friends of many ages
Eye drops – no blindness
Orthotics in my shoes – no foot pain
Family photos on the walls
Friends new and old
Walking sticks
Wool socks

Thumb drive
Digital photo displays
Wheelchair assistance in long airport transfers
Insulated metal water bottles
Companionable silence

Skyping with family and friends around the world
Watching birds in the backyard
Christmas caroling parties
Long walks

THE CHORUS WITHIN

As a child I often went to the Tuesday night novena with Aunt Mary, a service honoring Mary, the Mother of Jesus, with a few hymns, a few words from the priest, and a recitation of the rosary. Aunt Mary's rosary beads were worn smooth from their frequent passage between her fingers. I knew that after church Aunt Mary would say, "Should we stop for I-C-E?" I'd nod my head happily and we'd turn down Halsted Street to stop at Mitchell's Ice Cream Parlor with its twisted metal café chairs and sculpted glass dishes.

Much as I enjoyed the ice cream, I even more loved hearing Aunt Mary's voice, usually sure and confident: "Mother dear, oh pray for me, while far from heaven's shore." At home I also loved hearing Dad's clear tenor voice, alone singing *My Wild Irish Rose* or *Ave Maria* or in harmony with Mom singing *Harrigan, That's Me* or *A Little Red Barn on a Farm*. The familiar sounds comforted and reassured me.

Within myself I have various voices of my own. Sure and confident or wavery and uncertain, in combination or alone, harmonious or discordant. I picture them sitting together in sections, like the parts of a chorus. Each has its input. Some sing only minor supporting parts. Some muscle their way in for solo performances and others wait to be invited.

The soloists of my first forty years moved in with a vigor that often overwhelmed me. Their uninvited and unauthorized conductor, Comparing Mind, urged them on to ever-greater passion. Dora Despair began by intoning, *I keep repeating the same mistakes, I'll never get ahead, Everything seems lost.* Critical Callie chimed in with her favorite, *You always do it the hard way* (sometimes improvising with *You always do it the wrong way).* Hannah Hurt and Lena Leftout crooned their latest complaints. Fanny Unfair wept as she soared into high indignant fury with *She has a better-paying job, Her children didn't go through a divorce, Her employer pays full medical insurance.* Dolly Do It Right often sang duets with Critical Callie. Kathy Keep Them Happy raced – often frantically – from one tune to another.

One happy day a new voice presented itself. "I am your Knowing Self," she said directly to me. "I've been here for a long time but you're only now beginning to hear me." Turning to Comparing Mind, she said, "The baton, please." Turning to the previously undisputed divas, she said firmly, "Clear the stage, please, all of you. Yes, I am talking to you too, Fanny. I hear your protest – sit down with the others please – now."

Something stirred within me, a fresh breeze. "Helena Hope, it's your turn," said Knowing Self. A clear voice began softly and grew stronger as it went on. Greta Grateful added a lovely harmony line of beauty and renewal. Abigail Abundance painted tones of earth and sky, energy and rest, nourishment and friendship. Clarity, Kindness, Forgiveness, and Trust brought tears to the eyes of the seated listeners.

"And now I think you are ready for some new soloists. Let me introduce Letty Let Go and Eva Equanimity. Slowly I began to hear new lyrics: *Be gentle with yourself. Be kind. Let it go. Let it be. Wait a bit. Take your time. Growth is hard. Pain happens. Struggle is a choice. Listen with awareness. Be present with what is. See that slip not as failure but as good practice.*

And now? All the singers are there and new ones arrive sometimes. Knowing Self listens to each one and takes in their words. More importantly she takes in their feelings. She listens to every voice and makes an action plan based on what she hears and what she herself knows.

Most of the time Knowing Self maintains control of the stage. Occasionally when she is distracted, Comparing Mind picks up the baton. Dora or Fanny or one of the other displaced divas rushes onstage and bellows her tune. But shortly Knowing Self returns. "I'm back," she says to Comparing Mind as she retrieves the baton. "I hear you, Dolly. I'm taking your point into account. My turn now."

The Chorus Within grows surer every day, comforting and nourishing me like the beloved voices of my childhood.

* * *

Night in the San Francisco Airport

"You have been upgraded to business class for your flight from Santo Domingo, Dominican Republic, to Newark." My husband Bob and I sink into luxury: wide seats, leg room, fresh orange juice, Mixed Grill and a rare mid-day glass of wine.

Short connection in Newark. I get a wheelchair because we must cover long distances between terminals, get luggage, go through customs, drop luggage, go through security, manage carry-ons, and all at top speed. Challenging at age 73.

At security I take out two computers and the bag of liquids, remove belt and passport pouch (metal zippers), show the empty water bottle. We make the San Francisco connection on time: Thanks, wheelchair escort!

We settle into our seats – aisle and window – the middle seat between us empty. We hold our breaths until the cabin door closes. No one comes to claim the seat between us. Luxury again!

Long connecting time in San Francisco. Our small regional plane to Medford leaves at 8:10 the next morning.

Last year I Googled "spending the night in the San Francisco airport" and found a convenient gate that had seats without arm rests, perfect for sleeping. We chose a secluded spot and settled in, with blankets and pillows from United Airlines.

This year we land past midnight in a new section of the airport and walk, tired but confident, to "our" gate in the old terminal. Alas – shiny new seats with arm rests, an airport upgrade. No place to sleep. No blankets and pillows.

A helpful gate agent directs me to the service counter down the moving walkway. Result: two clean blankets, no pillows.

The only place with flat seats is the new terminal, so back we trudge with roller bags and back packs. We find several oddly shaped but nicely padded long space station-shaped things, like soft tinker toys – four foot wide circles connected by foot and a half wide links. Children probably use them to climb and jump.

No children now and few other passengers. Bob and I each select a circle. No seclusion here in the bright glare of always-on lighting. Shops are scattered about, the nearest an open-air coffee bar.

As the baristas complete their closing tasks, we settle in for the night. The temperature is quite cool, so I add long underwear over my knit slacks, lycra hooded vest, wool turtle neck sweater, fleece jacket, and crocheted cap. I use the backpack as pillow and the roller bag as nightstand for alarm clock and water bottle. I get my mouthguard, ear plugs, eye mask, extra shawl for my shoulders, and blanket for my legs. Bob goes through a similar ritual, adding wrist guards. He comes over to say "Good night, dear," and we do our usual bedtime hug and kiss.

A barista grins quietly at us, catching the eyes of her two partners as if to say, "Look at the old couple settling in for the night – sweet!" A pleasant ending for their day, a pleasant beginning for our night.

* * *

Speaking for My Future Self

At some point I may become confused, irritable (okay, more irritable than usual), belligerent, withdrawn, unable to say what I mean, or unable to understand what you mean. I offer here some suggestions, gleaned from years of self-observation, to guide you as you support me and those around me.

Arrange a good medical assessment for me. Do I have a bladder infection or allergies or seizures or blood sugar issues or anything else causing changes in me?

Help me keep active. Take me for walks outside. Set me up with my Tai Chi and Chi Gong videos. Send me on little errands like putting something in the kitchen or into the mailbox.

Make sure I get enough water. I drink 1 - 3 quarts from my water bottle each day now, less in winter, more in the heat of summer.

Watch what else goes into my body. Keep caffeine out and yes that means even hot chocolate and green tea. And no bananas. Give me herbal peppermint tea with skim milk between meals and hot honey-lemon water at bedtime with a dab of vodka for special times. I do best with vegetable protein (corn, rice, beans, whole grains, potatoes, broccoli), a couple nuts in my oatmeal, an occasional egg with my mashed spuds, peanut butter toast for dessert. Remember that too much sugar makes me antsy. For treats give me parsnips or an ear of corn.

Find me a nice sitting place where I look out on some natural beauty, preferably a tree that I can watch through the seasons, but even a big potted plant will do.

Let me do things that soothe me even if they aren't "age appropriate." Maybe I'm just the right age to snuggle a teddy bear and listen to preschool jingles that have laid down deep and happy tracks in my neuronal pathways: "Open, shut them, open, shut them, give a little clap." Play the CD of lullabies and folk songs I recorded for our grandbabies. Let me twist a bandanna or play my small harmonica repertoire – you can set a limit of ten minutes a day.

Play music with some rhythm and melody. I love Bach, Beethoven, Dvorzcak, Vaughn Williams, Mozart, traditional Christmas music (so it's June?!) Please avoid hard jazz, elevator muzak (I am TOO listening), and repetition of the same thing over and over, except for Dvorzak's New World Symphony – I can hear that as often as you play it.

Enjoy my giggles when I watch favorite movie scenes over and over (the car chase at the end of *What's Up, Doc;* the shredder scene in *Jumping Jack Flash;* the gate and jeep scene in *The Gods Must Be Crazy;* the airplane over the ocean in *Hopscotch.*) Hey, how about the whole movie? You don't have to watch.

Tell me comforting stories, using pretty much the same words each time, to reduce my anxiety about things coming up, to ease my distress about things that have changed, to remind me of happy earlier times (yurts, scavenger hunts, brown sugar raisin bread). Show me pictures or photos with the stories you tell.

Talk to me directly but slow it down a bit to give me time to make sense of what you're saying. Wait while I figure out how to respond. Sing a song in your head while I get ready to take my turn in the conversation.

Set up the kinds of communication devices I use as an autism consultant to help "my kids" who are confused, belligerent, withdrawn, unable to connect satisfactorily.

• Give me a communication system with pictures so I can ask for what I want by pointing or looking. Show me pictures with an X through them so I'll know you understand that I want ice cream or popcorn but you're telling me it's not available right now. Help me show you pictures that tell you, "I have an itch," "It's too noisy," "I don't want to do that right now."

• Tell me and show me what's going to happen with pictures and familiar words. Point to the pictures of *walk* and *eat* and say, "First we'll walk and then we'll eat." Write lists and check things off as we do them.

• Use a *visual* timer to show me how long I can do this thing or must wait for that thing. Show me how many times I can re-tell that story. Please don't use a ticky-ticky kind of timer – I don't like the sound and I may throw it at you and then I'll be in BIG trouble.

Hug me. Pat me. But do it from the front so I can see you coming. I don't want to hurt you if my startle reflex over-reacts.

Keep a close eye on my body temperature. My basal temperature is low, about 96.8 degrees rather than 98.6. My body adjusts to temperature changes very poorly. If my body shrinks in on itself, I'm probably freezing. Put a bandanna around my neck, wrap me tightly in a shawl, tuck me in snugly. If my body is moving back, shrugging out of my wraps, then I'm probably hot. Remove the layers, untuck my blouse at the waistband, and let my neck "breathe."

Take care of yourself as conscientiously as you're taking care of me. Eat well, exercise, take time off. Pace yourself, ask for help, let some things go, remember that it's okay to say no to a good thing. Watch out for each other with a periodic "How ya doin'?" and answer honestly.

Know that I appreciate all you are doing. Please tell yourself regularly for me even if I can't.

* * *

PRESENCE

I get up each day and say, "This is a new day. I will live it well."
Then I do some things and let other things go.

I gratefully embrace each new breath of existence
and live humbly in the presence of Mystery.

I know that what I am and what I do are good enough
because all is embedded in the One.

I strive to live as a blessing in the world
and see my mistakes and my successes equally
as part of the fabric I have been given to weave.

I speak my needs clearly and simply,
knowing that they will be taken care of.

I relish every bit of love and beauty that comes my way
and gratefully acknowledge
the power of loss and emptiness as well.

I spread my shawl of trust over
all the realities I encounter on my path,
embracing the conflict and differences
that keep the universe in creative balance.

###

THE WOMAN WHO WEPT
EVOLUTION IN THE 21ST CENTURY

JANET BOGGIA

*"The whole structure of the universe is not merely an arena.
It is a domain of collaboration."*
Rudolf Steiner

In an old, well-used hotel in Tblisi, Republic of Georgia, on a warm summer morning in 1998, fewer than two-dozen people come together in a roomy conference space. Collapsible tables are set up on the linoleum floor, familiar to conference-attendees worldwide. Individuals find the room and enter, some in small groups, some alone. There are greetings, handshakes, smiles, even hugs, among the post-Soviet adults, ranging in age from 20's to 70's. This is astonishing. Only a few years ago, all of these people experienced grievous loss because of the "other side," the enemy in the room. Some here escaped with only their lives in the face of indiscriminate shelling of civilians, rape and other savagery. And yet, they are here in an attempt to eradicate *the image of the enemy.*

Azerbaijan and Armenia were absorbed as part of the Soviet Union in the early 20th century, and for 70 years the Russian language became their second—the language they use now with one another here in Tblisi. Both countries have been independent since the early 1990's. They have also been at war. Because of the Armenia/Azerbaijan war—even during this season of troubled cease-fire—it is dangerous for citizens of either country to travel to the other, and so this meeting is held in neutral Georgia.

The atmosphere of friendly anticipation is vastly different from the anxious hostility of six years ago. This, their fifth dialogue over a six-year period, demonstrates a level of cautious hope and commitment not usually found among those who feel intense animosity and fear. These women and men, volunteers from countries at war, are willing to undergo discussions and painful encounters in order to free themselves from their own feelings of enmity. They are the "intelligentsia," as European professionals call themselves, from many walks of life—journalists, teachers, psychologists, engineers, philosophers, economists, documentary filmmakers, scientists, writers and human rights organizers. Their individual stories on the following pages paint a picture of their lives, losses, and the motivation that makes each willing to undergo a process, often tedious, even hellish.

The three U.S. Americans in the room are the final contingent, here to facilitate. My colleague has been part of the project from the beginning.[1] Our team started in 1992 when the Ambassadors to Moscow from both Armenia and Azerbaijan invited involvement of non-governmental organizations to find creative solutions to the intractable conflict. The 50 year-old, all-volunteer nonprofit of which I was a part, *Foundation for Global Community* (FGC)[2] in Palo Alto, California, had an established track record with conflict work. The third American is a conflict expert from George Mason University.[3] (A few observers and a translator are here also.) We are warmly greeted. My heart beats quickly when I think of the week ahead. I want our team to do well for these courageous people.

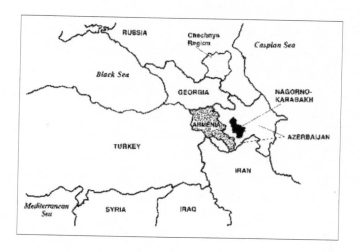

FOCUS OF THE WAR

Armenian and Azeri participants are here also from the focus of the war, Nagorno-Karabakh (Karabakh), geographically located in Azerbaijan, but mainly populated by ethnic Armenians. Tiny Karabakh is an area half the size of Los Angeles County in California. With noble mountains, purple and green, protecting its valleys, Karabakh's terrain is covered by forests and is home to bears, wolves and great eagles. Even though Karabakh is in Azerbaijan, the region is home to 138,000 ethnic Armenians scattered in its cities and towns. Before the fighting began, Karabakh was populated 75% by ethnic Armenians. Now, as a result of the war, it is 100% Armenian. The Azeris were driven out of Karabakh during the hot war—1988 to 1992—and have lived as refugees and displaced persons in makeshift arrangements elsewhere in Azerbaijan ever since.

BRIEF HISTORY OF THE CONFLICT

The deep history of these areas is complex, involving war, conquest and shifting alliances among a "greater" Armenia, ancient Albanians, Turkey, Iran (earlier, Persia), old Russia, the USSR, Europe and the Armenian Diaspora (a strong social and economic force). All cite history, ancient and modern, to justify grievances, actions and positions. Russia, the United States and France are the official negotiators, known as the *Minsk Process*.

Armenia, a modern post Soviet country, was among the earliest countries to become Christian in the fourth century. Azerbaijan, also a post Soviet country, is mainly Muslim with religious freedom. In its large cities, fashionable jeans and mini skirts are evident. Armenia and Azerbaijan share a border. They became independent from the USSR in the early 90's. At about the same time, the majority Armenian population of Karabakh voted to become independent from Azerbaijan and consolidate ties with Armenia.

Azerbaijan, incensed at the idea of losing a chunk of territory the size of Rhode Island from the western part of its country, justified its position by citing the Helsinki Accords on *Territorial Integrity*. Karabakh (supported by Armenia) justified its desire for joining Armenia, citing the Helsinki Accords on the *Right of Self Determination*. The hot war began in 1988 with demonstrations escalating to brutal military actions, with troops from Armenia, Azerbaijan, and the USSR. Hundreds of thousands of people fled from both countries.

According to *Human Rights Watch/Helsinki*, 25,000 people died in the fighting. Hostage-taking and torture of prisoners were reported on both sides. The cease-fire, still in effect in 2015, was signed in December 1994.[4]

THE DILEMMA OF INTRACTABLE CONFLICTS

The early meetings of this group of willing people occurred in 1993 and 1994 in California in a rustic lodge. (See *Endnote2* for a history of the project.) On the fourth day of the 1994 conference in California, the dilemma of intractable conflicts raised its ugly head. A dynamic intellectual from Karabakh, an engineer and Member of Parliament, Karen Oganjanian, an ethnic Armenian about 35 years old at the time, exemplified the dilemma of on-going, unsettled conflicts.

This intelligent, good-hearted man has the ability to influence the minds and hearts of his countrymen. Several years prior, when the hot war was raging, he had a personal experience of profound significance. "From the window of my apartment I watched colleagues making forays into the street to get cigarettes, water and other necessities," he says. "Some were hit by rifle fire. Then, I saw something so horrible..." He pauses, and in a low voice continues: "I saw a dog running down the street holding a human leg in his mouth." In that instant, Karen had a transformative experience in which he vowed to work for peace from that moment forward.

However, with a cease-fire declared several years later, and the ethnic Armenians there in control of the government, he feels safe, and at times, even euphoric. Karen moved from a time of profound realization to the realities of the day. His side is victorious at the moment. The status quo is comfortable. Karen's very human dilemma lies at the heart of intractable conflicts—those that are long-lasting, deeply embedded in history and seemingly hopeless. He experienced a deep moment of change during the hot war when he saw the running dog. However, with victory, Karen and his fellows can use their own language, choose their form of government, pursue their lives. He no longer fears that he will be subjugated. In his view, not only is he free from the former USSR, he is free from Azerbaijan.

"I will still work for peace as before the cease-fire," he said. His difficulty is profound: What does peace look like? Defined by whom? At what cost? On the fourth day of discussion, well-meaning Karen eagerly began to show a video about his peace work. The scenes of the verdant hills of Karabakh filled the screen. This is the land where many of the people in the room cannot return—their former home. To the Azeri Karabakhis, now refugees, the film is not a celebration of peace work, but an insult and vehicle of pain. They are watching images of a homeland from which they had to flee. Tempers flared as they shared their hurt and anger. Karen left the conversation and did not return for the week's final ceremony. He expressed that he felt misunderstood. His existential dilemma is clear. On one hand, he revels in new freedom. He sees a bright future for himself, and an outlet for his intelligence. He can have security, position and influence if he joins with the majority.

His inner psychological and spiritual conflict might continue to cause pain, or he might justify his actions and feel less inner turmoil. He can justify his position by "a history of oppression against my people" (and not think too much of atrocities perpetrated by his side). He is pushed from behind by fear and recent events, and pulled by the lure of the freedom that lies ahead. On the other hand, he remembers his transforming experience, the cost to those who have been made refugees and their ongoing agony. To go through the "eye of the needle" is difficult for any individual of status and ascendancy. To speak out now for reconciliation and inclusion against the prevailing position of victory brings intense animosity from his fellow citizens—even reprisal that could endanger his life.

271

I wondered what I would do in his circumstance. I wondered what choices all of the participants would make. The choices actually made in the intervening years are astonishing. They are presented below from the point of view of the 1990's and then updated to 2015.

FOUR POINTS OF VIEW REPRESENTATIVE OF PARTICIPANTS

The devastation and loss are best illustrated with personal portraits of four committed participants. (Not all participants were at every annual meeting, but many kept in touch in between.) These short snapshots exemplify four points of view alive in the region.

ZARDUSHT ALIZADEH (52 years old in 1998) Azeri

Zardusht, a soft-spoken, politically savvy, powerful intellectual with a gentle heart, is editor of a newspaper. He supports the unpopular view of reconciliation with the Armenian enemy. In times of war everywhere, outspoken peacemakers are often seen as traitors. His reconciliation stance threatened the power structure. Twice, because of his commentaries, he was attacked, intimidated, beaten, kicked, smashed on the head and in the face with the handle of a gun, and finally arrested and jailed for a time.

Intimidation does not stop him. He continues to write and editorialize. In 1990 Zardusht with Leyla Yunus (another 1998 participant—see *Update 2015* below) formed a political party with a goal of establishing a moderate political voice. His plea at the discourse is to "truly touch each other and work as individuals to move beyond the conflict, at least at the table, so that we can have a unified message when we leave." He believes that many people need to be involved, not just the intelligentsia, for reconciliation to become a reality.

Zardusht means *Zoroaster* in the language of his ancient religion. As part of this tradition, he feels identified with a higher purpose. He has been willing to face danger to his personal survival, as well as to live his life for peace.

KERIM KERIMLI (35 years old in 1998) Azeri, formerly from Karabakh

Kerim and his wife escaped Karabakh in front of the invading armies (Armenian and Russian) with only the clothes they were wearing. They left behind their home, possessions, and their established life. Now he is a refugee living in Baku.

He has an engineering degree, and in the 1980s before the war, worked in his profession in Shusa. (Most of the Azeri refugees lived in the Karabakh city of Shusa, now mostly destroyed.) Kerim, who started in journalism in 1990 is a dedicated editor. He published a booklet containing pictures and stories of people personally known to him who were killed or are missing. (All sides in this conflict have admitted committing atrocities.)

In every meeting, with every new group of people, he asks for help in finding those still missing—this is now his life mission. "We must have guarantees to allow the refugees to return safely to their homes." He also asks the world community "to allow a leader of the Azerbaijani Karabakhis to summit with the other presidents and leaders involved in official peace talks." His two brothers are among the missing.

AGHASI AYVAZYAN (73 years old in 1998) Armenian

Aghasi, a famous fiction writer in Armenia, was read and loved in Azerbaijan as well. He has made films, written short stories and novels. "I suffered under the oppression of the Soviets, then was filled with hope under peristroica and glasnost. Gorbechev is an intelligent and great man," he explains.

Aghasi spent many years in USSR Georgia where Joseph Stalin was born. When perestroika came, he started to work on a film about Stalin's life. "The new freedom would allow me to publish with no fear," he said. "Then the war came and it collapsed the Armenian economy. I sold my home, all my possessions to survive. And now there is no paper for writing, no light at night, and life is impossible." (When the war erupted, Azerbaijan placed an ongoing energy embargo on Armenia.)

Not so convinced at the start of the citizen process that it could accomplish anything, in 1998 he said: "I find it easier to agree now. I find something has changed. If changes continue, this will be ending positively."

KARINE OGANIAN (About 27 years old in 1998) Armenian from Karabakh

Karine, a journalist, hates the war and the blockade causing huge shortages—no water, a lack of transportation and most importantly, a cessation of normal life. She had felt oppressed under Azeri rule because "they tried to erase my Armenian identity. When I was growing up, I could not even learn my own language and history in school. Everything was controlled by the Azerbaijan government." During the war, her best friend disappeared. She was only 22 at the time. When she returned, she was pregnant, having been repeatedly gang-raped. "She lost her mind," Karine explained.

Karine's big fear is that the Armenian victory (in Karabakh) will be lost. She is proud of the advances made in living conditions such as schools and hospitals since the cease-fire. Yet she feels compassion for the Azeri refugees who were chased out of their Karabakh homes, and she does not want retribution. Her heart was touched by another

274

conference attendee, a Karabakh Azeri refugee. "There should be room for everyone in Karabakh, and all should live good lives and not be suppressed," she believes.

MEETING IN TBLISI, REPUBLIC OF GEORGIA – 1998

TALKING TOGETHER: LIVING ON AN EDGE

In our conference room in Tblisi, the participants are in the third day of dialogue. Reports have been made, opinions expressed, discussion engaged, laughter shared, feelings flared, and heartfelt exchanges have occurred. Progress since the first dialogue six years ago is evident: this time, one side allows the other side to chair. There is almost no return to "historical accuracy" issues, a history that Armenians and Azeries do not interpret in the same way. There is less "speech-making." The process has been taken over by the members rather than the third-party facilitators. Tangible progress is evident when they plow through setbacks that, in earlier dialogues, would have brought the discussions to a standstill. Conversations are often heartwrenchingly difficult and emotionally grueling, but the participants have grown more resilient.

It occurs to me that this is a spectacular phenomenon. These individuals willing to endure one another are walking a tightrope, living on an edge. The edge can be lonely, precarious. Not many are willing to be in this spot. They are living in the "evolutionary spirit" as defined by scientist Erich Jantsch in his book *The Self-Organizing Universe*: "To live in an evolutionary spirit means to engage with full ambition and without any reserve in the structure of the present, and yet to let go and flow into a new structure when the right time has come."[5]

The group decided earlier that since they as citizens are not making policy regarding the future of nations, they will accomplish together five projects across the political divide. In this meeting, they will continue to plan and work on the projects. These range over many fields and have the makings of Ph.D dissertations involving joint surveys in psychological, social and democratic development, ecological research (pollution across borders), and producing a children's book advocating peace. Accomplishing the projects requires close communication. This is a long way traveled since the early distrusting, despairing meetings.

But even now, difficulties are evident. Between two participants a personal, heated exchange is occurring. Svetlana, an Armenian Karabakhi (head of the youth division of the *Helsinki Citizens' Assembly* in Karabakh) is working with Hagani, an Azeri, formerly from Karabakh, now a refugee activist in Azerbaijan.

Tears come. Svetlana puts her head down. Tears are not "professional," and her embarrassment is acute. I pretend not to notice that she weeps. Compassion wells up in me and, when a few minutes pass, I give a smile of encouragement in her direction. Hagani has gone to another part of the room.

The human genome is encoded with the impulse of "fight or flight" as an important response to trouble. Traditional responses, appropriate when the predator leopard approaches, may not be appropriate in a room where the conflict comes from the mind: differing viewpoints, beliefs, interpretations, fears, memories. Evolution has honed tools of mind and consciousness that provide the capacity allowing Svetlana to cry but not to leave or strike back past a point of no return. The response of conscious choice is a novel human response made at particular nexus points.

Svetlana and Hagani each choose not to continue the conflict. Perhaps it was something the chairwoman said earlier, perhaps it was Hagani's decision to speak quietly and not defensively, perhaps it was an insight that moved Svetlana, a shift within. In a little while, Hagani returns, sits next to her again. Between the two, understanding grows. They begin to plan their joint project. They move their chairs closer. Their enthusiasm keeps them involved for the rest of the afternoon, laughing together from time to time. Everyone in the room is working in the same way in small groups.

There are many toasts at dinner that evening.

UPDATE TO 2015

In 1999, one more meeting, the last, was held in California. There were embraces and tearful goodbyes. Has anything changed in the 16 years since? At the level of nations, final settlement of the conflict has not been accomplished. It is labeled "frozen" in official language. Armenia and Azerbaijan are in deadlock, an uneasy truce. The one million refugees have not returned to their original homes. Few want out-and-out war, but leaders threaten, and on both sides, the military has been bolstered. There are border incidents. The official Minsk Process continues. Karabakh is not recognized by the international community.

PORTRAITS: CHOICES MADE

Did discussions over a seven-year period—the first in 1993 and the last in 1999—change the participants? Did they influence peace-making in the region over a period of 16 years? Many from the conclaves are prominent citizens within their countries and internationally known. Eleven members are profiled here as of 2015. I believe these individuals—all supporting a peace point-of-view—make a difference as many courageously continue to support human rights in their own regions, and reconciliation between countries. They risk everything.

AZERIS

ZARDUSHT ALIZADEH (69 years old in 2015)

Zardusht (discussed above, see 1998) retired from politics in 2000, but not from writing and speaking out. As a harsh critic of the administration, he feels he is being harassed. He believes that by arresting his son, the government sent him a warning for describing the Azerbaijan ruling elite as an "organized criminal ruling class that uses oil money to assert its authority over the population." He delivered this speech to the European Parliament two months before his son's arrest.[6]

LEYLA YUNUSOVA (known as Leyla Yunus, 59 years old in 2015)

Educated as an historian, Leyla is passionate about human rights. In 1990, she and Zardusht (above) founded the *Social Democratic Party*, and she published an article arguing for a democratic middle course that rejects extreme nationalism and violent repression. In 1995, she launched the Institute dedicated to fighting corruption, unlawful evictions and violence against women. In 2009, she and her husband were tried for libel for alleging that police, in a recent kidnapping trial, had been complicit in further trafficking the two young girls involved. Authorities bulldozed Yunus' Baku office the same day an interview appeared in the *New York Times* in which she criticized forced evictions. In 2014 she compiled a list of 98 political prisoners in Azerbaijan.[7] She and her husband were arrested in July 2014 and accused of espionage. They face charges of fraud and treason that supporters say are punishment for their long years of activism and Yerevan-Baku peace efforts.[8] In the last months of 2014, Leyla received several international peace and freedom awards and is named by

Amnesty International a prisoner of conscience. She is still a prisoner in Azerbaijan.

ARZU ABDULLAYEVA (61 years old in 2015)

Arzu, a tireless human rights activist with an academic background in history, is passionate about reconciliation. She was a prime mover at our annual meetings and pulled the projects together under the umbrella of *Peace Service*, an NGO she created for that purpose. Already the winner of numerous international awards including the 1992 Olof Palme Peace Prize, in 2008, she joined a hunger strike with other brave individuals to free journalists imprisoned by the Azerbaijan government. In May 2011, the European Parliament passed a resolution condemning "oppression of opposition" in Azerbaijan. The resolution mentions concern for the "increasing number of incidents of harassment, attacks and violence against civil society and journalists in Azerbaijan."

Arzu coordinates the *Council for the Settlement of the Karabakh Conflict*. Their current project is the independent *Civil Minsk Process*, a civic-driven, proactive peace initiative.[9]

RAKHMAN BADALOV (78 years old in 2015)

Rakhman Bandalov in 1998 was the department head of the Institute of Philosophy and worked with the children of refugees. He is a member of the Azerbaijan Academy of Sciences. "Understanding and compassion are harder than hatred, especially when we are humiliated. Only understanding can change the world," he said in 1998. Today, Rakhman writes scholarly articles analyzing the deep changes necessary in the fabric of his own government to become fully a member of the global world. He writes of corruption and the need to establish basic rights. Recently, he courageously wrote: "Azerbaijan still fails to guarantee its citizens such fundamental human rights as freedom of speech and assembly."[10]

AKRAM AYLISLI (78 years old in 2015)

Akram has been greatly punished for his peace point-of-view. His fame as a writer, cinematographer and playwright extends around the world. He was recognized by Azerbaijan with prestigious awards in 2002 (for "independence") and 2013 (for "honor"). His novel *Peoples and Trees* has been translated into more than thirty languages. He served as a Member of Parliament from 2005 until 2010.

In 2013 Akram published a novella, *Stone Dreams*—a story he (an Azeri) wrote from an Armenian point of view. The characters experience the terror of the 1990 planned slaughter of Armenians in Baku. He depicts also sympathetic Azeris who hide Armenians.

Soon after *Stone Dreams* was published, the honored writer was proclaimed an enemy of the state. Rallies were organized and slogans chanted: "Death to Akram Aylisli," and "Traitor." Legal actions were taken against him. He was stripped of his prizes and of the title *People's Writer*. His plays were banned from theaters, and his works withdrawn from the school curriculum. The *Union of Azerbaijani Writers* expelled Aylisli. He was publicly insulted and humiliated in the press and by the government who said, "Azerbaijanis must express public hatred towards these people." His books and portraits were publicly burned. A political party offered $13,000 to any person who would cut off Aylisli's ear. His wife and son were fired from their jobs. He lost his pension and his citizenship.

In an interview he defended himself. "Armenians are not enemies for me. How can they be? I am a 21st century writer. A solution to Nagorno-Karabakh is being delayed, and hostility is growing between the two nations. I want to contribute to a peaceful solution."

Some brave writers and others spoke out in his defense. Leyla Yunus (in jail now, see above) said, "Only Aylisli defends the honor and the dignity of our nation after the story of Ramil Safarov." (Safarov, an Azeri army lieutenant, hacked to death an Armenian army officer in Hungary and was lauded by the Azerbaijan government as a hero. This, in part, motivated Akram to write *Stone Dreams*.)

In 2014, Akram was nominated by fourteen public figures from around the world for the Nobel Peace Prize for "courage shown in his efforts to reconcile the Azerbaijan and Armenian people." "His willingness to sacrifice all for the sake of truth, is encouragement to each of us to be brave. His personal courage and moral impulse can change a nation's fate."[11]

KERIM KERIMLI (52 years old in 2015) Azeri refugee from Karabakh

Kerim is the Karabakhi engineer-become-journalist (see 1998 above) who fled in the night with his family ahead of the invading army. Still a refugee living in Baku, he is a respected spokesperson. Kerim has received international awards for journalism, reporting under extreme conditions. In October 2011, he was interviewed by *Commonspace*. The interview profiles Kerim as an intelligent, mature individual, with wide and deep knowledge of the Caucasus region, his burning purpose to allow refugees to return to Karabakh. He puts forth possible solutions. His in-depth analysis leads him to believe that peace with coexistence is possible if built with guarantees of safety.[12]

ARMENIANS

AGHASI AYVAZYAN

The well-known and loved Armenian writer and cinematographer (discussed above, see 1998) died in 2007 at 81 years of age.

ANAHIT BAYANDUR

Anahit Bayandur, human rights activist, Member of Parliament and Armenian literary translator, died in 2011 at the age of 71. She and Arzu Abdullayeva, the Azeri mover-and-shaker (see above), became close friends and shared the Olof Palme International Peace Prize in 1992. The Prize commends them for outstanding activities towards the establishment of peace in the region by the power of grassroots diplomacy.[13] Arzu eulogized Anahit, her Armenian sister-in-spirit.

"Anahit was sincere and honest, bravely upheld her point of view, looked for compromises and always tried to provide her opponent with opportunity to make steps forward. She was not imbued with stereotypes, remained open for new ideas and mutual understanding. Our first joint action was visits to our countries [each other's countries] at the height of the war and calls to cease combat operations. Huge strength and courageousness was hidden in her outwardly fragile figure. I remember how we, jointly with brave others, led Armenians and Azerbaijanis to meet on the border of the two belligerents across minefields. We confided our lives to each other. I shall keep her in my mind forever."

TIGRAN SARGSYAN (55 years old in 2015)

Tigran Sargsyan, an economist, was a banker and Member of the Supreme Council of Armenia in 1998. In 2008 he became Prime Minister and held that post until

2014. In November 2014, he was appointed Armenia's Ambassador to the US. President Obama welcomed him: "The U.S. places great importance on relations with Armenia based on mutual respect and interests…" President Obama said, "The US highly appreciates Armenia's commitment to reaching a peaceful settlement of the Nagorno-Karabakh conflict." Sargsyan is in a position of influence, but he faces the dilemma of intractable conflicts. How he will use his position will unfold in the years ahead.[14]

KARINE OGANIAN (early 40s in 2015) Armenian from Karabakh

Only about 23 and a journalism student when she started meeting in 1994, she has become a successful journalist (see 1998 above). She attempts to bring her fellow journalists into joint projects with Azeris. In 2007 Karine convened a conference, *Journalism and Peace-Making*. A difficult subject that most do not approach, she queried: "Does peace-making journalism exist? How much does Karabakh media need it?" Government people and media specialists took part. The outcome: "Dialogue will allow softening of tension among the parties; it is necessary to continue dialogue with Azerbaijani colleagues."[15]

KAREN OGANJANIAN (in his 50s in 2015) Armenian from Karabakh

The young engineer discussed above as exemplifying the dilemma of intractable conflicts (who had a profound experience when he saw the running dog) was a Member of the Karabakh Parliament in 1998. He had vowed that he would continue to work for peace. He told the truth. Karen was, in the 2005 election, leader of the *Social Democratic Party*, one of seven parties in that election. Most political parties in Karabakh have strongly economic and nationalistic emphases. Oganjanian's party platform, on the other hand, stated as their goal: *The Social Democratic Party "concentrates on man, the fundamental values of justice, kindness, love, and morality."* His party received 1.3 percent of the vote and failed to capture any seats.

Besides his attempts to work through the political process, Karen Oganjanian continues to work for human rights in his capacity of coordinator of Karabakh's *Helsinki Citizens' Assembly*, an arm of the international refugee advocacy NGO. He has held this position for 20 years.

In 2007, a German journalist described Karen Oganjanian's "astonishing viewpoint."[16] His viewpoint is noteworthy because as an ethnic Armenian from Karabakh, he supports Azeri refugee return and joint governance. In conflict resolution, the ideal solution is not the enforced outcome of one side. It is a "third way." Both sides agree to give up total victory, but each gains something vital. They create new ways to move forward together with security and future possibility. Against the herd, Karen's is a courageous stand. This visionary and daring proposal is only one idea. It demonstrates the creativity necessary to reach a solution.

WHAT IS SUCCESS?

Crucial are the acts of individuals with vision. The fundamental task is to create an image of peace that includes the "other." This is accomplished by proposals that recognize a shared destiny and shared governance (such as the one proposed by Karen). We have learned from prior transformed "intractable" conflicts what is of essence: Individuals who transcend hold a view of a larger picture and are not trapped on one side in a polarized, frozen event. Transforming events are created by individuals, and they make the difference.

How do we create transforming events? *First* we do it in our hearts and minds. We admit to ourselves that many of our former enemies are truly human, just as we are, and we act on this knowledge. This is what Akram Aylisli risks with *Stone Dreams*. Because society is not yet ready, he is heavily punished for his vision. If the culture chooses to deepen the fear and distrust, there will be ever-escalating hatred—hostilities that can only increase in intensity, and the present will become the history that can never be erased.

The *second* step is to form bonds of trust to eliminate the image of the enemy in our own lives. I watched the trust build among those who shared similar interests such as ecology, security, governance and human rights, education, and journalism. I watched heart connections form among those who shared similar experiences, especially suffering. I watched respect build when one recognized the depth of another.

Finally, to create transforming events, it is essential to recognize the deep interests held in common. In common for each participant are at least two: the first is a profound abhorrence of violence, cruelty, war and revenge. Each has a desire for security, liberty and access to a creative life. Most of the participants in this project continue to be deeply immersed in, and passionate about two related issues: reconciliation and human rights.

In common also is love of the children. By the decisions we make, we can endow our children with cycles of violence (by giving them memories only of atrocities to be avenged), or we can bequeath to them a vision of people who have reconciled, forgiven, and who recognize that the future is one of shared destiny.

Breakthrough: We Are All Connected

When I ponder the vast 14 billion year history from the Big Bang to *Homo sapiens*—you and me—I am in awe that we have reached the revolutionary evolutionary capacities of choice and compassion. Other species have a narrow capacity to a limited extent, but humans can access these in each moment.

In evolution, *emergence* means an entirely new phenomenon has arisen. These have always come from the edge. Most ancient fish developed into magnificent, sleek swimming forms, not clunky quadrupeds, the edge-living ancestors of the new: amphibians and reptiles. Huge dinosaurs became extinct—except one group, smaller than the others, became the magnificent birds of Earth. Most reptiles did not become warm-blooded mammals, but one did. And one line of mammals, the primates, gave birth to *Homo sapiens*, a group that now have the evolutionary capacity of choice and forgiveness.

Irving Kristol, a neoconservative American journalist, wrote in 1997: "It is hard to find a peace process that has accomplished anything, anywhere." I disagree with his cynical observation. Most who attended the yearly convocations made heart connections with "enemies" as defined by their politics and identity, but not by their deep humanity. These individuals are indicators that the human species can adapt to the Earth as it is today; that the species can adapt its outdated and no longer functional operational modes. They will make the difference, step by small step. A creative peace plan that includes: the enemy as partner (as did Nelson Mandela's), apologies from all sides for atrocities, and finally forgiveness and demythologizing the enemy—offers vital possibility for change. Every member of our citizen's dialogue group when they risk everything, even their lives, in an effort to eliminate the image of the enemy, demonstrate that we are all connected.

I think of you still:

For me, the month in the Caucasus was profoundly inspiring. I will never forget you.

I believe that you, 34 brave souls who participated in the project—seven years of meetings between Armenians and Azeris—succeeded.[17] You, who create events to aid reconciliation, risk your reputations, liberty and lives. You continue to influence and impact your own societies through your networking and individual acts. I am deeply moved that you risk your lives to raise the level of freedom. You are definitely living on the edge—the evolutionary edge. Evolutionary change happens in individuals first. Then, groups transform. It has been so for as long as life on Earth.

ENDNOTES: THE WOMAN WHO WEPT

[1] Samantha Schoenfeld, Conflict Resolution Trainer, was central to the project.
[2] Foundation for Global Community/Stanford Project: 1992 to 1999
With Stanford University as a partner (and with support from the *Carter Center* and others), a group from FGC visited Yerevan (capital of Armenia) and Baku (capital of Azerbaijan) and made many of the contacts that resulted in the first dialogue in 1993, held in FGC's rustic lodge in Ben Lomond, California. A signed document of shared goals was achieved. After the difficult first dialogue, FGC members traveled to the region to secure support from the belligerent countries to allow more attendees in future meetings. A second meeting was held in the Ben Lomond lodge in 1994. We took walks in the woods, ate and washed dishes together. Dr. Harold Saunders, former US Assistant Secretary of State for Near East Affairs, facilitated the first two years' meetings with support from FGC volunteers. In 1996, FGC members spent six months in the region to help prepare for joint collaborations. Following the six-month visit to the region, the third meeting was held there, and a fourth in 1997. I was involved in the California meetings and fortunate to be invited to this, the fifth dialogue in 1998, which lasted for one month, including a week in Baku and a week in Yerevan. I was involved also in the last dialogue in California in 1999, where, at the end of the week, we said final goodbyes. The participants were working together as one team

established as the NGO *Peace Service*. Their projects had in common one primary goal: to reduce the "image of the enemy" in their own societies.

[3] Dennis Sandole

[4] Figures from: Rieff, David. "Case Study in Ethnic Strife. (Nagorno-Karabakh)." Foreign Affairs v76, n2 1997: Council on Foreign Relations

[5] Jantsch, Erich. *The Self-Organizing Universe: Scientific and Human Implications of the Emerging Paradigm of Evolution*. Pergamon Press. 1980

[6] http://en.wikipedia.org/wiki/Zardusht_Alizadeh

[7] Coalson, Robert. "Azerbaijan Tightens Screws on Civil Society, Independent Media."
Radio Free Europe, Radio Liberty. December 29, 2014
http://www.rferl.org/content/azerbaijan-squeezes-civil-society-media/26574692.html

[8] Sindelar, Daisy. "Together a Lifetime, Azeri Activists Now Apart and in Jail." Radio Free Europe, Radio Liberty. December 29, 2014
http://www.rferl.org/content/azerbaijan-yunus-couple-apart-in-jail/26551508

[9] http://www.hyd.org.tr/?pid=613

[10] http://www.idea.int/europe_cis/upload/Badalov+Mehdi_en.pdf

[11] Most information regarding Akram Aylisli is from Wikipedia

[12] http://commonspace.eu/eng/debate/6/id883

[13] http://www.reseau-ipam.org/spip.php?article2281

[14] http://armenianweekly.com/2014/07/16/amb-tigran-sargsyan

[15] Ayrumian, Naira (Correspondent). "Problems of Peace-making Journalism Discussed in Nagorno-Karabakh." Caucasian Knot. 20 October 2007
http://eng.kavkaz-uzel.ru/articles/6520/

[16] Brenner, Andreas. "It's Time to Forget This War." 2007. Deustche Welle/Qantara.de. Translated from the German by Nancy Joyce

[17] There were other participants who contributed as much as those about whom I wrote. All of you are included in my message of appreciation, admiration and love.

###

LIFE IN GERMANY
GINGER RILLING

The following narratives are based on Ginger and Dieter Rillings' experiences in Germany; Dieter, born in 1938 in Berlin, as a boy during and after the Second World War, and Ginger, born in 1944 in El Paso Texas, as a new bride who came to live in Germany in 1966.

A GERMAN BOY'S PERSPECTIVE ON THE WAR
DIETER

I was born in 1938, and the country was already at war. Germany had invaded Poland, and everyone was gearing up for the war effort, including my father, who was in the military. He worked in headquarters in Berlin, and continued to do so throughout the war. He worked as a courier, and traveled often carrying important papers from one place to another.

If I looked out of the window from our 6th floor apartment where we lived, I could see an air defense station with a cannon erected on a high concrete bunker. By the time I was four in 1942, we often spent long periods of time in the cellar because the siren would indicate that an air raid was coming. We would then also hear the cannon being fired if the air raid was any place close to where we lived. It was common practice for everyone to have a backpack with essential things in it; some food and water, and some information to identify yourself.

On the positive side, I also remember my father, Philipp taking my sister, Rosemarie, and me to the nearby stadium to run around the track. Berlin had excellent sport facilities because the Olympics had taken place there in 1936. There were also bicycle trips into the beautiful forest areas within the city, which were preserved for the people's use.

At some point an incinerator bomb hit our house in Berlin, and it was no longer safe to continue living there. Soon I found myself in my grandparents' home in Glogau (which is now in Poland) with my mother, my sister, 3 years older, and my brother, Gernot who was 3 years younger than myself. Glogau is situated on the Oder River. My grandmother had a flower shop on the bottom level of the house where they lived. Many of her customers were Jewish people, and I would hear about some people disappearing, a thing which clearly upset my mother. She was definitely not a friend of Hitler. How my father felt, I don't really know. He never talked about it. He was in the military, but so were all men. There were very few exceptions for this; farmers and men involved in manufacturing for the military, for example, did not have to join the military.

One activity I remember well is helping my grandfather with his sauerkraut production. I would put on my rubber boots, and climb up a ladder to get into a huge vat where we would stamp down the cabbage. The processed sauerkraut he then put in smaller barrels, which he distributed to all the shops in the town. His sauerkraut was a most sought-after vegetable, because it could be eaten all year round. He would sometimes take me on his bicycle to the large garden area they had outside the town. His bicycle had a little seat on the handlebars, and when we set out for the garden, he would always stop at the Gasthaus (pub) for a beer. This garden was where the flowers were grown for the flower shop, as well as vegetables for the family. My grandfather also raised rabbits and doves to eat.

I started school in Glogau, and according to my mother, I was a very inattentive student. The school was directly next to the Oder River, and I was constantly at the window looking at the big tugboats going down the river with all kinds of military equipment, like tanks and cannons, that was much more interesting than the ABC's. Glogau, being much closer to the front line, was a place where the sirens often sounded, and since there was no place to go for shelter in the school, they would just send us home. So my first year of schooling was not very instructive for me. I don't think I got much out of it.

In '45, I remember I was sledding on a little hill, and the person who worked with my grandmother came and picked me up. I just changed clothes and an hour later we were all at the train station. The order had come down from Hitler's headquarters that mothers with small children had to leave Glogau. I remember we had to be lifted through a small opening into the toilet of the train, because the train was full to overflowing. My brother was just three years old at the time, and I know it was quite an ordeal for everyone. The train went off in the direction of Berlin, and we left everybody else behind, including my grandparents. We never saw them again, and never found out what happened to them. Some people had the intention of setting off on foot toward the west but since '45 was one of the coldest winters, who knows what could have happened. Besides, everything they had was in Glogau. Perhaps they felt they had to stay. The front line was very close to this town, and at night you could see the tracers of the cannon shots and there was a lot of noise. Eventually, Glogau was pretty much gutted. My mother went back in the early sixties, and there was nothing left, and nothing had been rebuilt, either.

That train ride was quite eventful. We were getting close to Berlin, I think it was in Potsdam, and they stopped the train because not all the railroad tracks were in working order. There had been many attacks and bomb raids everywhere. The British and the Americans were coming in from the west, and the Russians from the east with big bombers. Since the German Air Force was pretty much decimated at that point, there had been much destruction by the Allied air strikes, including railroad tracks.

We all had to get off the train and they told us that there was a fast moving military train coming, and we all had to lay down flat on the ground. I remember going over this large railroad yard, many, many tracks, to the city train station, which was part of that whole complex. With the help of lots of people we actually made it there. As we were waiting to get on the train, my brother was in a little carriage with some of our things. The city train came, one of those where the doors automatically close, and my brother in his carriage was first pushed inside the train, and the doors closed. My mother Herta and my sister and I were left standing outside the train as it left. There was a lot of commotion, and somehow my mother convinced the station manager to call ahead, and when we arrived at the next stop, someone had taken my brother out, and there he was, waiting for us. I cannot imagine how frightened my mother must have been.

We ended up in the Kaserne (military base) where my father was stationed. Everything was very tense; you had to go through a guardhouse anytime you went in and out. There was not enough food; everything had been rationed for some years. This must have been February or March in Potsdam, and as we all know the war was coming to an end in May 1945. All was in an uproar, out of control. The military tried, but they all were scared, knowing that the Russians were coming. Everybody feared the Russians – they had a very bad reputation.

Somehow, I remember, we all got into a military truck, and there must have been another family, because my father did not know how to drive. We drove on that famous Berlin-Hamburger highway. The intent was to cross the Elbe

292

River because my father was convinced that the Elbe would be the dividing line between the western allied forces and Russia, which turned out to be correct. But we didn't get that far. I recall that an airplane attacked us and we had to get out and take cover. We wouldn't have been able to cross the Elbe anyway, because later we learned that all the bridges has been bombed.

We ended up in Grube, where my Onkel (uncle) Gustav, who was a teacher there, and Tante (aunt) Erna were living. It was a very small town, 600 people. We first stayed with them, but it didn't work out very well. They were very well off as far as food goes. They had slaughtered a pig and had smoked part of it, and they had sausages and bacon and meat and potatoes, and we had nothing. They weren't really willing to share with four hungry mouths. I think they ate at a different time than we did. I was also annoyed by the fact that my aunt didn't allow me to go upstairs and use the play stuff that had been left behind by her son who had been killed several years prior in a car accident. His name was the same as mine – Hans Dieter.

Sometime in June '45 a Russian battalion came into the town and settled there. They were Cossacks, and they were all on horses, pulling their equipment with horses as well. There were only a few command trucks there. They settled and they ruled the town, and according to my mother, there wasn't a single woman who hadn't been raped during this time except her. She had put cow manure in her hair and a big pillow in her clothes, and when she went out, she always had my little brother with her. Nevertheless, she did have one experience; she was home, had cleaned up, and the Russians came, and she jumped out the window with my brother, went through the forest, and right behind the forest was a potato field. She threw herself down between the rows of potatoes, and the Russians came after her and shot signal ammunitions, which lit up the whole sky, but they didn't find her. Eventually she came back.

I also remember that when the Russians came, we left the house and stayed in a bunker about one kilometer out of town where there was food and water. With us was a young woman, a neighbor, and two young Russians came and found us and took the girl. We heard her scream, and later she came back, all bloody, and I think they raped her at that time. As terrible as the Russians were to the women, they treated all the children well. They were always friendly and smiling, and shared some food with us. I liked it when I could ride one of their horses.

The Russians had been there maybe three weeks, and somehow the commander found out that my father had been in the military, because members of the community had seen him in uniform, visiting my uncle. So, they came and picked my father up and he disappeared. He ended up in Siberia and didn't come back until '48, three years later. We received one or two postcards from him in those three years, giving us hope that he was still alive. While he was gone we were forced to move into some housing which was horrible. It was infested with rats and mice, and there was no way to control them because there were just too many of them. I remember that the mice were running over our faces in the middle of the night. Of course all three kids slept in one bed.

Eventually we got a place with a farmer, and the farms were built in such a way that they had what was called the 'old people's portion' so when the old folks were not working in the fields anymore, which was pretty hard work, they would move into this old people's place at the farmhouse and take care of the chickens and things like that. All the farmers were forced to take in these refugees who had all streamed in from the east, and we were designated to stay in this place. It was much nicer. We had a regular kitchen, and there were no rats and mice and we had a wood burning stove. There was a living room, kitchen and one bedroom. We moved in there in '47, and when Vati (father) came in '48, we all had to sleep in that one bedroom. It was awfully cold in that bedroom – it wasn't heated. It had double windows, but they were leaky, so we filled them up with moss against the cold. At night we would put a brick on the stove and heat it up, and Mutti (mother) would put a towel around it and that's what you would put on your feet because it was so damn cold in there.

Since it was a farming community we did not hunger. There was food. After the harvest, we collected small potatoes which were left behind, and we would find what was was left over after the rye harvest, and convert it to flour. So we had some potatoes and flour. Then of course, everything was rationed, so you had so many grams of sugar, butter, bread and milk that you were entitled to, and usually these were available in stores.

The Russians eventually left, but before they did, we were all forced to watch one of their tournaments, which I thought was quite impressive. These Cossacks put on quite a show with sabers, showing their dexterity by racing around on their horses cutting up apples secured to the tops of poles. They had made places for all of us to sit, and I remember hand carvings that were quite beautiful. It was interesting that they were able to do this work in such a short period of time.

Life returned to normal on some level. Mutti would work with the farmers, and she also made wreathes for funerals and flower arrangements for weddings at which she was very talented. Somehow we were able to survive. Mutti had to make all the clothes, mostly from old military uniforms – there was nothing else available. She would knit all the socks, very scratchy socks. Shoes were always a problem. When my father finally came back home, he would take shoes that had holes in them and remove the soles and replace them with wooden soles, which were very hard and stiff. There was a lot of stress on those shoes, and I would always get in trouble because I would run and the shoes would come apart and my father would have to fix them again.

Yes, I was in trouble a lot. Not being a very good student, nor being interested in helping out, it was easy to get into trouble. Vati began to raise rabbits for food, and one of my not so enjoyable jobs was to provide grass for the rabbits. I would go to the meadows that the farmers hadn't mowed yet, and there I could get a sack full of grass and transport it back on my bicycle. But many times I would forget and be late, and quite often I got a licking.

I learned that equality didn't really exist. When we would go out and help the farmers in the fields, they would provide such delicious sandwiches with homemade bread and slices of smoked ham or sausages. At home we didn't have anything like that. We did have eggs and butter, and some meat, all rationed, but never smoked ham. We were not allowed to have our own chickens, because the chickens were all running around loose, and how could we identify which ones were ours? So we did not get permission to have chickens. I did however, sometimes help the old woman who would collect the eggs and there were times when she couldn't go up into the hayloft and get the eggs. She really had no idea how many eggs were up there. They were located over a drive-through, which was used when they would bring in the hay when rain was pending. So that's where my brother would be and he would have a hat and catch the eggs in his hat. I would make a one-third to two-thirds distribution; one-third for us, two-thirds for her.

We did have a little garden way out of town, and I had to go out every second day in the summer and water everything; potatoes, tomatoes, cabbages, and radishes. Radishes were the first thing in the spring that you could put on the bread with a little bit of butter, and it was most delicious.

I also knew where all the different fruit trees were in town; apples, plums, cherries and one single walnut tree. I got my share of those walnuts, too. The way I usually operated, I would know always where the good fruit was, and when it became ripe. And I would also know exactly when the farmers were eating, or when they were out in the field, and then I would go and harvest. I would wear a big shirt and a belt and I put whatever I would harvest into the shirt and belt would keep it from falling out. Then I would reluctantly share with my sister and my brother.

The farmers always had fruit stored in the cellar, placed on hay. On Saturday mornings they would open up the small windows to let air in, and you had this terrific aroma, which came out of that cellar of those apples on hay! It was unbearable. So I put a nail on the end of a long pole like a little harpoon, and I would go and carefully take one apple from this tray, and another from that, one from that and brought them out. I thought they had plenty but they were never willing to share, so I had to force the issue.

In this little town, all eight grades were in one room and the teacher was my uncle. I found some interest in school later on, and I remember in the eighth grade, there were three boys and two girls and we were all sitting on the same bench. We were writing with goose feathers in the beginning, and the paper was horrible – it was like blotting paper. You had to make a very thin line with the ink because if you made a big line, it would just spread out, keeping you from ever making a nice looking paper. We would come in the morning, and everyone would have to stand and my uncle would pose a math question – a chain; 15 times 10, divided by 5, take away 8, add 5, take away the number of days in this month and so on. As soon as you knew the answer you could sit down. I was pretty good at this. I was never the last one standing. At writing, however, I was not so good. When the weather was nice, the seventh and eight graders would take the first and second outside and do math or reading with them.

When I graduated after eight years of school in 1952 with my class of three girls and two boys, I actually only had seven years of school, because my first year was really lost during the war. My sister was much more diligent in studying, and liked school, and had already left home after the fifth grade to go to school in a nearby city, Bad Wilsnak, where she lived during the week. (Note: in Germany, after the fifth grade, students who are doing well are directed into continuing high school. The other students finish eight years of school and go into apprenticeships of one kind or another, or into vocational programs. This is still true today.) Later she attended the 'Internat", which is a kind of boarding school where she lived and went to school all in one place. She finished thirteen years of school, which is typical in Germany for a high school degree.

I started right away as an electrician apprentice after the eighth grade. Actually I wanted to be an auto mechanic, but of course there were no cars and no repair stations where we lived. I helped out a little bit at the blacksmith's in town, which was quite a busy place. At that time you had to make your own nails. Most of the wagons were wooden wagons with wooden wheels, and iron rims around the wooden wheels. I used to help the blacksmith with this – he was Rumanian – his German wasn't very good, but I enjoyed being with him. He was treating me very nice.

My apprenticeship was also in Bad Wilsnak, where my sister was going to school. I had to work 48 hours a week. That meant every day eight and a half hours and on Saturday until one o'clock. It was required of me, as the youngest guy of the team, to be at the workplace first, especially important in the winter, because I had to fire up the stove. Bad Wilsnak was eight kilometers away from Grube, and it took me fifty minutes to go the eight kilometers there by bike on a dirt road with cobblestones. I rode mostly on the dirt because it was not so bumpy. These eight kilometers went through large sections of forests, and I knew a lot of history involving these forests. My father used to tell stories at bedtime that made me so frightened that I would curl up in a fetal position, of course enjoying it at the same time.

But then, the next day, when I had to drive back and forth by bike through those same forests on my way to work, those stories had a powerful effect on me. In the morning when there was light, it wasn't so bad; (although in the winter it was dark both ways) but in the dark on my return, it was a different story. I tried to pedal as fast as I could, but the generator for the lights slowed me down. I would take the generator off and continue in the dark. The place I was most fearful of, and always tried to hurry by, was called Glocken Stein, meaning 'Bell Rock'. This big rock was at an intersection with a signpost indicating how many kilometers to Bad Wilsnak or Perleberg or Grube. This was the location where many of my father's stories took place.

One such story happened during medieval times when merchants traveled down this quite well known road. At this intersection, the knights would wait for the merchants to pass, and demand money and goods from them. If they didn't agree they would decapitate them and throw the bodies by the side of the road into a swamp, where they disappeared for all time. According to my father, their souls were living on, and so at night, when I passed by this place, ahh, I could just feel all these souls. My hairs on the back of my neck would stand up. I would go faster and faster, and more than once did this damn chain jump off the drive and get stuck, and all I could do was take the bike and run until I thought I was far enough away from it so I could get the chain back into working order. Also, at the same place, after the war, somebody had hanged himself, so, this was a double-banger, I thought. It was very frightful for me.

I had to be at work at 7:30, and I would drive by the place where my sister was in a nice warm cozy house, getting ready for breakfast and school. I would whistle and she would look out the window and we would exchange some greetings and I would go on. Here she was, so much better off than I was, going to school, and I was working. Forty-eight hours a week made for long days, plus driving back and forth, pretty much a ten-hour workday for a fourteen year old. It must have been stressful, looking at it now, but back then, I don't think I gave it much thought. That's the way it was. According to my parents, it had been MY choice not to go to an advanced school. Well, they offered me that choice in the sixth or seventh grade and I would have had to keep up with people who had had Russian since the fifth grade, and physics and biology and all that, which my sister was able to do. So I ended up being trained as an electrician. My first year of working I didn't do much; I just handed the tools to the journeyman and I traveled with him and carried stuff. I was productive for him but I didn't seem to learn much. I was always so tired I had to hold onto the ladder not to fall asleep.

Work was hard, but there were many things that I did enjoy. When I graduated in 1952, after the eight years, I was to go visit my aunt in Hanover, in West Germany. I finally got some decent tires for my bike, which was a single-speed bike. I got a permit to cross the border, and the only way you could cross the border was to go on the autobahn. I had never driven very long distances by bike, and on that very first time, I covered 120 kilometers, which is almost eighty miles in one day on that single-speed bike. I don't know how I did that. I would have a hard time doing it now.

Anyhow, I ended up visiting my cousin who lived in Wolfsburg where they build Volkswagens. She was a teacher there, living by herself. What a difference coming from East Germany, and knowing very little about what was going on in West Germany. We had a radio, but we were afraid to turn on the radio to a West German station. The fear that somebody might identify that and report you to the party or the police was big. Fear was a constant. There was always fear of some sort, during the war especially, and later on because of the Russians. Fear has always been a partner in my life – it just didn't seem to leave.

From Wolfsburg I went to Hanover, which was another eighty kilometers, and I stayed with my aunt. In the same apartment building there was a young guy who had a turntable, and he had some jazz music. It was the first time I heard jazz. It was unbelievable! I wanted to hear the same piece again and again. Those were the little 45 records, which I had never seen. I think he finally got tired of me.

I listened to different radio stations, whatever I wanted to listen to. My Onkel had work, so there was a lot to eat – quite different - things that I had never had before – chocolate, oranges, bananas, noodles. Everything smelled so different. When I went into the city by bike, I was amazed that I could do that by myself. I almost got killed because I wasn't aware of how to cross the streetcar tracks. There was a streetcar behind me and I was supposed to get out of the way, and I got stuck in the tracks and fell. The streetcar had to stop, and I was able to get up and out of the way. Nothing happened but it was a close call.

There was a sweet smell in the air in the city that I had never experienced before. It turned out that it was the exhaust from the cars! In Grube the only car that was ever in town was the milk car, and it was running on wood. Most big trucks during the war ran on wood, because we didn't have any oil production. Hitler's aim to get to the oil fields in

Bulgaria and Saudi Arabia never was possible, so many cars and trucks were converted to run on steam. The steam was generated by burning small pieces of oak, which certainly smelled quite different from the exhaust in the city.

I came back from that trip and I was the center point of attention for the time, because I had replaced the generator for my bike with a new one, and I had bought a new light with a lot of power. I could turn the bike so that the light was aimed at the church tower, rotate the wheel and I had enough light to illuminate the tower. Nobody else could do this. I also had bought a new jacket with a zipper. No one in town had ever seen a zipper – they didn't exist for us. I also had shoes, leather shoes!

Two days a week during my apprenticeship I had to drive to Perleberg, which was almost twice as far away as Bad Wilsnak, in order to attend school. You have to hand it to the Germans – they had to divide it up so that we could work and go to school, too, and the school was eight hours a day. Part of the curriculum included physical education. We would go regularly out to the fields, summer, spring and fall, and do running, long jump, hurdles and so on. There would be competitions, and during the competition some people from the political party's education branch came and evaluated how we were doing. If anyone had potential of being a good athlete, they would try to convince you to work in a "People-Owned" factory, where you had meals and transportation. You could live there, work half a day, and train half a day. That was in 1953 -54, when already East Germany was doing a broad search for Olympic talent. And as we know, East Germany was extremely successful in many Olympics. A nation of only seventeen million was, I believe, third in the world at one or two of the Olympics, which was unbelievable.

Eventually things happened with my father's work. He was working in the mayor's office, and the farmers had to complete a 'Zoll', meaning they were forced to deliver to the state collection agency a certain amount of all the food they produced: milk, butter, rye, potatoes, meat (usually pork), eggs. If they didn't fulfill their Zoll, because they just couldn't or they didn't have it, they didn't get permission to kill a pig for themselves. My father used to manipulate the data such that they were able to have their pigs, and he was then reported for that. Luckily there was a friend there that heard that my father was in trouble and he notified him. So the very day he got this notification from this man, my uncle, my father and myself went by bike to not the closest, but the further away train station and both my uncle and father went to Berlin by train. (The reason I went with them was so that I could bring the bikes back home.) That was in December 1953. They had to leave because they knew they would be picked up. Sure enough, a couple of days later, the SSD, the Statts Sicherheit Dienst, (security service) came to pick up my father and luckily he was gone.

My aunt moved in with us after that; her husband was gone and she was very scared. She wasn't a very independent person, and so there was my mother with us three kids, and now my aunt. My sister was at that time already at the University in another town, and she had a boyfriend at the University in Potsdam, and through him we heard that my father had a good chance of being recognized as a political refugee. That was the signal that we should leave as well. Early in 1954 we all went to the train station with a minimum amount of luggage, went to Potsdam and got on the city train. At this time, the city train would go through East Berlin and West Berlin (West Berlin being in the middle and completely surrounded by East Berlin). There was always the chance of being picked up by plainclothes police, because they would inspect all the passengers. We couldn't sit together as a family. We had to separate and we just had to make sure that everybody got off at the same place. Sometimes they wouldn't stop the train in West Berlin when they thought they had somebody who wanted to escape. The train would just go through. We were lucky. It stopped, we all got out, and we were re-united with my father who was in a displaced person's camp. It turned out to be the Dutch Consulate Building. We slept in a big room, with the men and women separated. The beds were three stories high, and as a young kid, I had to be on top. All the guys were smoking, and there I was on top, the youngest kid around.

Luckily enough we didn't have to stay very long there because of the recognition that my father was a political escapee. We were to be transported to a different place where we as a family would have our own room. Eventually we were flown out of West Berlin to Hanover. I found out my mother had been in terrible pain for the whole flight. It was a DC3 two-prop plane, and it wasn't pressurized. She had cavities and under those conditions the air in the cavities expanded with tremendous pain for her.

We didn't stay long in Hanover. We went by train all the way to Traunstein, in Bayern (Bavaria). We arrived there very early and my father woke me up to show me the mountains. I had never before seen mountains in my life. The Alps! With snow on top, two thousand meters, six thousand feet! What a delight!

In this displaced persons camp, one of the goals was to get all the young people into a working environment as quickly as possible. University students came to tutor us, and lucky for me, my sister took a liking to a young man named Gerhard who liked to climb mountains. I had a strong desire to do this as well, but he could see I needed some training first. I was put through a tough regimen of running up hill, push-ups and pull-ups using weights, and more. Eventually he invited me to go along on one of his trips, and so we biked from Traunstein to the foot of the Alps, about sixty kilometers.

The goal was to climb up one of the walls of the Watzman, one of the highest mountains in the Alps, three thousand meters (nine thousand feet). There were three of us climbing together, my sister's friend Gerhard and another young man named Karl, the son of a forester who was supposedly well prepared. As for myself, I was in good shape, but I had no experience climbing, let alone using climbing equipment. I remember how challenging it was to climb that wall. We did it though, and reached the top, but by then it was starting to get dark, and we had a long ways to go to reach the hut. We descended another route that was not as difficult, but nevertheless in the dark and in rainy conditions, hard enough. Karl who was in front, fell through the snow, and we had to pull him out. After that he was so frightened he did not want to continue. He wanted to return to the top where there was a small weather hut and spend the night there. But that building had no insulation and we were soaked. It would not have been a good decision. Gerhard squeezed some lemon juice into his mouth and threatened to slap him until he agreed to go on, and luckily he pulled himself together and we continued.

We finally reached the hut, so cold and wet through and through. There were people who were already in the hut, and they wrapped us in blankets and gave us hot tea with rum. It was a harrowing experience, but exhilarating to me. I wanted very much to continue learning more about climbing. I learned from that experience that the mountains had such beauty and power, but that one needed to have great respect for them as well.

Traunstein was only a transitional home for me unfortunately. Soon after that, I had no choice but to go north to a town to continue my apprenticeship. There were no mountains there, and I regretted not being able to pursue my desire for climbing. My brief exposure in the Alps had given me an awareness of the value of camaraderie and teamwork, as well as the importance of having a common goal. Ten years or more passed before I had another opportunity to climb in the Alps. I was stationed in Munich, in Bavaria, with my new wife, Ginger, and she and I, together with our sons, Toby and Chris, began climbing mountains together.

Some Honeymoon
Ginger

The last thing I ever expected to see as the plane descended in Cologne was green, everything was green. And it was the middle of November. Coming from El Paso, Texas where I had lived all my twenty-two years, and where the first hint of cold turned carefully watered lawns to brown overnight, I was astonished at the abundance of green.

It was only the first of many surprises that awaited me as a young American woman arriving in Germany to be re-united with her new German husband. Our first stop was to meet his family, who, I was to hear later, pronounced me to be 'all right'. Their main concern was that this new bride of their son's came complete with two children, which was not considered a plus in their eyes. But I think they were relieved that I seemed normal enough, and that my boys' behavior was not too unseemly. For my part, I was mostly oblivious to their careful examination of us. I was excited about beginning my new life in this beautiful country.

Leaving Dieter's parents apartment in Stuttgart, we drove on to Freising, where Dieter was stationed at the time.

We had temporary housing there, as our apartment in Munich had suffered building delays. On my first day in Freising, Dieter literally took me around to meet the butcher, the baker and, not the candlestick maker, but the milk man, explained that I could not speak German, and instructed them to treat me nicely. After that I was on my own. I had taken a few weeks of German at the YMCA in El Paso, and had learned a few useless phrases that I never heard a single person actually say. I was confident enough, however, as I already could speak Spanish, and they say the third language is a cinch. (Ha! Whoever first said that clearly had not tried to learn German as a third language.) I mastered enough words to get by – "Ein Liter Milch, bitte", (One liter of milk, please) at the milk store, and "Drei Hundert Gramm Leberwurst, bitte", (Three hundred grams of liverwurst, please) at the butcher's. I did a lot of pointing. At the grocery store, I was surprised to learn that the shoppers were not allowed to pick out their own fruits and vegetables, and if you did pick anything up, I quickly realized, you would be sharply reprimanded. There was an attendant on hand who was told the amount the shopper wanted, say, a half of a pound of tomatoes, and then the attendant picked them out and handed you the package.

Too soon, we needed to vacate the apartment in Freising, and as ours in Munich was still unfinished, Dieter had to ask his parents if I could come live with them for a few weeks. It was a six-hour drive between Freising and Stuttgart, so of necessity Dieter could only be there on weekends. So there I was with my very few words of German living with my in-laws who had no words of English. I carried my pocket dictionary with me everywhere, and my mother-in-law was very patient with me, but it was a trying time.

Now December, it was increasingly cold, and central heating was almost unknown in Germany at that time. There was a Kachelofen (a large, built-in clay tile coal-burning oven) in the living room, which had the potential to warm the entire apartment, but it was only lit once a day, in the evening. My clothing was woefully inadequate – southwest Texas style – and in those days, slacks on women were not permissible. I was freezing most of the time, and Toby, age 5 and Chris, age 3 had constant runny noses. To make matters worse, my mother-in-law was always airing out the rooms. Just before going to bed, she would open wide the windows in the room where we slept to let in fresh air. The only saving grace was the blessed feather bed, which, when my feet finally thawed out, was so delightfully warm. I wanted to keep it draped about me all day.

My mother-in-law shook her head with dismay, seeing me use toilet paper for runny noses and I was soon given a few handkerchiefs. There was no Kleenex. I supposed I owned a few handkerchiefs, but they were back in El Paso, something one tucked into one's purse before going to church. Handkerchiefs were a nicety, not a necessity, until arriving in Germany.

In spite of the trials and tribulations, I was bonding with my new in-laws, after a fashion. I won brownie points with Mutti by always clearing the table and washing dishes, as she patiently demonstrated, using much less water than I was accustomed to using. Each evening after dinner Vati would take out his mandolin and play some songs he knew, which included 'God Save the Queen', which is the same tune as 'My Country Tis of Thee', which we knew and could sing along. He sang some simple children's songs to the boys that we quickly learned as well. It was a sweet time, and we were in a WARM room! On weekends we would take long walks in the forest, and Mutti and Vati were experts at finding mushrooms. We often would come home with a basket-full to prepare for our supper.

By Christmas of 1966 we were finally in our own place, in Munich. It was lovely, brand new. I realized that Dieter had been concerned that I might not feel comfortable with some of the housing that most people lived in. We did have central heating, and plenty of hot water, which I appreciated, of course. But I really had not had any expectations that I would be living in such a nice apartment. I was in love, and would have been happy in just about any flat!

Christmas gave us our first real argument. The German custom is for the Weihnachtsman, or Santa Claus, to come on Christmas Eve. The children go out for a walk with mom, and dad brings the tree in, decorates it, and puts the presents around it. I firmly believed that children should wake up to their Christmas presents on Christmas morning, knowing that Santa Claus comes during the night. I was convinced the boys would not buy it. Take a short walk, and presto, Santa has paid his visit, and has decorated the tree to boot. Besides, I wanted to decorate my tree with my kids! Well, Dieter won – when in Rome, and so on. Did Toby and Chris believe it? If they had any doubts, they sure didn't show it. They learned early on that where presents were concerned, ask no questions. It was a lovely Christmas, and I felt blessed, indeed.

TREFFAUER STRASSE 48, PART 1

I don't remember much about the actual move from Dieter's parents' apartment to our new flat in Munich, on Treffauer Street number 48. What I do remember is the sense of excitement at having our very own place, in a captivating new city. It was an adventure. Upon reflection now, though, I realize that I gave no thought to how my in-laws were feeling as we left Stuttgart. Relieved, I'm sure, to have their apartment back to themselves, but probably also very concerned about how this little 'adventure' was going to turn out for their son. I can imagine they had heavy hearts.

I now reflect back as well to that day, when I departed from the El Paso airport, with my mother outside on the tarmac, waving to us, until the airplane was just a dot in the sky. I know I cried, but I didn't spend any time imagining what my mother was going through as her only child was leaving, perhaps forever, to live in a country half way around the world, and I had taken her precious grandsons to boot. I wouldn't see her or speak to her again for two whole years.

Only much, much later as my own children left me, each to make his own way in the world, did I look back to how brave my mother had been. She celebrated my adventure, never once hinting at her own feelings, which I know, must have included sadness and heartache. She faithfully wrote me long letters each week, as I did to her, and my life and hers went on.

We arrived in Munich and moved into our apartment. We had barely moved in, however, when I was faced with dealing with Frau Sommersberger, the Hausmeisterin, apartment manager who was responsible for the goings-on in our apartment building. Frau Sommersberger was a strongly built woman with a thick Bavarian accent. She always wore an apron and a kerchief on her hair, and her cheeks were a deep flushed pink. She was skeptical from the start that this young American girl could pass muster.

With my limited German, I struggled to understand all the rules and regulations she recited to us. One point of contention became an almost daily issue. The hallways and stairs in this building were made of beautiful white stone, which she meticulously swept and mopped when needed. There was a grate and a rug in the entrance to the building where one was supposed to clean one's shoes before proceeding up the stairs, and my two boys seldom thought to make sure their shoes were dry and clean enough before running up the stairs. Each evening Frau Sommersberger would stop by after Dieter came home and explain once again (in Dieter's presence, to make sure I fully understood) that the boys MUST clean their shoes properly before coming upstairs, because she was far too busy to have to be constantly cleaning up after them. I was strict with my kids, but they had not been raised in surroundings where cleanliness was more important than godliness, nor had they been stringently drilled daily to mind their P's and Q's. In fact, the three of us had never before been exposed to apartment etiquette. Goodness knows I tried, they tried, but it soon became apparent that it was going to be very difficult to measure up to her yardstick.

Toby and Chris wanted to be outside as much as possible, it was winter and cold, and their clothing, to say the least, was less than adequate. We were from El Paso, Texas, for heaven's sake! Their shoes and gloves would become wet, and the two freezing boys would come bounding up the stairs to get warm and dry out. Under the scrutiny of Frau Sommersberger's watchful eyes, I knew I was being judged. My boys were not dressed appropriately for the weather (very true – we did not have nor could we afford proper clothes), they were not supervised adequately, and were allowed to come and go anytime they wanted (not true – but there was a vacant lot adjacent to our building and they loved to play with other little boys there), and they certainly did not know how to greet people, but we were working on that. "Gruss Gott, Frau Sommersberger". (Gruss Gott, a common greeting in Bavaria, means "May God greet you".)

Gradually I was becoming more comfortable in my new neighborhood. The boys and I did our daily shopping at the bakery, the milk store, and the butcher. One day, feeling a little bored and at the same time very brave, I decided to take the streetcar, a first for us, into downtown Munich. The whole family had taken this trip numerous times in the car, and I had memorized where I must transfer from one streetcar to another, as well as where I should disembark. Dressed as nicely and as warmly as we could manage, we waited at the stop for the streetcar to come humming around the corner. As it slid smoothly to a stop, we climbed up the steps and I handed some money to the driver. He waved me on, and I looked at him questioningly as he had a glass box with money in it next to him. He waved me on again, impatiently, and we dutifully took our seats. I looked around, wondering if we were to pay as we got off, and saw another official-looking man who was stationed at the rear door of the streetcar. And he was glaring at me. He marched down the aisle to where we were sitting and began telling me in no uncertain terms what I had done wrong. I couldn't understand a word he was saying, but I did know enough German to say "Pardon me, I'm sorry," and I gave him my money. He spun around and returned to his station, shaking his head.

I was shaking quite a bit, myself, feeling many eyes upon me, and still not sure what I had done wrong. At the next stop, however, I noticed that most people boarded the streetcar at the rear entrance, and if someone did enter in the front, they would proceed to the man in the back to pay. At each stop I confirmed that this was indeed the proper procedure. Unless, as I determined at a later date, if there is no one stationed at the rear door, one should indeed pay in the front, hence the box with money in it.

When we reached our destination and climbed down the steps of the back entrance, the lovely man barked a few more words of advice to me, which of course I didn't understand. I gave him a big smile, and nodded, realizing that was one mistake I would not make again.

In just a few months I had my own translators at my side for such future predicaments. The boys quickly picked up German from their playmates, and were a big help to me when I couldn't understand what was being said. According to Dieter, a big part of their vocabulary was swear words and Bavarian slang. But they were learning to take care of themselves in the language department. It took a good year before I began to feel like I could express myself.

We never had enough money to make ends meet; our rent alone consumed two thirds of Dieter's paycheck. I scrimped and cut corners wherever I could to get through the month. I soon became adept at finding the cheapest cuts of meat, and the biggest loaf of bread for my money. I could appreciate how Dieter described his younger years living on bread and potatoes, because they were the most inexpensive things one could buy. Toward the end of month, we often had bread and gravy for dinner. The boys were so hungry they even learned to appreciate liver, which was the cheapest meat I could find. I hated it myself, and was grateful to a German friend who taught me to prepare it with spaghetti sauce and serve it with spaghetti. It was nobody's favorite but at least it was a hearty meal.

Our visits to Dieter's parents helped get us through the leanest times. Mutti canned everything and would give me a jar of this or that, and she always had a big crock of sauerkraut that she generously shared with us. Mutti and Vati voraciously hunted for mushrooms, and we would go with them to collect baskets full, which in turn, provided many a meal. Dieter's sister and brother-in-law had a big garden with fruit trees, and in the summer we would come home with our little VW Beetle crammed full of cherries, plums and apples, potatoes, carrots and cabbage.

My mother's care packages were eagerly awaited as well. She occasionally sent me cans of green chile and dried pinto beans which I missed terribly. There were many ethnic groups in Munich and stores in the downtown area carried items from around the world. I would search up and down the aisles, but there were no pinto beans and no tortillas to be found. She often included a dollar for each of the boys in her letters, which allowed us to celebrate. We could spend these dollars at the American Military Commissary where we would go on the weekends and treat ourselves to a 25 cent hamburger and a 10 cent coke. I learned a song from the Americans at the commissary, which was fitting:

"Dankeschoen, Bitteschoen, Auf Wiedersehen,
I wish I could sprechen zee Deutsch."

In spite of the financial hardships, which honestly did not have a big impact on us in most ways - we were just doing what everyone was doing – being as frugal we could and still enjoying our lives to the fullest. Not just looking back years later, but then, in the moment, I remember being acutely aware of living such a good life.

I will never forget the moment when I realized that I was home, home in the sense of being completely contented deep inside myself. It was the day that I climbed my first mountain all the way to the top.

It was our second fall in Germany and we spent almost every weekend hiking in the Bavarian Alps. I was in lousy shape, and the trails were steep. After a few hours I would give up. But the exercise paid off and one day I made it. The sensation of standing on top of a mountain, looking down in every direction and seeing a panorama of mountains surrounding me brought a profound sense of satisfaction and joy. Added to that was a keen sense of having done this before in some previous lifetime. It was as if I were coming home after a long, long time.

TREFFAUER STRASSE 48, PART 2

I look back with so much gratitude to my mother who not only wrote me weekly letters during those three years in Germany, she kept my letters as well. It is because she so carefully bundled together those one hundred or more letters and gave them to me at some point, that I am able to write these stories with so much detail. There is much I had forgotten.

Reading these letters, I realized how much support I received from my mom during my stay in Germany as a young army wife. I wrote her almost every week, long letters, describing the goings-on in our household, and I also included a lot of information about our needs. Our boys didn't have enough warm clothes, or shoes or slippers; I was starving for Mexican food; the boys missed comic books and I missed the El Paso Times; I needed a uniform for work and material to sew a warm nightgown and on and on. And sure enough, care boxes arrived frequently with all the items I had told her we needed.

As we all settled down to our new life in Munich, I was busily making sure my boys would be cared for if and when I found a job. As an x-ray tech I thought I might be able to find a position with the Americans on the large kaserne (military base) that was in the city. There I met a German radiologist who invited me to work for him, part-time, in his private practice instead, because as I learned, the jobs on the base could only be had by American military dependents. And by then my German was at least good enough to say "Atmen Sie tief, bitte, und einhalten!" (Take in a deep breath and hold it!) I eagerly accepted his offer.

Understanding my responsibility in my children's education was a big learning curve. The school day, from kindergarten through high school, was finished by lunchtime, or by 1 PM at the latest. Children packed a 'second breakfast' to eat at about 10 AM. All were expected, from first grade on, to do hours of homework at home, rather than put in a long school day. It took time for me to realize that even as a kindergartener Toby had daily assignments that he conveniently didn't tell me about. I assumed he was doing well in school until his first report card. I went to see his teacher and she told me that he was very bright, but just wasn't completing his assignments. So we began spending several hours a day together establishing a homework routine. It paid off. By the time we returned to El Paso, after only a couple of years in the German school system, both boys were a year ahead of their classmates in the US.

Each weekend we were on the go – hiking, swimming, floating down streams on air mattresses, riding bikes, skiing, mountain climbing – summer or winter, it mattered not. One winter weekend there was an especially hard freeze, so we decided to go ice-skating. I don't remember how or where we managed to procure skis and ice skates and the like for the four of us; perhaps borrowed from friends? We had a good time ice-skating and even watched a group of old men playing a game of curling; sliding flat discs across the ice with just the right amount of speed so that they end up near a target. The sliding disc can be induced to "curl" (curve) by a player vigorously sweeping the ice in front of the disc as it moves across the ice. What a strange sport.

By the end of that ice skating day in the frigid temperature, I was frozen to the core. Never really adequately dressed for any winter occasion, I was shivering and shaking. We had been invited by our friends, Rainer and Hildegard, to their flat for dinner, and even after a long ride in the car with the heater blasting, I felt like a piece of ice. A wood stove, which had gone out, heated our friends' flat and the rooms were icy. I only warmed up much later when

Hildegard served a green bean, potato and bacon soup. To this day, this is my favorite recipe on cold winter days.

Clothing, or not enough of it, was always an issue for me. In those days women did not wear pants, ever, except to go skiing. And the miniskirt was in style. Most women wore leggings (thick stockings) and boots. Since short skirts were in, so were short coats. Add to this my desire to look good no matter what, and the result was I was always cold. The boots I had bought when the first winter weather arrived looked good, but I had unwittingly bought some that fitted well with stockings, but not with the thicker leggings. They were too tight, and there was no money for a second pair. I quickly ruined all my heels because the sidewalks were cobblestone-like and heels would get stuck between the rocks. (I had wondered in the beginning why I never saw any women with high heels.) Thankfully, my mother-in-law perceived my plight, and as she was an excellent seamstress, she began making me 'more appropriate', warmer clothing.

A memorable event every fall in Munich was the Oktoberfest, a very big deal, indeed. Large beer halls were constructed on the fair grounds, and the excitement of everyone was palpable. Suddenly, the normally reserved and proper German folk were transformed into rowdy, hard drinking, boisterous people. I wrote in one letter that during the 16 days of the Oktoberfest 25,000 liters of beer were consumed. Wikipedia tells me that in recent years, beer consumption is up to 7 million liters! It was the only time of year that I have ever seen couples necking in public. Crossing the fairgrounds was hazardous to a young woman, or a woman of any age, especially if she was unescorted. Even with an escort, I couldn't avoid the grabbing and pinching.

Children in Germany were much more into Indians and Cowboys than American kids. Toby and Chris loved playing Indian, and I made them outfits out of burlap and constructed headdresses for them. Their Christmas wish lists looked like a complete inventory of an Indian camp: spears, peace pipes, tomahawks and moccasins. A series of popular novels by the German writer Karl May, 1842-1912, about a Native American called Winnetou, was later made into several movies. The boys spent hours listening to our Winnetou records and begged me to take them to a movie. The German version of the American Indian was much more romantic than the American one. Winnetou was the true hero of these stories, and was beloved and trusted by all those who knew him. It was filmed at the gorgeous Havasupai Falls near Grand Canyon, and Winnetou had the most beautiful blue eyes you ever saw.

Frau Sommersberger and I had reached a truce of sorts after some time. One day, however, she showed up at our door in the middle of the day, her cheeks even more flushed than usual, and she was livid. She had found her daughter, Brigitti, under the front steps playing 'doctor' with our little Chris, and she demanded that we let our son know that he was never to do that again. I wanted to ask her "do what, exactly? For Gods sake these kids are only four years old!" but my German was not up to that conversation. Later when Dieter was home we met with Frau Sommersberger and her husband and we were able to assure them that we would let Chris know that playing doctor under the steps with Brigitti was not a good idea.

One of the biggest stumbling blocks for me in Germany was my lack of ability to communicate effectively when I committed a faux pas. I looked like a German and I had little or no accent with the German I could speak, and therefore people assumed I was German. Many times when I unwittingly did or said something that crossed a line that I was unaware of, I would be the recipient of a barrage of German that I could not understand. Germans have a strong obligation to let you know when some rule of etiquette has been breached. I finally learned to switch to English and say, "I'm an American, and I don't understand what you are saying." Then they would back off, usually. But for the most part, I found my immersion in a new culture to be rich, fascinating and delightful. I recognized how lucky I was to learn about a different culture from the inside out.

ON THE BISCHOFSTEIN

The Muenchen Polytechnikum engineering students were on strike again for the second semester in a row. For Dieter and me, this action confirmed the decision we had recently made to leave Munich and return to the US. This had not been an easy decision to make. We were torn between leaving the life we had created together in Germany, and starting over yet once again on an uncertain adventure.

It was my third year in Germany and Dieter had finished his twelve years of commitment to the German Air Force, and was now studying engineering at the Polytechnikum University in Munich. The German equivalent of the GI bill was paying ninety percent of his salary plus providing health insurance for us, while he completed his education, but this would last only three years. Now he was losing another semester because of this strike. The students were striking because their engineering degrees were not recognized in countries other than Germany, while virtually identical degrees from other countries such as Britain and France were. The students wanted a level playing field and thus were compelled to go on strike.

For us, however, it meant a paycheck going away before Dieter would be able to finish school, so Dieter applied at the University of Texas in El Paso, my hometown, and was accepted. Then we booked passage on a freighter that was to leave Germany on December 1, 1969

It was a mixed blessing, though, as we would be leaving behind his family, and the beautiful countryside of Bavaria. At the same time, Dieter would welcome parting from an educational system where the students could not fail more than two of thirteen subjects without being forced to completely repeat the whole semester. Thirteen subjects every semester! It was a grueling task, and the pressure was enormous, especially for Dieter who had only completed eight years of grammar and middle school anyway. He was looking forward to the Ami's (German word for American) system of six or seven courses per semester, and where, if you did flunk something, you simply repeated the course you failed.

Soon it was December, and we found ourselves in Hamburg with all our earthly possessions waiting on the dock to be loaded onto the *Bischofstein*, the freighter we were sailing on. Our household furnishings, our VW camper and our family were all going across the great blue water together

The first week on that freighter was most exciting. We had a large stateroom, and in the beginning we were the only passengers. There was a baby crib in our room because somehow they thought Chris was a baby. It had wheels on it and I can remember it rolling around the room as the boat rocked back and forth. We were treated like first class passengers, and dined at the captain's table with the captain and a couple of the officers. The food was excellent and much too abundant. There was a baker on board, and true to German custom, coffee and cake were served every day at four PM.

We spent our mornings up on deck exercising as much as possible to work off the extra calories. Then while Dieter was studying, I did school work with the boys until lunch and then the boys set off to explore the ship. In a few days they had gotten to know the entire crew, and spent all their time with them. One sailor in particular, Elto Janicke, took them under his wing, and his every free hour was devoted to showing them around the innards of the ship, and playing cards and monopoly with them. I am convinced that the main reason Toby and Chris became fishermen was because of the early influence of this sailor. They corresponded with him for many years.

Our first stop was in Rotterdam, where we were able to disembark and explore for a day. A new passenger joined us there, a young Texan named David. Likewise in Felixtowe, England, we were able to go ashore. It was a quaint little seaside resort, which reminded me of Main Street in Disneyland. We even got to ride on a double decker red bus. Next stop was Edinburgh in Scotland where we visited the castle of Edinburgh, an ancient fortress that dominates the skyline of the old town. I remember noticing how the walls were blackened with the grime of centuries. And of course it was cold and snowy that day, which added to its' beauty and mystery. Later in the old town, I loved looking at the thousands of different plaids in the little shops, and we even saw quite a few men running around in their plaid skirts. We sampled steak pie, shepherd's pie, cheese and tomato pie, and of course, kidney pie.

We learned that the reason for our stop near Edinburgh was to take on Scotch whisky, of all things! Soon the decks were filled with large containers full of whisky, destination Nassau in the Bahamas. Whisky was the main cargo being transported by the *Bischofstein*. In Edinburgh a lady passenger came aboard, a schoolteacher from California who was on sabbatical for a year.

The captain loved to tell us stories about his many years on the seas, and he assured us that the *Bischofstein* was one of the most seaworthy vessels to cross the Atlantic, had made the trip hundreds of time, and that it was perfectly suited for the kinds of seas we were about to encounter. His 'about to encounter' statement made me suddenly aware that we were beginning to cross the north Atlantic in the middle of December. I guess when we had booked our passage in August, we really hadn't thought too much about that.

As we continued our journey around the northern tip of Scotland, I began to develop a queasiness in more ways than one. We awoke one morning to the realization that the boat was groaning and creaking as it pitched both forward and backward, right and left, or more correctly, fore and aft, starboard to port. Holding on for dear life, we peered out the portholes in our room. All was black outside – the sky, the sea – as I wrote to my mother, "You've surely never seen anything like this!" The waves were not waves, they were mountains and valleys, and we were traveling up and down them at an alarming rate. Add seasickness to the mix and it was not fun. We discovered that lying down we did not feel as sea sick, and besides, moving was a major undertaking.

After a couple of days of this, we began to get our 'sea legs', as they say. Even though we all desperately craved fresh air, going outside would have been suicidal, so we mostly just endured the discomfort. Eating was no longer a pleasure. We had become accustomed to gathering in a little anteroom outside the dining room before meals where a chart was posted of the Atlantic that showed our progress across the ocean with a pin that the captain moved each day to a new location. That pin was moving painfully slowly. It was interesting to see the captain, who never needed to hold onto anything, maintain his balance by moving perfectly in sync to the slant of the ship.

An added challenge for me was the funky smell in our bathroom. The *Bischofstein* was an older vessel, and since the water used in the bathrooms was seawater, the old pipes took on a strange smell, and thus the water did too. It hadn't bothered me too much until I felt seasick, but then it was awful. The worst of the whole ordeal, however was

322

nighttime, and trying to go to sleep as the ship climbed up one wall of a wave and crashed down into the next trough. It literally felt like it was hitting the bottom of the ocean each time. We had to brace ourselves diagonally across the bed, holding on to the sides. I don't know how we ever slept. It was terrifying, feeling the ship rise and fall like that. I was convinced, that regardless of what the captain had been trying to assure us, this time the *Bischofstein* was not going to make it, and that the Rilling family was going to end up on the bottom of the sea.

After a few endless days of this, the seas became calmer, and we tentatively poked our heads out the door to the deck. The air had become warm! It seemed a miracle, as we were still far from our destination of Nassau. We asked the captain and he showed us how, as we moved into the same latitude as North Carolina, we were now part of the Gulf Stream, which gave us warmer air and water. And calmer water as well, thank God. Soon we were stretched out on the deck in chaise lounges, wearing shorts, unbelievably.

Our fellow passengers were quite engaging shipmates, and we got to know them well in a month's time. Each evening after the boys were asleep, we would play cards and drink Canadian Club with Coca Cola. On board, we could purchase all the alcohol we wanted very inexpensively. If I remember correctly, Canadian Club was $2 a bottle. It is safe to say that some evenings we probably drank a little too much. The evening I will not forget our schoolteacher friend was more than a little inebriated and needed some help getting to her room. The Captain had joined us that evening and he would have been happy to escort her, but she shooed him away and asked me to accompany her. In her room she lay down on her bed and when I came over to say goodnight she grabbed me and tried to pull me into bed with her. I managed to extricate myself from the situation, and suddenly realized why she was not eager for the captain to go along with her to her bedroom. She clearly preferred female company in that department.

In a few short days we were in Nassau, whisky safely delivered and passengers intact. We spent a lovely day on the beach and then hung out in some clubs listening to the drum rhythms of Junkanoo, the lively music of the region. It seemed like arriving in paradise after our harrowing passage across the north Atlantic.

We sailed on to Miami on Christmas Eve, and what a Christmas it was! Germans celebrate Christmas on Christmas Eve, so our Christmas started about 5 on that afternoon. There was even a tree someone had put up that evening. We were invited by the Captain for cocktails, and then had a lovely dinner. We were directed into the smoking room where gifts were arranged for each of us: a plate of nuts, fruit and candy, and a present. Toby and Chris received a toy ship just like the *Bischofstein*, and from the sailors they each got a sailor doll. We were taken aback by the delightful, unanticipated hospitality.

At nine the sailors all came upstairs and joined us, and there were at least twenty of them. Each and every one of them could sing beautifully. It was such a pleasure listening to all those deep voices sing Christmas carols. They sang every Christmas carol I had ever heard of and then some. And though it was all so beautiful and unique for us, we couldn't help thinking it wasn't much of a Christmas for all of them.

As the evening progressed and more wine was consumed, they began singing sailing songs. What fun, and right in the middle of it all were Toby and Chris, sitting on Elto's lap and taking it all in. Some of them had guitars, and we sang and sang until the middle of the night. A Christmas to remember, indeed!

Christmas day we spent wandering around Miami, which was quiet on that day, no traffic at all. I remember thinking that everyone who lived in Miami was over the age of sixty, at least. By the next day we were sailing on to New Orleans, which took a couple of days, and we had a weather change again. It became cold and snowy and we had the rare experience of seeing the French Quarter blanketed in snow.

A day or two before we reached our final destination, Houston, we celebrated New Year's Eve, or Sylvester on the *Bischofstein*. This time we were invited by the sailors to hang out with them in their cantina. It was apparent that the boys were quite familiar with that cantina, and seemed to know all of the sailors by name. I remember feeling so grateful that these young men had given our sons the experience of a lifetime. It was sad to think that we'd all have to part. The evening was spent with the sailors regaling us with their tales of adventures at sea, more singing, and lots of hilarity. It was clear that while Christmas Eve had been the Captain's party, New Year's Eve was the sailors' opportunity to show us a good time.

Finally, we reached Houston, sometime in the first week of January. My immediate family was not there to greet us, but my father's family lived in Houston and several cousins were on hand to welcome us graciously to the good ole' USA. We stayed with my cousins as we figured out how to get all our belongings through customs, and within a week we finally were back in El Paso.

What an experience, and what a blessing to have had such an adventure with my husband and sons. It was a most exhilarating way to end our years together in Germany and to prime us for our slide into a new life. After all, if you think your ship is sinking and you manage to survive it, then you can handle anything. Bring it on!

###

ESSAYS

Don't Lose Heart
Anne Batzer

The City Council in a nearby small city is giving consideration to legislation that would set common-sense limits on activity with loaded guns. So far, some council members have directed the city attorney to delete and dilute the wording of this mild legislation. Suggested by a thoughtful grassroots group of constituents, these proposals are already law in other Oregon cities.

I don't envy the City Council. As usual, some people opposed to any conversation about gun control legislation have walked through town and shown up at council meetings wearing guns on their hips, exhibiting wild west behavior most of us hoped had long since been relegated to history's dustbin. This behavior is meant to be intimidating. And it's working.

I pondered this when I watched the coverage of the latest mass shooting at Fort Hood, Texas.

A man in a suit and tie fills the TV screen. He's the spokesperson for the National Rifle Association (NRA) and he's been invited to broadcast his thoughts. He talks about the second amendment, but I've grown cynical since the lack of Congressional response to the Sandy Hook Elementary School tragedy a year ago. I know this NRA man speaks for the $6 billion-a-year gun industry.

When the anniversary of the Sandy Hook killing was noted recently, I watched as this same man said, "We can't make decisions based on emotions, we must be rational."

I still can't believe this statement. Twenty young

children and six adults who taught them are senselessly murdered and we are to ignore our hearts?

I remember one of the most poignant stories I heard about the tragedy at Sandy Hook. It's about a young victim who would sit on the bathroom counter every morning before school while her mother brushed her hair. The little girl would entertain herself by drawing pictures on the steam-covered window. The morning of the shooting — the last morning of this little girl's life — she drew a peace sign.

The following morning, when a family member took a shower, the drawing of the peace sign emerged when the hot steam covered the window. It was still there.

The little girl's mother relates this story to a broadcaster. She says she takes heart from this sign. She takes heart.

The NRA man drones on.

I force myself to listen. He's citing statistics and spouting data. But he's not mentioning the over 11,000 homicides and 19,000 suicides by firearm that have occurred since the murders at Sandy Hook. And he doesn't talk about the NRA's opposition to surgeon general nominee Dr. Vivek Murthy. They are blocking this nomination because Dr. Murthy has identified gun deaths as a significant public health issue.

The NRA man is not acknowledging that his group successfully lobbied Congress to pass a law that stymies scientific research on shooting deaths in America. And yet, in spite of this, a recent Harvard University study revealed that the areas of our country that have the strictest gun control laws have the least amount of gun violence.

As I listen, my heart hardens toward the NRA man. But I'm wise enough to know this won't help, so I repeat to him and to myself: Have a heart. Have a heart. Have a heart.

###

TRUE PATRIOTISM

KATHIE OLSEN

From *The Lithiagraph*, Ashland, Oregon, July 1999 Column

I was raised to be a patriot, in the deepest sense of the term. I was taught to love my country.

My father was a Ukranian immigrant, who came here with his parents when he was only one year old. His parents were Jews, more revolutionary than religious, more intellectuals than peasants. They were followers of Tolstoy, and they were part of the humano-vegetarian movement. This means that they not only didn't eat meat, but also that they wore no leather, because their vegetarianism came from a belief that all killing was wrong. (Do not be misled, however. My grandfather was something of a dandy. He dyed his canvas shoes and belts and suspenders black so they would look like they were leather. He also waxed his mustache, and always smelled like men's cologne, but that's another story for another time.) His parents' beliefs are important because it meant that my dad was not only always at home in a tight-knit community, but in a community that was at odds with everything around him.

Daddy didn't feel bad about this. He was proud. He was an optimist born of optimists, surrounded by good friends who knew they were right. The adults in his parents' home cheerfully went about the business of trying to change the world, and Daddy was one of their beloved young.

My mother also came from a Ukranian Jewish radical family. Her father, also an émigré, was a leader of the Socialist Party in Nebraska. Mama was one of six children, raised in true poverty by a mother who spoke little

English. Mom's whole life was inspired by the fervent optimism of her parents and their friends. (She remembers, as a little girl, sitting on the lap of Eugene V. Debs, no less!) Again, they were different from the broader society, but part of a tight-knit group of forward-thinking friends.

Both sets of grandparents held organized religion in contempt, so neither of my parents were raised in the Jewish faith. Nonetheless, they had a different kind of faith. They were not so far removed from their own peasant grandparents, and fervently believed that those who raised the food and tended the soil should own that soil and its harvest. They had faith in the glory of the working person. All around them industrialism was rearing its mighty head, and factories and mills were filled with thousands of working men, women, and children. It seemed only logical that what held true for the tenders of the soil should also hold true for the workers in the factories.

They believed, then, that working people were unsung heroes. They believed that the work done by honest labor was glorious. It was in this context that both my parents became communists in the 1930's. They truly believed that communism would help to make this country even greater.

In the 1940's my Dad went to war. Serving on the front lines in France and Germany, as a member of the infantry, he fought the hardest fight against fascism, leaving behind my mother and three little daughters. He didn't come home until I was almost four years old. Mama spent the war years helping to raise money for the war effort, and taking care of us girls as best she could.

When Daddy came home, it was to a country getting ready to launch a fierce anti-communist period which came to be known as "McCarthyism." He and my mama were about to be outsiders again, only this time their wider community of like-minded people wasn't so wide, and the issues were clouded by familial responsibilities.

I was always aware that we were of Jewish heritage, in a time of the Holocaust. I was also aware of our radicalism in a time when Ethel and Julius Rosenberg were killed as traitors. As McCarthyism raised its ugly head, it would have been so easy for my sisters and I to retreat into our home, afraid and ashamed, or for our parents to ask us to keep our family values a secret. But it didn't happen that way. Not for us.

As I said, we were raised to be patriots. Our parents taught us, every day, that the American people were good. That the American worker had built an endless array of wonders -- like the Golden Gate Bridge and the Washington Monument and the highway to our grandparents home, and on and on. They taught us that all the people of the world cared about their children and laughed and sang their own songs that were as fun for them as ours were for us. They sang us lullabies from many lands. They read us fables from all over the world. They exposed us to European classical music and rhythm and blues and to rockabilly. They gave us the world, and a context for hope.

When I was in the third grade, they took us by train to Washington, D.C. to see our grandparents, and to see the Bill of Rights. (I don't know which was more important to them.) All the way across this beautiful land, they pointed out how people lived, and what they had built. All the way they told us stories about both the slaughter of the Native Americans, and the bravery of the families who came west. The contradictions weren't confusing -- they simply were the truth.

When we got to Washington, the cab driver insisted on driving us through a slum neighborhood, all the while loudly spouting racist untruths. We were horrified and turned to our parents in hopes that they would make him stop his rant. My parents made us listen. It was part of the truth of our country that racism existed, and that there were people who could look at such misery and not "get it." They wanted us to love our country, but also to know what ailed it and what had to get fixed. We were to listen and learn.

When we actually got in to see the Constitution and the Bill of Rights, my mother stood in front of them and cried with joy and admiration. We purchased copies of the Bill of Rights and the Preamble to the Constitution in the gift shop, printed on paper made to look like ancient parchment. We carried them home all the way back across the country, cradling them like they were the Crown jewels.

I have never forgotten the lessons. I still love my country. I still marvel at all that is wonderful about it. And I still rage at what ails it and have hope that we can fix it. I'm a patriot in that way. And I thank my parents for those gifts.

###

In Praise of Laundry

Lois Langlois

As a young girl, I noticed that the mothers of some of my playmates were not always busy. They would sit down in the evening and be done. But not my mom. She had a constant To Do list, and it wouldn't leave her alone. She took occasional breaks, of course – longer and more often as she got older. In fact, the little breathers turned into major naps as the years sped by. But she never did finish all that work.

Mom led a full life. She was a good mother, a devoted wife, and active in her church and community. She raised four children – two sons, two daughters. Naturally, managing a household and raising a family entailed plenty of chores. There was always mending to be done, greeting cards to be written, meals and desserts to be cooked and baked, weeds to be pulled. And laundry – there was always laundry to be sorted, washed, dried and ironed. Mom was always busy. Sometimes being constantly busy gave her pleasure, but sometimes it was a source of frustration to her. No matter how much got done, there was always more waiting to be done.

As to mom's four children, I observed a remarkable phenomenon as we grew up. Her two sons did not inherit the busy gene. Her two daughters definitely did.

Up front, it must be noted that being busy is not the same as being productive. Being productive means having finite goals which lead to results that can be measured and celebrated. Mom probably meant to be goal-oriented. In reflecting on her life, though, I see that the act of doing was more important and satisfying to her than the result of accomplishing. I fear I am the same way. I need to be busy. My sister Rosalie has the same affliction. Brothers Keith and Dave clearly did not receive the genetic message that they must be busy all the time. They approach time and life quite differently from how my sister and I do. If something needs to be done, they are likely to do it. But if nothing presents itself, they don't fret about it.

I, however, have a seemingly endless supply of Things to Do. Some are little tasks, and some are bigger, what you would call projects. I keep lists. I cross things off lists. My mind leaps ahead and finds more things to add to my lists, faster than I can cross off the done things. And when I do complete a major project, I feel lost and empty for a while. *Oh, no, I just bundled up the income taxes and took them to the accountant. I am so depressed!*

Yes, that is the scariest part of having the busy gene. When I am not being pushed or pulled around by my list of Things to Do, I slither into instant depression. *What is the meaning of life? IS there a meaning to life?* Without a list, I'm not sure how to assess or prioritize the value of things -- of space, of time, or lack thereof. I know right now would be a good moment to direct this treatise into deep metaphysical contemplation, to ponder the purpose of life and such related topics as silence, being, doing, or the void. And of course I would love to do that, once I'm not so busy.

Fortunately for me, the problem of deep thinking usually takes care of itself. A few minutes of raging depression and of questioning the very essence of existence, and then a new list starts forming itself in my brain, begging to be written down. Soon, there are Things to Do, and *voila*, the depression abates. At least, it does for the present moment.

As I noted earlier, being busy does not exactly equal being productive, and, frankly, the state of being busy seems rather undesirable to me. Thus, when friends comment, "Oh, you have so much going on. You are such a busy person," I take it as a snarky swipe, not as a compliment. I assume they are putting me down after making note of my frequent wheel-spinning state. I would much prefer being productive over being busy. I would like people to say, "Oh, you accomplish the most amazing and wonderful things." Yes, sometimes I do. But often, I merely keep busy. And I can't always tell, when I start out, whether I shall end up being productive or merely busy with any certain list of activities.

Because I am afraid life will have no meaning if I don't have events, travels and projects to anticipate, I plan far into the future. I even plan to plan things. This requires compartmentalizing in order to keep from being completely overwhelmed. I'll say, "Yes, I can start thinking about that matter in two days from now, after I blah-blah-blah."

Sometimes I use lists to limit what I intend to do, as in, "I am only going to do the seven things on this list today. Then I'll be DONE."

Other times, though, the lists, like sci-fi robots, gain the upper hand and start running my life. I fall ever-farther behind. I plan my garden in July and write Holiday cards in January. A friend of mine looked at me in horror a few months ago when I declared, "I'm only three months behind in my life right now." I was equally horrified to discover that this is not exactly normal.

Years ago, when I lived in Kauai during my mid-life crisis, I had a roommate who said one day, "I'm going to wash that window. It's dirty, and it's bothering me." She jumped right up and washed the window. I was shocked. I didn't know one could do that. I thought you had to notice the dirty window, notice all the dirty windows, decide they all needed washing, plan to wash the windows, worry that you didn't have time to wash the windows, and eventually – maybe weeks later – haul out the buckets and brushes and ladders and paraphernalia to finally wash the windows. *What? You can just have an idea or see something to be done and act on it instantly? Amazing.*

Clearly, busy-ness is a learned behavior, whether consciously taught, or not. That my sister and I both feel impelled to pursue an impish devil of doing, while our brothers are not so possessed, is quite fascinating to me. And while our brothers – and our husbands – stand back in awe and dismay when we get into our doing frenzies, Sis and I find ourselves unable to stop, dancing under the spell of bad fairy-tale witches, as if caught in a scene from *The Red Shoes* or *The Sorcerer's Apprentice*. The expression *Do or die* takes on new meaning when there is a large black cloud of depression chasing me if I don't keep busy.

And this brings me, at last, to the topic of my treatise: why I love laundry. Any time I do a load of laundry, I feel I have accomplished something. The reward is instant and pleasing – a nice, clean, good-smelling pile of clothes, all folded and ready to put away. Not only have I been busy; I've also been productive. Even the dreariest day can be perked up by one completed cycle of the washer. Even a day when nothing seems to go right can be rescued by those clean shirts, or socks, or sheets.

Thus, I celebrate laundry. I sing its praises. It is the one certain antidote to slackerly despair, to empty busy-ness. Long live laundry.

###

TEACH YOUR CHILDREN WELL
ANNE BATZER

The photo of a dolphin with a sea sponge on her nose grabs my attention. It's from a yellowed newspaper clipping stuck into an old paper file I keep of stories that intrigue me. Stories of wonder or invention.

I sometimes pull the file out after I've waded through the dark waters of daily news, where stories of bomb blasts in Afghanistan, glacier melt in Antartica or people carrying AK47s at anti-Obama rallies in Arizona have instilled a murky mood.

No wonder the article with the clownish photo of the dolphin, her sleek head pointed toward the surface, a rumpled sea sponge stuck on her nose, interests me. Makes as much sense as anything else I've read today.

Turns out it makes more sense. The animals wear the sponges on their snouts while foraging for food along channels in the sea floor. The sponges protect them against cuts from the sharp coral or nasty stings from stonefish.

But here's the best part: this trick appears to be almost exclusively passed from mothers to daughters. Mama dolphins teach their baby girls to wear the sponges like a shielding glove.

Some years ago when my own daughters graduated from college and moved to bigger cities I gave them the gift of a newspaper subscription in their new hometowns. I sent it with much hope that it would help bridge the underrated difficulties of transitioning from years of school with its predictable challenges to the more erratic trials of adult life.

Looking at the dolphin photo, I hope I passed along much, much more. Our world seems increasingly like the ominous-sounding Shark Bay in Australia where these dolphins live. These mammal mothers---more like us than we had previously known---ventured into shadowed depths, into deep mysterious waters and discovered something there in the dark that could protect and shield their descendants.

Now I hope *we're* more like the dolphins than *they* had previously known, and that we can do the same.

###

GRANT WRITING AS METAPHOR

KATHIE OLSEN

Among her other jobs, Kathie often teaches classes on fund development for non-profits. This is a flier that she hands out.

***

What follows are eleven rules for successful grant writing (not necessarily in order of importance). They are also rules for successful living. Take heed, go forth, and conquer.

RULE ONE: KNOW WHERE YOU ARE GOING.

If you don't, who knows where you'll end up. The problem is hungry children. But it's not the problem you need to focus on. It's vision. Focus on creation of a world where everyone is well fed and healthy. If you hold that vision, you'll keep your energies about you, inspire others, and make it happen. Go ahead, inspire the grantors.

RULE TWO: DON'T LIMIT YOURSELF.

If you could do anything in the world to make your vision real, what would you do? Figure that out. Don't hobble yourself. If you had all the resources in the world to make the vision come true, what would those resources buy or create? Make a plan to buy or create what is really needed. Build a real budget.

RULE THREE: SPEAK FROM YOUR HEART. TELL IT LIKE IT IS. BUT DON'T GO ON AND ON.

Figure out how to articulate the problem and your vision for solution. Learn how to say it simply and clearly and without a lot of extra words. Once you do, then say it – often – to whoever will listen. Sooner or later, someone will be as excited about the vision as you are. They will want to help. Which leads to,

RULE FOUR: LOOK FOR SYNCHRONICITY.

Who is more likely to help you -- the grantor who shares your vision and priorities, or the grantor who doesn't?

RULE FIVE: DO YOUR HOMEWORK.

Whether it is researching a likely grantor (see Rule Four), or creating a realistic budget (see Rule Two), take the time to be thorough (phone bills, transportation costs, installation fees, etcetera). It will save everybody precious time and make everything work better.

RULE SIX: CREATE COMMUNITY.

Work from your values. Do you know what they are? Walk your talk. Be the world you want to create. Make your organization that world. Look for those who walk the same path, or want to walk with you. Honor them with your partnership.

RULE SEVEN: TELL THE TRUTH.

Treat your partners (including grantors) with respect. This means that you tell the truth, share your successes, share your difficulties, ask for clarification.

RULE EIGHT: DON'T BE GREEDY.

We are all sharing the same world —all dipping into the same basket of resources. The fat in your budget (the fat in your *life*) could help meet someone else's need.

RULE NINE: NEVER GIVE UP.

A rejection may have nothing whatsoever to do with you. Maybe there wasn't enough to go around this time. Maybe there were three similar requests on the table at the same time, and one of the others had a more perfect fit for now. Maybe the program officer just split up with the third cousin of one of your board members. If you believe in your vision, if you care about your problem, keep trying. And remember, it's okay to ask for feedback.

RULE TEN : KNOW THYSELF.

You might be a brilliant mentor, or you might be a passionate visionary leader. You may not be a grant writer. You may have way too much to do. If that's the case, sit your brilliant, passionate, over-worked self down with somebody who knows how to write and research grants. Teach them about your project, give them *all* the information they might need. Then, let them do it. Pay them fairly (never as a percentage of any dollars earned). It's an investment that will pay off. If you simply can't do that, then take yourself to a grant writing seminar and take good notes. Listen. Talk to possible grantors and get their assistance. Listen. Be brave. But make sure you apply. Remember, this isn't about you – it's about the work, the vision.

RULE ELEVEN: SAY "THANK YOU."

If someone gives you their time. If someone gives you their money. If someone makes you feel good. If someone has simply tried very hard. Say it from your heart. This is called recognizing relationships, acknowledging your partners, being a *mensch*.

.

HOW WE WORK

How Our Writers' Group Functions

SHARON SCHAEFER

1. KEEP THE GROUP SMALL AND DIVERSE

   We have 11 members, all published, all women. At any given time some of us will be absent. We routinely have 7-8 attending. We have writers of poetry, short story, memoir, travel, novels and non-fiction.

   It has been the experience of several of us that having men in the group changes the give and take atmosphere. Most of us rely upon the men in our lives to be the first reader and first editor. We feel that's enough testosterone.

2. DECIDE WHERE AND HOW OFTEN TO MEET.

   Our group meets weekly for 2 hours. We meet in the same place each time unless otherwise arranged. Meeting that often allows each of two readers to share for 45 minutes. Most of us are on some sort of self- imposed deadline and this weekly advantage lets us read often. We have a six month schedule of readers prepared by one of the members. This columned schedule shows: date, readers, members absent, place.

3. PROVIDE COPIES OF WHAT YOU ARE READING FOR EVERYONE.

   The author reads her work out loud and the listeners mark the manuscript as they listen. We mark kudos as well as question marks. At the end of the session, the author takes all the pages back home and contemplates. These notes on the page are very valuable for the author to use when re-writing. We tried sending out work in advance, but that just didn't work for us.

4. THROW AS MANY BOUQUETS AS BRICKS. DON'T BE MEAN WITH YOUR CRITIQUE.

Two or three of our group are former editors and do the tenses, grammar and punctuation. Everyone reads for content and plot. "Does it make sense? Does it flow?" We honor the author's voice and intent. The author will often ask for the kind of input she needs. "Forget the commas, I want to know if it accomplishes what I meant." To go along with this rule, the reader does not spend her time in the spotlight making excuses, and we all remember that we are there to be supportive.

5. ALLOW ENOUGH TIME FOR EACH MEMBER TO OFFER A CRITIQUE OF THE WORK.

Sometimes it's best to go around the table, allowing everyone a chance to contribute. Each of us will have something to say as time permits.

We are polite and let everyone who wants to contribute do so.

6. IF YOU ARE SCHEDULED AND FOR SOME REASON CAN'T READ, FIND A SUBSTITUTE.

If no substitute can be found, bring a writing exercise.

7. HAVE ONE OF THE GROUP BE THE TIME KEEPER/LEADER.

Usually this is the hostess, but it can be anyone who is obsessive enough to keep the group under control.

8. HAVE A CHECK-IN TIME BEFORE THE READING BEGINS.

Our group has met for so long we usually have updates regarding our families or publications or general information to pass on. We try to not get carried away though. The time keeper/leader is responsible for calling a halt. Unless there is an unmitigated disaster to discuss, fifteen minutes of check in time is enough.

9. I<small>F</small> <small>POSSIBLE,</small> <small>MEET AROUND A TABLE.</small>

We are writers after all. And tea, coffee, water and a light snack never hurt.

10. H<small>AVE A</small> W<small>RITERS</small> R<small>ETREAT</small> <small>ONCE A YEAR.</small>

It is so much fun to go away together to a bed and breakfast and do nothing but write and talk about writing. Two days is good. Three is heaven. We try to find someplace close, so we don't have to waste time traveling. We try to plan this event a year in advance so that as many members as possible can attend.   We schedule time for writing, time for socializing, and time for eating. Someone usually takes the initiative and plans a writing exercise and/or an activity.

###

AUTHOR BIOGRAPHIES

ANNE BATZER is retired from her full-time career that included roles as diverse as news reporter and autism consultant. She enjoys exploring the Oregon wilderness with her family, volunteering to make education more accessible in Kenya, and working with friends to put nonviolence into practice. A published fiction and nonfiction writer, she has always lived the writing life. Her work includes short stories, essays, poems, articles for arts and natural history projects, speeches for politicians, scripts for documentaries and in-depth profiles of women who live with intention. Anne loves the clarity, insight and humor that comes from sharing the written word with her cherished writing group.

FAYEGAIL MANDELL BISACCIA is the author of *Dancing in My Mother's Slippers: A Journey of Grief and Healing* (a Nautilus Book Award Finalist) and of *Circles: Prayers for the End of Life*. Her story "The Anniversary" appears in the anthology, *More Kisses*. Fayegail writes primarily about aging, the end of life, grief and healing in a way that is uplifting, moving, insightful, and sometimes playful. Her work points to the sweetness, courage and inspiration that often accompany sorrow in times of loss. Fayegail has done program development, facilitation and training for non-profits which focus on bereavement, and end-of-life education and preparation. She lives in Ashland, Oregon, with her husband Lance. Visit her website at www.GriefandHealing.net.

JANET BOGGIA followed two career paths that provided an array of remarkable experiences. Her deep interest in global education resulted in world travel with citizen diplomacy projects in Armenia, Azerbaijan, the USSR and Beijing. Grants took her to India to create curriculum, and South Africa to deliver a project on the Universe's 14-bilion-year history. She co-founded two successful consulting groups focused on the transformation of conflict. For her bread-and-butter career, she created and managed risk management divisions for Palo Alto Schools and the City of Mountain View. Jan has published professional manuals, articles and stories. Situated in Ashland, Oregon with her husband, she researches, writes and teaches her passion: the evolutionary story.

LOIS LANGLOIS loves to travel. She is drawn to remote and scenic places, and she prefers to get there by foot. For over forty years she has hiked, camped, trekked, and backpacked with the "Ladies Backpack Group" and others. She also likes colorful cities such as Cusco, Oaxaca, Barcelona, and Ljubljana. In recent years she has participated annually in a volunteer dental project in Jamaica. Lois lives in Ashland, Oregon, where she is most lucky to have a caring husband, Dan, who always welcomes her home with open arms after each of her adventures.

ELLEN DAVIDSON LEVINE, author of "Captain Flash and the Moon Illusion," and "The Awkward Runner" enjoyed a successful career as a community college instructor and administrator, receiving several state and national awards for excellence. She has written for various education and professional journals and has also prepared white papers and reports for the

U.S. Department of Education and the Oregon Legislature. A winner of the Bloomie Award for her short story "My Mother's Closet," Ellen's short story "The Dog War" was recently published in an anthology of Oregon Writers – *The Wind, The Rain and The River* (Forest Avenue Press, 2014) She is also the author of two novels – *Looking for Karma at the Eden Café* and *The Importance of Bulldogs* (Terroir Ink, 2010).

KATHIE OLSEN. In her 70+ years, Kathie is most proud of (1) raising two incredible daughters; (2) going to jail for civil rights; (3) breaking out of the steno pool and becoming a CEO and board president; (4) publishing her book on the women's movement of the 1970's, *Take Me To Mercy;* (5) being a columnist; and (6) keeping her sense of humor in spite of it all. You can find samples of her writing at www.kathieolsen.com.

GINGER RILLING worked for many years in the field of conflict resolution and is now retired. She has turned her passion for peacemaking into singing in a peace choir. A lifelong organic gardener, she spends much of her time growing the family food. Living in beautiful Southern Oreogn, Ginger and her husband take advantage of the many opportunities it has to offer. She writes mostly for fun.

SHARON SCHAEFER learned to read by age 4 and won an award for a poem when she was 8 that sent her on the road for a lifelong love of words. During her 30 years as a nurse she published medical/scientific papers and essays, including a monthly health related newspaper column. After retirement she has found fiction to be her new passion. Sharon writes short stories and has two mystery novels waiting to be published. She is one of the founders of this group, and has served as the host since its inception.

DIANE M. SCHAFFER retired from an academic career to pursue her twin passions: mystery novels and good wine. A member of *Sisters in Crime*, she lives in Southern Oregon with her husband and extended family. Included in this anthology are chapters from her forthcoming mystery novel, *Mortal Zin*, written under the pseudonym Dee Maxim.

DOLORES HOLMES SCHEELEN has been a lifelong teacher of students from newborn to octogenarian. Much of her teaching has focused on child development, especially the progress of children with autism, their parents and their teachers. Writing has been part of Dolores' teaching in imparting information and practical skills. Writing is also a means of befriending ideas, fears, successes, losses, and the ongoing experience of beauty. Dolores' writing is non-fiction – memoir with a smattering of poetry.

LOIS SCHLEGEL has an MFA in Creative Writing from Antioch University. Her fiction work has appeared in the West Wind Review and Margin Magical Realism and her story, *The Gate*, was nominated for a Push Cart Prize. She has published three collections of poetry, including the latest titled, *Intersection*. Lois is a therapist and group facilitator, specializing in depression, anxiety and communication. She also writes a blog for the Medford [Oregon] Mail Tribune called *Living a Life in Bloom* that explores mental health and well-being.

###

INDEX BY AUTHOR

###

Made in the USA
Charleston, SC
05 June 2016